D0309135

SELF MANAGED LEARNING IN ACTION

SELF MANAGED LEARNING IN ACTION

Putting SML into Practice

Edited by
Ian Cunningham, Ben Bennett
and Graham Dawes

Gower

This edition published by
Gower Publishing Limited
Gower House
Croft Road
Aldershot
Hampshire GU11 3HR
England

Gower
131 Main Street
Burlington
Vermont 05401
USA

Ian Cunningham, Ben Bennett and Graham Dawes have asserted their right under the Copyright, Designs and Patents Act 1988 to be identified as the authors of this work.

British Library Cataloguing in Publication Data
Cunningham, Ian
    Self managed learning in action : putting SML into practice
    1. Organizational learning   2. Organizational change –
    Management
    I. Title   II. Bennett, Ben   III. Dawes, Graham
    658.4'06

ISBN 0 566 08214 4

Typeset in Century Old Style by IML Typographers, Chester and printed
in Great Britain by the University Press, Cambridge

Contents

Preface

This is the third book to address the Self Managed Learning (SML) approach. All three followed in the wake of a trail of papers (for conferences and journals), chapters (in anthologies) and articles (for a wide range of periodicals) stretching back to 1978, the majority of which were written by Ian Cunningham. The first book on the topic was Ian's *The Wisdom of Strategic Learning* where the SML element announces itself in the subtitle: 'The Self Managed Learning solution'. The book is more or less equally divided between advocating a strategic approach to learning and presenting Self Managed Learning as an example of applying such an approach. The strategic learning focus is important in taking a much wider view of organizational life and proposing the kind of thinking required in today's challenging environment (for both private and public sectors). In doing so, it gives a rationale for using the SML approach. In turn, the material on SML makes concrete the notion of taking the strategic view throughout the organization, which is what is required if the concept of a learning organization is to have any meaning.

The second book, *Self Managed Learning: Selected Writings from 1978 1996* (edited by Ian Cunningham and Graham Dawes), collects together material starting from the first theoretical expressions of the approach as it is differentiated from other educational approaches. There are examples of SML being put into practice for a variety of organizations, sectors and groups of people. Along with consideration of more general issues bearing on the kinds of developments frequently accomplished on SML programmes are interspersed short extracts from participants conveying their own impressions of SML.

The above literature concerns Self Managed Learning as it has been practised since 1978. At that time a database search showed no previous use of the term. In more recent times the term has been taken up for approaches that have little bearing on the subject of this book. This is due to contemporary developments in organizational life to which we will refer shortly. The upshot is that the term has become popular with people who have no knowledge of the existence of SML as we know it. Alternative uses of the name range from the principle that it is sufficient to provide, at most, a bunch of learning resources and leave managers to get on with them on their own, to programmes that are based on SML but do not apply the approach wholeheartedly. Chapter 2 will detail what we mean when we refer to the Self Managed Learning approach, and will show why variants tend to fall into the kinds of problems SML has been designed to avoid.

As the third book, this volume enlarges and extends the literature relating to SML as it has been applied by ourselves and our colleagues for over twenty years. As will be evident, the approach has been deeply 'thought through' and any developments and refinements over the years have evolved from the concrete experience of running SML programmes.

Part I of this volume locates Self Managed Learning against the backdrop of changing global trends and organizational responses to those trends. Chapter 1 covers some of the ways in which both cultural trends and organizational logistics have led to the need for people to be self managing in general. Chapter 2, as already mentioned, provides an overview of the structure of an SML programme.

Part II begins (in Chapter 3) with four brief case studies to complement the longer cases in the chapters that follow. These cover a range of applications, from a consortium programme in Chapter 4 to the use of SML in changing the orientation of the personnel function in Chapter 5. Chapter 6 addresses the use of SML in a culture change initiative within a local authority and Chapter 7 links SML to wider organizational change issues. Chapter 8 surveys three SML qualification programmes to illustrate the challenges of working with academia, and Chapter 9 shows how SML can translate to other national cultures. Chapter 10 makes the case for SML as the best approach to lifelong learning. Chapter 11 shows how SML can address the needs of those professionals undertaking Continuing Professional Development (CPD).

Part III covers specific aspects of the use of SML in more depth than was possible in the overview given in Chapter 2. Chapter 12 looks at Strategic Learning Contracts, showing how important they are to the overall SML process and, in the process, points up the frequent failings of less rigorous forms such as Personal Development Plans (though they can easily be strengthened by applying the methods outlined here). Chapter 13 covers another crucial element of SML, the learning group. Again, factors discussed here can be usefully applied to other contexts. Chapter 14 examines the elements surrounding an SML programme, which can provide a more profound learning context for those on the programme. Chapter15 concludes, fittingly enough, with a view to the future, not only the future of SML but also the way in which the approach is relevant to the wider debate about education and its purpose.

Ian Cunningham, Ben Bennett and Graham Dawes
September 1999

Acknowledgements

This book could not have been completed without the support and assistance of many people. Our families and friends have been important along with the many people in organizations with whom we have worked. Some of these latter are represented in chapters in this book. Throughout the text we refer to 'we'. That covers not just the three of us but also our colleagues in Strategic Developments International especially Anne Gimson and André Mailer. We also want to say a special thank you to Julia Scott and her colleagues at Gower for making it easy for us to work with them.

Part I
Setting the Scene

INTRODUCTION TO PART I

This book focuses on Self Managed Learning. It provides, in Part II, an array of case material and evidence of the success of well-organized Self Managed Learning (SML) programmes. This part introduces the background to SML and the thinking that underpins it.

It's flattering that many organizations make claims to be doing Self Managed Learning. However, when we investigate such claims we often find that the term 'self managed learning' is used as a label for various approaches that do not provide really effective learning. The reasons for this include:-

- the organization has seen the term 'self managed learning' used and decides it would be a nice title for some self development activity that it plans to offer;
- the organization reasons that stopping formalized learning activity would save money and effort and so labels what it is doing as 'providing opportunities for people to manage their own learning';
- consultants decide to re-label their packaged learning offerings as self managed learning in order to increase sales.

We also come across people who have read about effective SML programmes and try to replicate their success without learning what SML really means. We hope that this text will stimulate people to think about the SML approach but we make no claims that it provides an instant recipe book for running programmes.

In Part I of the book we provide an introduction to the approach so that readers can approach Part II with sufficient background on SML. If you have already read some of our previous writings (for example Cunningham 1999) you might want to dive straight in to Part II – or use Part I as a quick reminder about SML.

Chapter 1 makes a generalized case for thinking along SML lines. Its twin themes are the social and organizational context and the learning issues that underpin SML practice.

Chapter 2 outlines the basic structures of SML programmes. These are explored in more detail in Part III. The main aim in Chapter 2 is to make certain that readers have enough background knowledge about Self Managed Learning to read the chapters in Part II.

REFERENCE MATERIAL

References in the text are deliberately biased to our own writings as these show precise links to SML practice and readers can track back if they want to explore specific issues more widely. We have overlapped little with previous writing except in Part I where we need to provide a basis for people to read Part II.

1   **Background and introduction**

Ian Cunningham and Graham Dawes

INTRODUCTION

Here are some comments from participants on Self Managed Learning (SML) programmes. First from ICL:

- 'The benefits were enormous'
- 'It has heightened my self awareness'
- 'Broke out of my comfort zone'
- 'Really helped'
- 'Thinking time'
- 'Very useful peer network'
- 'A process and framework to improve my skills'

The second series of quotes are from managers in Cable & Wireless:

- 'The group encouraged me to try things I wouldn't have thought of – and they worked'
- 'It's highly beneficial to work out goals with objective listeners and get feedback'
- 'Members of my group accomplished what they set out to achieve – and more'
- 'SML brings the benefit of candid and confidential opinions'
- 'Other participants push and motivate you to achieve the impossible'
- 'SML helped me to prioritize my goals and values, and to check my progress'
- 'Through SML I came to realize that learning is not tied to attending school'
- 'Very helpful in teaching me to take charge of my career growth'
- 'Found it easier to resolve problems'

These statements (from two in-house evaluation studies) show a variety of benefits of Self Managed Learning. Later chapters will explore how these benefits can come about. We hope to show readers that these benefits are not unusual – and that they exceed what can be achieved through other approaches to helping people to learn.

SML has developed over a period of more than twenty years and is now becoming widely used, as the cases studies in Part II will show. Self Managed Learning grew, in part, out of a reaction to the waste and irrelevance of much of the didactic and authoritarian education and training of the 1960s/1970s. As its name suggests, SML has provided people with the wherewithal to take charge of their own learning. It has also provided a basis for connecting individual learning to organizational needs. What the name does not convey is the collective dimension of the approach – the notion that real 'self managing' requires collaborative learning and not a wholly individualistic approach. In this respect SML is also a reaction against sloppy, poorly designed self development methods.

LEARNING AND DEVELOPMENT – PROBLEMS IN ORGANIZATIONS

Top managers, HR directors and trainers may be starting to accept the simple truth that people are self managing anyway (though some 'self manage' better than others). For instance, people can be sent on courses, and to that extent controlled, but they will choose what they learn. Time and again in evaluation studies it's evident that this is so. Research going back to the 1950s has shown, for example, that managers may go on a course about being better leaders (more people-oriented, etc.) but within a few weeks they are behaving in exactly the same way as they did before attending the course (see, for example, Fleishman 1953). The reasons for this are various, including personal cynicism, superficial learning and the influence of the person's boss ('forget all that fancy nonsense you were told on that course – this is how I want you to manage your staff').

Often trainers, on finding that training does not work, have redoubled their efforts to control people. In one organization the trainer in charge of presentation skills courses was able to show from his end of course feedback how extremely popular the courses were with attendees. However, evaluations of people's performance six months after the course showed little change. His solution was to offer top-up courses, advanced courses, etc. The notion that more training might not be the answer never entered his head.

The problem here is not that helping people to learn presentation skills is a bad thing, but that individuals were being *sent* on the course; it was too generalized to respond to individual needs and it did not fit with people's personal strategies, for example in their careers. Many organizations have tried to overcome these problems with the use of personal development plans. Here the person is expected to meet annually with their manager to agree a development plan for the coming year, often based on an appraisal or performance review.

Indeed the organization mentioned above had such a process in place. However, as with most organizations, the scheme did not work very well. The personal development plan was usually a superficial, last minute part of the appraisal interview and was often driven by personal weaknesses already identified in the interview. Hence the notion of learning was attached to a need to address one's deficits and had severe negative overtones.

A final point on appraisals is that, despite attempts to make them more user-friendly, they are more often than not controlled by the appraiser. Hence they are out of keeping with a more self managing/empowering culture.

THE CONTEXT OF SELF MANAGED LEARNING

We hope to show in later chapters how we have made the SML approach work. The rest of this chapter provides some background material as a basis for those later chapters. It specifically outlines issues under the following headings:

- social and organizational factors that support the use of SML
- learning issues.

We have not attempted to make a comprehensive analysis of all the factors that have influenced our thinking. Rather we have tried to give a few pointers as to why we believe that SML provides what is needed – by individuals and by organizations.

SOCIAL AND ORGANIZATIONAL FACTORS THAT SUPPORT THE USE OF SML

Part of our thesis is that SML fits both the mood and the needs of the times – and it is based on timeless qualities. Some social historians have argued that many of the social arrangements of the last two centuries are just a temporary aberration brought on by, amongst other things, the Industrial Revolution. Bridges (1995) has taken a specifically critical stance toward our concept of a job, the word used to refer to a task, as in when your plumber says 'I can't come today – I have another job on.' Today we take a job to mean a paid position of employment; in effect, aggregating a range of tasks into a package (often defined in a 'job description'). In the future, Bridges sees tasks as being important but not the notion of a job. Hence he makes an explicit challenge to the future of employment, as we may see less jobs (in the twentieth-century sense) and more emphasis on paying people to carry out tasks.

Some commentators have argued that just to be employed is too risky in a changing world and that people need to be employable. If you take Bridge's critique seriously then being employable is not sufficient since employment as we know it may reduce severely over the coming years. Even less trenchant critics of 'the job', such as Charles Handy (1994), argue that there will be less full-time employment available in the future. What people do need is the ability and the opportunity to work. Such work can be, for instance, on a self employed basis or as part of a partnership. The ability to be able to work in the new world may be related to the ability to self manage.

Put simply, as shown in Figure 1.1, we are moving from a focus on employment and employability to a focus on self managing. This is therefore one obvious link to SML – the process of learning needs to match the needs of the work environment.

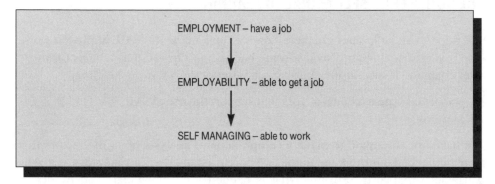

Figure 1.1   Work trend

Interestingly the balance of research seems to show that self managing and the move away from 'jobs' can have beneficial consequences for individuals. For instance, research at the Institute of Work Psychology at Sheffield University (quoted in *The Times*, 10 January 1996) shows that workers on short-term contracts tend to be psychologically better adjusted than their colleagues with so-called permanent jobs. Temporary workers were more certain about their future, more satisfied with their jobs and in better psychological health than their 'permanent' colleagues in the same line of work.

The idea of 'self managing' seems to be becoming ever more appealing to organizations. At the individual level, people are being exhorted to manage their own careers and their own development. On a wider scale, there has been a growing demand for individuals to take on a 'self employed attitude' (for example in the RSA's Tomorrow's Company project: RSA 1994). Such an attitude could be seen as consonant with the notion of self managing.

Some of these ideas are outcroppings of the 1980s concept of 'enterprise' – the idea of people standing on their own feet and looking after themselves, and not being mollycoddled by the organization. However, there are some who wish to avoid the overly individualistic overtones of ideas like the 'self employed attitude'. One dimension of this is in the growth of self managed teams. Here, in its ideal form, we can see a balance of the individual and the collective. The person manages themselves in the context of collaboration with others to achieve collective goals.

Self managing, in many ways, seems superior to the idea of empowerment. For example, there is little agreement on what 'empowerment' means despite its extensive use in the popular management literature. Everyone is, to some extent, self managing and SML mobilizes this natural orientation. The use of self managed teams is becoming more common yet organizations often struggle to facilitate the effective functioning of these teams. A key reason is the continued reliance on training methods that do not allow individuals and teams to 'self manage' their own learning. Figure 1.2 shows some connections between self managing teams and SML. The specific ways in which SML meets these principles are discussed more fully in Chapter 2.

- People are always to some extent self managing – total control is not possible, even if bosses try.
- People can be positively and more fully self managing, given the right circumstances.
- Self managing does not mean without structure - it needs a different kind of structure.
- We need to balance the individual and the collective.
- We need to help people break out of a dependence/counterdependence cycle into an independence/ interdependence cycle.
- Assisting people to work/learn in new ways is crucial.
- Self managing occurs within a context – arrangements have to be negotiated and contracted. Sympathetic leadership is important.
- We need to use the language of self managing to help to make systems and structures work. We need to stop using 'command and control' language and move to 'collegial language'.

Figure 1.2   **Principles common to SML and self managed teams**

A WORLD THAT IS MOVING TOWARD SELF MANAGING

The term 'Self Managed Learning' conveys to most people only the process by which a person goes about learning something. Within this view, it differs from other ways of learning something, most noticeably in that the 'something' that is learnt is chosen by the learner. Those who have had experience of Self Managed Learning programmes are likely to recognize another outcome of the process – that participants become self managing learners. That is to say, there has been another level of learning. By going through the SML process they have learnt not only those things they chose to learn but also a lot about learning.

When there is something they need to learn in the future, they will no longer have to rely on training departments or their managers to provide a course or workshop; they will be able to take the initiative themselves and go about their learning in an active, systematic and effective manner. This is of great benefit to anyone. It is especially valuable today when the explicit or implicit messages coming from organizations are that people need to look after their own careers, their own development, and to do so in an ever-changing context where there always seems to be something new to be learnt. In some cases organizations are simply abdicating their responsibility to those who work for them; in other cases, organizations are at a loss to know how to enable people to keep up with the changes, and the consequent need to learn new things. Either way, those who are able to manage their own learning are at an advantage.

The 'self managing' theme is also being sounded in those organizations that have cut management layers while changing over to team working. In some cases, the brave new world of self managing work teams is heralded with a rhetorical flourish as a strategic decision. In others, it is the inevitable result of there being too few managers to go round. In both cases, the working experience is very different from what people have been used to. It has been said that, in democratic societies, many organizations contained the last vestiges of a feudal culture. The national culture may be democratic but the organizational culture is not. However, at greater or lesser velocities, organizations seem to be moving toward the self managing concept. Many have a very long way to go, and are moving with glacial slowness. No matter, the direction is implicit within the external environment to which organizations will have to adapt or succumb.

The flowering of self managing within work teams is still fairly new for many organizations and it is novel enough to still be contained within those work teams. None the less, the anomaly of being within self determining work teams yet within an organization where strategic decisions take place at altitudes high above your head will become increasingly oppressive. Sacrifices are being expected, with fewer people to do the same amount of work, and many benefits, including security of employment, have disappeared. These will be resented unless people are convinced that the organization's strategy makes sense. With still only a very few precursors, the first faltering steps are being taken toward the self managing organization – an organization where everyone is involved in running the organization. This is a significant step in the evolution of organizational forms and promises a greater variety of forms within a context that encourages innovation and imagination.

These may seem overly optimistic words, particularly for those in sclerotic organizations showing every sign of clinging to their rituals and rigidities to the very last. None the less, it gives pause for thought when we consider that only twenty years ago the idea of organizational forms evolving would have seemed extremely fanciful. It is less so today. Over those years, new organizations have emerged that are organized on lines unknown before (see, for example, Semler 1993), while other more recognizable organizational forms have metamorphosed, slowly or suddenly, to the extent that it often seems as if only the organization's name has remained the same.

These kinds of shifts are not restricted to the organizational world. The social world has changed also. The expectations that people bring to their working life no longer match what old-style organizations are providing. The emphasis, here, has been on one aspect of that change in expectations, that which concerns self managing, with its blend of greater autonomy with more co-operative working. This is supported by other social currents, for example greater consumer power, concern for the environment and the use of new technology.

At a social level, there is a parallel sense of the exhaustion of social forms. As characterized earlier, organizations have often been the strongholds of past social forms such as feudalism. Today, organizations can be seen as the seedbeds for social experiments in organizing. While they may have stayed the hand of social change in the past (after all, they conditioned much of day-to-day life), they may prove to be harbingers of the future. People who spend their working lives in self managing work teams, perhaps even playing their part in self managing organizations, may no longer be content with the rather vapid and remote involvement they currently have in their democratic society. While the case has been made for free market, liberal democracies as the most advanced social form, such a form leaves, as Fukuyama (1995) emphasizes, a wide range of options for each specific nation.

OTHER ASPECTS OF SELF MANAGING

The concept of self managing is finding favour outside organizations. An example is in the area of mental health. The Manic Depression Fellowship found that promoting self managing, through a more self managed learning process, has produced positive results. As Guinness (1996: 21) comments

> people who self manage have less frequent and less severe mood swings, fewer hospital visits, stable relationships, more tolerance of stress, more self confidence and are more able to hold down a job ... When members were asked to prioritise various three-year goals for the Fellowship, 'promote self managing' had the largest number of first choices.

While the further reaches of this argument may not concern us immediately, many points have been made to suggest that the self managing theme will have increasing importance. While the kinds of qualities attached to self managing will be of increasing value to people and their organizations, they are not that easy to develop. For instance, they tend to resist the application of a competencies approach, with its inherent reductionism and lack of attention to the integration within the person of what is learnt. Self Managed Learning is one way such qualities can be developed, as has been proven over and over again. This suggests a continued and increasing relevance for Self Managed Learning as the aforementioned external factors indicate the development of self managing learners will have a high priority. While this might be cause for optimism, organizations often find it difficult to recognize that they need self managing learners or, if recognizing it, find that having them in the organization makes those who would preserve the status quo somewhat anxious. Both factors can lead to organizations resisting the logic of the times – to what consequences for themselves we can only speculate.

THE CONVERSATIONS OF ORGANIZING

Whenever an organization, almost any organization, conducts a staff survey you can predict that 'communication problems' will feature as one, if not the most frequent, of the complaints. This is so predictable that it is often ignored on the grounds of inevitability – everyone always says that. Is it inevitable, or is it only inevitable in organizations where only a few senior staff have any say in what goes on in the organization and where levels of trust are low, that is where people continually feel things are being kept from them? Whatever the case, the continual concern about communication can be taken as an indication of the importance of communication within organizational life.

Indeed, communication can be said to constitute the organization. The organization comes about through the conversations people have. An organization is not defined by its buildings or equipment, or its products or services; it has a formal, legal existence but, in essence, the organizing of an organization takes place through conversations. It is through conversations, whether they be in formal meetings or in corridors (or in writing as memos or e-mail), that plans are laid and agreements are made that this or that person will take this or that action, or get someone else to do one thing or another. These conversations result in products or services, in actions being taken, but the organizing of all this takes place in conversations.

Formal systems within an organization can be seen, in this light, as fossilized conversations. In fact, such systems only work when they imply conversations that are so routine as to no longer need to be spoken. People often consider conversation too ephemeral to be of so great an influence. The tendency is to look for 'organization-ness' in things that are more concrete. Search for it as you may, though, it slips out of your grasp, leaving only the conversations and relations between people. This is what tends to get missed and this is why the concept of 'organizational culture' has value. A culture cannot quite be tied down to artefacts, it means something more. We may have thrashed around vainly in our attempts to capture that 'something more' but at least the notion of organizational culture reminds us that it is there.

We find it so much easier to focus on concrete things than what we can't see.

People, as concrete individuals, are easier to focus on than the relationships between them. Yet the people you can point to as major players in the organization are usually not able to play their roles alone. They are significant because of their relations with others. And those relations are constituted in conversations. No wonder there is such emphasis on communication when people are asked to reflect on their experience of their organization.

Conventional approaches to learning tend to ignore conversation, until you get to tutorials. Prior to that, conversation may be frowned upon. It is either noise in the classroom or, even worse, cheating. Tutorials almost seem to be a vestige of an earlier oral culture. (A vestige generally excised from most training courses and other organizational forms of learning.) Yet when people report back from such learning activity you will frequently hear them say that 'The best bit was talking in the bar.' Indeed, this is frequently given, somewhat apologetically, as a reason for holding a residential event. Bar talk is recognized as something useful, but kept firmly on the periphery, outside of the learning event proper. And what does the learning event proper consist of? Inputs; the content that has to be learnt; whatever it is that features as the theme of the learning event – this is given the privileged position and this is what is most important. At least, it's most important to the train- ers.

Yet anyone who has spent some time involved with organizational learning events knows that while much of the content is forgotten, or never put to use, the conversations in the bar (or over a meal or around the coffee machine) are often remembered. This is one of those facts that is well known yet at the same time has little impact on what anyone does. Content remains king and conversation is pushed to the periphery – after hours.

A crude characterization of Self Managed Learning would be that we have switched the two around. We put conversation in the centre, and push inputs out to the periphery. Admittedly, the talk in an SML programme is a good deal more focused than much that takes place in the bar. But what is it that people appreciate about bar talk? There seem to be two main elements. Firstly, people gain great comfort from hearing that others are wrestling with the kinds of difficulties they sometimes thought were theirs alone. Secondly, they benefit from hearing how others are dealing with those difficulties. Even when they are hearing from some- one in a situation distinctly different from theirs, people still find that this stimu- lates their own thoughts about their situation. Such conversations can be very beneficial.

The two elements people most appreciate about bar talk are transposed into SML programmes. It is through focused conversations that much of the learning on SML programmes takes place.

Peter Senge, in his *The Fifth Discipline* (1990), has brought attention to a parallel process which utilizes focused conversation. Its developer, the physicist

David Bohm, called it Dialogue. For the practice itself, Bohm drew on the work of social psychologists but the original stimulus had been his long involvement and friendship with the Indian philosopher Krishnamurti. Both were concerned with the quality of our thought. In their view the problems of the world, while manifest in people's behaviour, stem from how people are thinking. Consequently, in their desire to bring about beneficial changes they place their emphasis on thought.

The Dialogue process, taking place in groups of varying size, entails, as Bohm puts it, 'holding our thoughts in front of us' so that we (and others) are able to examine them (Bohm 1985; 1994). The aim is thus to enable us to recognize and thereby explore our underlying assumptions. A very similar process takes place in SML programmes.

This emphasis on the quality of conversations is mirrored in other work. For instance, the researchers at Xerox's Institute for Research on Learning have argued that 'communities of practice' constitute the basis for much learning that goes on in organizations (see Brown and Duguid 1991). Such communities are naturally occurring social entities that share common language and values. Copier technicians in Xerox would discuss problems with each other and learn from each other's 'problem solving', especially where novel solutions were required. These conversations were more important than company training for the learning of the technicians. Indeed official company ways of doing things were often inefficient and people learned to be more effective in their work through the telling of stories within the community of practice.

We have seen that conversations have a far more important place in organizational life than is usually supposed. Also that, while all manner of conversations are constitutive of the organization, it is in focused conversations that the most profound examination of the bases of action takes place. Senge promotes the use of Dialogue within organizations precisely to bring this level of exploration to bear on the thoughts behind those activities being undertaken in and by the organization. He considers that the depth of conversation taking place in Dialogue generates innovation and removes blocks to change. We have suggested that Self Managed Learning provides much the same possibility for participants. To the extent that an organization utilizes SML it is promoting a process which, through its development of deep conversation and the questioning of assumptions, both brings people into contact with one another and establishes the kind of conceptual movement that encourages change. These are the kinds of factors that, when widespread within an organization, bring about a learning environment. This is what needs to be present for any organization to call itself a learning organization.

Much of the literature on the learning organization, while exhorting its development, often fails to convey a strong sense of what would constitute such an organization. So far in this chapter we have touched on some of the concrete factors that need to be in play. We next look at some issues about the nature of learning itself.

LEARNING ISSUES

LEARNING PRINCIPLES

Discussed below are just a few examples of the learning principles that support an SML approach – further material can be found in Cunningham (1999).

If people in organizations are to improve their performance then they have to learn how to do so

The simple equation to summarize a person's abilities and attributes is

$$U = G + P + L$$

By this we mean that you (U) are the sum of the other three factors. G stands for what we get from our genes, P stands for physical changes that we experience over life and L stands for learning. The message is: we can do nothing about our genes and little about the physical processes of maturation (our bodies just do change over time, or we suffer accidents that limit our physical performance), so the only realistic strategy available to help people improve is learning. But we also want to say that it is learning and not necessarily education or training. Indeed from our research we have found that at most 10–20 per cent of what makes a manager effective comes from formal settings such as courses. Most learning comes from the conversations we have discussed above. Such conversations may be with peers, with more senior people or with those outside the organization. Other learning can come from a variety of sources such as reading or travel (though even in the case of travel, it's the conversations with others that often seem significant).

Learning is not just additive (e.g. gaining new knowledge or skills); it can crucially involve habit changes

We often find that senior people are quite knowledgeable and skilled. Their learning problem may be one of using what they have to better effect. For example, we come across many managers who say that they have a problem with time management. Frequently they have been on time management courses, and still have not improved. The issue is often one of inappropriate habits. They typically will have absorbed work patterns in their early work career (often from the manager they had at around the age of 27–29) and these may not now be very functional.

An extreme example of a poor work habit was a manager who told us that her problem was that she did not open her mail until late afternoon. This was hampering her efficiency as her colleagues expected her to have read things that she had yet to open. The basis of her habit was that she had had negative stuff come to her through the mail and she associated the mail with things she did not like. She was a knowledgeable and skilful person and she did not need additive learning. She needed to change a basic habit. And that kind of learning is not likely to happen through standardized didactic training events.

Learning can come as a 'whole piece' (from experience) or analytically

We need to explain this point a bit. The tendency when learning from experience is to take in the learning in a whole lump. What is learned may be a whole package of ideas, theories and assumptions. This point is related to the one above. People may learn to manage their time from past experience and they can find it difficult to unpack it in order to make any changes. So that is a disadvantage of learning from experience. However, an advantage is often the efficiency of learning – a whole bag of useful habits can be picked up in this way, as when a person has to learn a new organization culture when they join as a new recruit.

Analytical learning is that favoured by the educational and training worlds. The teaching mode is to impart knowledge or skills sequentially. This mode has some advantages. In learning to drive we tend to be taught each piece in turn and add it all together, eventually to become a safe driver. However, we do need to create that integration so that most of what we do when driving becomes internalized and unconscious. This allows us to focus on the road in front of us instead of worrying about how to change gear or use the brakes. Those movements come naturally.

The down side of analytical learning is when that integration does not occur. This causes what is often called 'the transfer of training problem'. Learning off-the-job does not get used on the job.

In SML programmes we want to see people address these issues in a productive way. It is part of what is often called 'learning to learn'. However, much of what is called 'learning to learn' stops at the 'learning skills' level. People are taught, for example, how to read more efficiently or how to take notes in lectures. This is all fine but if it stops at this surface level it can miss more fundamental aspects of learning. In Self Managed Learning we use structures and processes to encourage a varied approach to learning and these are outlined in the next chapter.

Learning needs to be holistic

Figure 1.3 shows diagrammatically what we mean by holistic. Given that 'strategy' comes from a warfare root, we have shown in the figure an imaginary 'corporate warrior' (strategist). We recognize that this macho image may not appeal to every-one (and perhaps especially women). It could certainly reinforce a male image of what a manager or leader should be, which we do not want to promote here. Rather we want to recognize the root of strategy as lying in warfare – and to face the metaphor head on. We hope that the analysis below supports a balance of what has been labelled as the masculine and feminine sides of all of us (men and women).

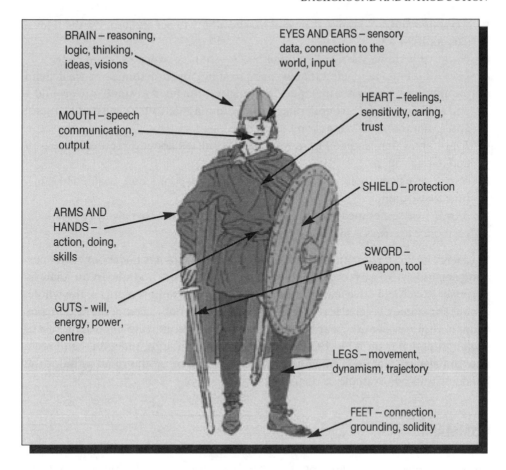

Figure 1.3   Corporate warrior

The person in the figure is meant also to respond to the notion of corporateness, that is that the organization can be compared to a human body. So in the figure you can see all the areas that a person needs to be effective in (and by extrapolation, what an organization needs to be effective at also). Moving around the figure you can see the idea that learning needs to accommodate the following factors:

- *Brain*   this signifies that rational, logical thought is necessary.
- *Eyes and ears*   this shows the need to learn how to take in information from the world around us.
- *Mouth*   this symbolizes communication capability; we have to learn to relate to the world around us.
- *Heart*   the notion of emotional sophistication has become increasingly recognized, especially from the popularizing of the idea of EQ (to balance IQ) from Goleman (1995).

- *Arms and hands*   signify the need for the ability to act and to have the necessary skills to act.
- *Guts*   this shows the need for qualities like courage, will power and energy.
- *Feet*   it is often neglected that we need to stand for something – or we'll stand for anything. This has a metaphorical quality – the need to stand our ground – and a real quality of 'groundedness' (see Cunningham 1999); we need a moral and a value basis for our actions.
- *Legs*   show that we need to move in the world; it's about direction, trajectory and dynamism.
- *Sword*   we need tools, equipment and maybe weapons – and we need to know how to use them.
- *Shield*   we sometimes need protective capabilities - life isn't always easy on us; resilience to stress is just one example here.

In real life all these elements need to work well together – it is not about each operating separately. So we recognize the danger of taking this 'body' apart for analysis purposes. Really effective learning has to recognize the requirements of the whole, even if sometimes precise learning activities focus on only a few of these domains at once. However, we are clear that all the domains indicated are important. Just to switch attention from IQ to EQ, for instance, is not enough. Indeed it can create new imbalances just as pernicious as the old. Reliance on the heart without the head and guts, for example, is dangerous.

SUMMARY

We have outlined here a number of factors that contribute to the idea of using Self Managed Learning. We have argued that changes in the world around us contribute to the notion that self managing is to be valued. We have then raised a few issues about the nature of learning in order to make a case for both the importance of learning and a particular approach to learning that is consonant with Self Managed Learning. We are aware that we have not yet explained much about what SML actually looks like and how it works. The next chapter fulfils that need. We are also aware that some complex issues are only outlined here. We will return to some of these in the closing chapter in order to round off the book.

2 Self Managed Learning in organizations

Ben Bennett

INTRODUCTION

This chapter starts to provide the answers to two questions, 'What is Self Managed Learning?' and 'How does it work?', linked with some important ideas about learning and development. Later chapters provide rich material on practical applications while this chapter concentrates on basic principles and on aspects of the design of programmes.

Self Managed Learning is an umbrella approach under which other training and development activity can be accommodated. SML can be used for the development of any staff at any level in the organization. It is intended to offer individuals and organizations an approach that is in tune with the world of today and tomorrow, by enabling learning that matches the seven S's below.

- *Strategic* long term with the big picture in mind.
- *Syllabus-free* driven by the real needs of individuals and organizations.
- *Self managed* people take responsibility for their own learning.
- *Shared* integrating learning with others' and the organisation's needs.
- *Supported* supporting people in achieving their goals.
- *Structured* provides a clear structure for learning.
- *Stretching* demands real, significant learning.

An SML programme would be most immediately recognizable from the fact that there would be no common syllabus or timetable to be seen. If there were 50 people on a programme there would be the equivalent of 50 syllabuses or courses in operation at any one time. Also, unlike competence driven programmes, there would be no pre-defined objectives to be met.

Self Managed Learning has been applied to, and rigorously evaluated for, a range of programmes and contexts. These have included qualification programmes from Diploma to Masters levels (see Chapter 8) and numerous in-house programmes (from those localized within specific areas of organizations or in relation to particular capabilities, to those which have been used as a means of culture change) in a wide range of organizations in the public and private sectors, in the UK and internationally (see Chapter 9). Our experience is that organizations have used SML in different ways and that each in-house programme has to be designed to suit the business needs and culture of the organization concerned.

Cable & Wireless used SML to foster development in a variety of regions of the world including Europe, North America and the Middle East. It found that the approach was especially valued by technical staff, secretaries and administrators as well as by managers (see Webster 1995). PPP healthcare similarly found that having launched Self Managed Learning with senior managers, its front line customer service staff valued having the same opportunities for development. On the other hand, Arun District Council started Self Managed Learning with middle managers and then extended the process to all senior managers and directors (including the Chief Executive). Sainsbury's used Self Managed Learning as a basis for a major shift in the role of Personnel and all their six hundred plus personnel professionals went through a nine-month programme. Later chapters in this book go into more detail on these last three cases.

A list of organizations that have used SML is provided in Figure 2.1. In each of the organizations mentioned, Self Managed Learning was part of a strategic approach to development, usually supported by the commitment of managers to make it happen effectively. As far as the answer to the question 'how?' is concerned, all the programmes had in common a number of structures and processes

Abbey National	Ladbroke Group
Allied Domecq	London and Edinburgh Insurance
Amersham International	London Borough of Lewisham
Arun District Council	Mid-Essex District Health Authority
Barclays Bank	Nestlé
BBC	Norwich Union
Birmingham Midshires Building Society	PPP healthcare
C.T. Bowring	Prudential
BP	RCO Support Services
British Airways	Rothmans
Cable & Wireless	St Helier NHS Trust
Debenhams	Sainsbury's
Eastleigh Borough Council	Scottish Health Service Centre
Electrolux	Shell
EMI	SOK (Finland)
Ericsson	South East Thames Regional Health Authority
Finnish Post	South West Thames Regional Health Authority
GKN	W H Smith
KPMG	Virgin Our Price

Figure 2.1   Organizations that have used SML

firmly rooted in a clear understanding of what Self Managed Learning is. In each case these structures and processes were integrated in carefully designed and managed programmes.

In this chapter we will explain what Self Managed Learning is by covering the essentials of the approach, so that you are in the best position to get the most out of the chapters that follow. Some of these essentials are represented by such key structural features as the Strategic Learning Contract and the learning group. As well as explaining what each of these features is, and how it works, we will also show how they are brought together in the design of a Self Managed Learning programme.

To go into more detail, we will first explain Self Managed Learning. Next we will look at the Strategic Learning Contract and the learning group in sufficient detail to prepare for the case studies in later chapters. The Strategic Learning Contract and learning group also each have a chapter devoted to them, Chapters 12 and 13 respectively. Having introduced these two key elements we will return to considering what Self Managed Learning is in more detail, but from the perspective of how it differs from other approaches with which it is often confused. Having done so we will introduce the other key elements of programme design in preparation for the cases that follow. We will conclude by re-visiting the seven S's in the light of what has been covered.

WHAT IS SELF MANAGED LEARNING?

Self Managed Learning is about individuals managing their own learning. This includes people taking responsibility for decisions about:

- what they learn
- how they learn
- when they learn
- where they learn

and most fundamentally

- why they learn.

All of this is carried out in the context of live organizational needs. But organizational needs cannot be met without individuals feeling a personal sense of commitment to what is required by the organization. You can compel someone to sit in a classroom, but you can't guarantee what they will learn. (If you could, almost everyone would be leaving school with perfect grades.) As the saying goes 'You can take a horse to water, but you can't make it drink.'

Although everyone manages their own learning to some extent, it's clear that just telling people to take charge of their own learning can be very inefficient. Research indicates that people who are effective at, for example, leading major organizations have managed their own learning very well throughout their careers. This does not mean, though, that they have been on more courses than others. Managing their own learning has meant the person using a wide range of opportunities for learning. These include:

- learning from others around them
- travel
- reading
- secondments
- projects
- being coached/mentored.

The examples quoted are only a few of the many experiences we can use for learning. Self managing learners use a range to suit themselves. The problem is that unstructured, unplanned learning is very inefficient. Our research on successful top managers and leaders shows that they set clear goals for themselves in relation to their learning. It is not purely random. In Self Managed Learning this is where the Strategic Learning Contract comes in.

STRATEGIC LEARNING CONTRACTS

A Strategic Learning Contract is more than just a fancy name for a personal development plan or an action plan. Such plans, often completed at the close of training courses, development centres or annual appraisal and review meetings, typically remain no more than interesting short-term wish-lists (the equivalent of New Year's resolutions). They are unlikely to involve any negotiation, agreement or regular and continuing contacts with others. A Strategic Learning Contract is different from a personal development plan for the following reasons:

- It is a written document created by the individual, after serious consideration, and then negotiated with the relevant interested parties.
- It is a living document that individuals refer to regularly.
- It covers long- and short-term development needs and spells out a programme to meet these.
- It has measures of achievement built in so that pay-off to the individual and the organization can be monitored.

The way we achieve the above is to get people to answer five questions – and to write down their answers to these.

THE FIVE QUESTIONS

The questions are taken in order, moving the person from the past to the present to the future.

1. **Where have I been?** (How has my career progressed? What have I learned from past experiences?)

This question helps the person make sense of past experiences. The reason for starting with this question is that we are today – all of us – a product of the past. We are 100 per cent created by the past – either we were born this way (the genes) or we had accidents that changed us, or we learned to be this way. Whatever the reason, it's 100 per cent due to the past. So in order to move on we need to explore where our current capabilities, values, beliefs, etc. have come from. And we may need to modify some of our ingrained habits if we are to move on.

2. **Where am I now?** (What kind of person am I? What are my strengths and weaknesses? What are my guiding values and beliefs?)

This question locates the person's current situation. The person may have evidence from a range of sources to help them address this. These are outlined in Figure 2.2.

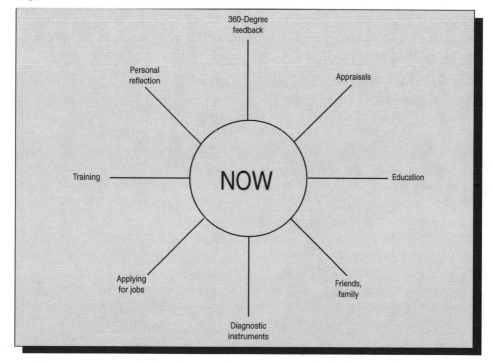

Figure 2.2   Sources of information for 'Where am I now?'

Sometimes people want to leap straight on to the next question (on goal setting) but we have found that getting a secure sense of the present is essential as a baseline for considering the future.

3   **Where do I want to get to?** (What kind of person would I like to be? What strengths can I develop? What weaknesses do I want to address? What are my short- and long-term goals?)

This question focuses on the future – and Figure 2.3 can help people see the need to balance goals at different levels. Too often people focus just on learning skills related to narrow job requirements. These need to be balanced with attention to longer term needs such as preparing oneself for often unknown futures. Many of the people made redundant in the 1980s had learned quite well how to do their current job, but when new technology or new organization structures hit them they were ill-prepared for the changes.

People may need to get a sense of their current abilities, qualities, values, interests, etc. in order to prepare for future career and life opportunities. Often they need to become clear about these issues before they can become more strategic. For instance, a person may say that they have problems with time management. However, it may be that an underlying issue is the lack of balance between home and work. So one might end up addressing this bigger life issue alongside the specific job-related needs. Figure 2.3 does not imply an either/or choice. It's often necessary to work on the problem at all levels. In the process a person can become more effective in work and have a more balanced life style.

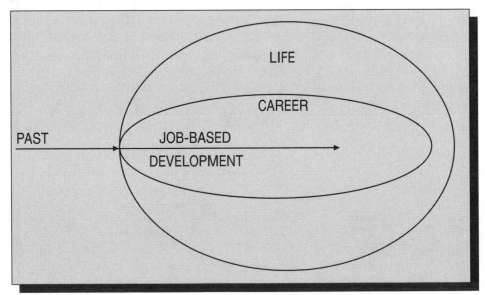

Figure 2.3   Goals at different levels

The learner's attention can be drawn to these different levels by indicating that answering question 3 can lead to three kinds of learning goals – job goals, career goals and life goals. The distinctions between these different goals are covered comprehensively in Chapter 12.

4. **How will I get there?** (What action is needed for me to progress from where I am to where I'd like to be? What learning do I need to undertake – and how will I do it?)

The answer to this question in essence provides the person's own plan of action and is equivalent to a curriculum (in a traditional educational programme). Learners may draw on a whole range of methods to achieve their goals including the standard training offerings (e.g. workshops, courses, seminars and conferences) as well as coaching and mentoring assistance, learning packages, secondments, projects and so on. There is nothing that need be excluded, except on the grounds of cost or organizational policy. In fact the major limit to what can be used is human imagination.

Where the person appears to be utilizing predominantly standard offerings, the development process can look like any other. Even here though, the big difference is that the learner will be working to the carefully crafted plan created in their Strategic Learning Contract. They will not be randomly going off on courses or haphazardly ploughing through learning materials. They will have clearly identified strategic goals and they will be aware that they will need to show progress to those with whom they have entered into the contract.

5. **How will I know if I have arrived?** (How will I demonstrate the achievement of my goals? What will be my measures of achievement? What evidence will I be able to show?)

This last question is vitally important. The learner is contracting to learn against specified goals and they need to show that this has happened (after a period of time – typically six months to a year). This question adds considerable bite to the Self Managed Learning process and is one example of a difference between Strategic Learning Contracts and less rigorous formulations of development goals. For example, on Self Managed Learning qualification programmes the answer to question 5 provides the assessment criteria that will be used in the assessment process leading to the award of the qualification.

LEARNING GROUPS

In Self Managed Learning programmes individuals come together in learning groups of about five or six people. The group is the primary place where each person negotiates their learning contract and reports progress on it. The learning group usually meets every four to six weeks and provides an arena for both support and challenge. Meetings can last from several hours to a whole day. The process adopted in each meeting typically follows the five stages below (though this is not a rigidly imposed format):

1. Check in
   This is a brief opportunity for each individual to unload thoughts, cares, or whatever preoccupations are on their mind which might affect their ability to focus on the meeting.

2. Agenda setting
   This establishes what will be covered during the meeting. There may be some information about the programme itself to be provided or discussed. Most of the agenda will be taken up by individuals' time slots (the lengths of which may vary, see below). When the order of the agenda is established, the meeting begins.

3. Individual time slots
   These are the essence of the meeting. During each individual's time that person is in control. They decide how they want to use it and it is for them to adjust the direction if it is not proving useful to them. This is their opportunity to have the undivided attention of the others present. If someone has done a lot since the last meeting or is grappling with difficult problems they may need more time than others.

4. Process review
   In early meetings particularly, it can be useful for members to review how they are working together. How effective are they in assisting the learning of others? Are there ways in which they could be more useful to each other? Such questions can be addressed to ensure that everyone gets the most out of the experience.

5. Check out
   This can be used for a quick round of responses to the meeting, for example for individuals to capture particular things they have learned and/or shifts in perspective they have made since their time slot.

Participants in Self Managed Learning programmes comment that the learning group provides a unique, cost-effective forum that pushes them to learn in depth and to solve real business problems at the same time. In this way, attending a learning group is not like going off on a course. Learning group meetings only work on practical issues that have a bearing on the business and the needs of individuals in the group. Indeed, in an SML programme for Shell we were asked to ensure that the pay-off from the programme, in money terms, was measurably greater than the cost (which we did). However, organizations with whom we work are clear that the main benefits come over time: individuals really do learn to take charge of their own development.

This not only enhances their performance but can reduce training costs. It's not that training ceases with Self Managed Learning. It may continue, but people on an SML programme use it in a more focused manner. In companies such as Allied Domecq – which uses SML extensively – training events were only put on if enough people had specified the need for them in their learning contracts.

This example points to another distinction between training events and Self Managed Learning. Providers of the former will say that the focus and relevance of these events is ensured by undertaking thorough training needs analysis. However, this 'analysis' is undertaken by different people (trainers not learners) using data from different people (i.e. different from those who eventually partici- pate in the events to which the analysis leads). In Self Managed Learning, on the other hand, the people who do the needs analysis also do the learning. This means that the two processes are integrated rather than separated or disconnected and this ensures that the learning is relevant to learners' needs.

Evaluation studies show that participants highly value their membership of learning groups. As well as recognizing the practical business benefits that they and their organizations gain, they are often particularly appreciative of what has led to the sense of the 'uniqueness' of their learning group experience. This sense of uniqueness will be explored in detail in Chapter 4, where issues related to the development of senior managers will be discussed drawing on an evaluation study of a consortium SML programme. For the moment we can note that, typically, indi- viduals characterize their learning groups as providing higher levels of commit- ment, openness, trust and honesty than their everyday organizational experiences and relationships, and a better balance between pressure and support. This does not mean that the cultures of participants' organizations do not support the achievement of high levels of performance. The difference is that processes used to achieve high levels of performance combined with learning need to be different from those commonly used to promote and reward performance alone. Self Managed Learning provides the means to achieve both and is most appropriate for those organizations that desire the kinds of development outcomes typified by the seven S's outlined at the beginning of this chapter.

One crucial support factor, and contributor to the development of the kinds of productive relationships noted above, is the learning group adviser.

LEARNING GROUP ADVISER

The learning group adviser is someone with knowledge of the SML process. Much of the time they are likely to function as any other group member, although with- out a Strategic Learning Contract with the group they are advising. They are present in the learning group to assist it to function effectively. The role may be played by someone in HR or training or by an external adviser, but can also be effectively carried out by a good line manager or team leader. The reason for this is that the role is not one of teaching or training but of providing support for the learning group.

There are important differences between the adviser's role and that of teacher or trainer. For our purposes, their importance lies not least in some of the differences they highlight between Self Managed Learning and other approaches. Some of these distinctions will be covered here. More will be covered explicitly in the next section.

One issue around which a number of distinctions can be grouped is to do with responsibility. The person in the teacher or trainer role is often seen as the one who carries the responsibility for the individual's (i.e. their student's or trainee's) learning. This is because what constitutes learning is seen as already existing in the specialist or subject knowledge possessed by the teacher or trainer. They are the experts in what needs to be learned and, in these circumstances, have the responsibility to impart this knowledge to the learner. Because they have the knowledge and the learner does not they can be expected to know what it is that needs to be learned, typically represented by a curriculum or syllabus, and to be the arbiter of whether or not anything has been learned. In the practical world of managing in organizations, where the effectiveness of managers is seen in terms of their ability successfully to overcome problems, the learning managed by teachers or trainers is seen to be driven by the solutions offered by their specialist or subject expertise.

In Self Managed Learning the individual learner is responsible for their own learning. In particular, rather than the learning being predetermined by the solutions inherent in the input provided by the expert teacher or trainer (or in training materials), it is driven by the real problems experienced by the learner. These problems are real in the sense that they are unique to the individual and owned by them. Other individuals can be responsible to them to assist them to define and clarify what the problems are and to work out the solution or solutions for themselves. Being responsible to someone to assist them in their learning is what the best managers do when they are coaching the people who report to them. Such coaching is based more around questioning and support than around direction and control (see Cunningham and Dawes 1998). In the learning group the adviser provides such assistance and, importantly, models the process for learning group members.

The distinctions above do not mean that the resources of subject experts will not be relevant to the individual's learning. For example, such knowledge may be invaluable in the process of devising optimal solutions. However, in Self Managed Learning 'subjects', 'specialisms' and 'solutions' are the servant in the learning process rather than the master or mistress.

THE SELF MANAGED LEARNING APPROACH

The use of Strategic Learning Contracts and learning groups are essential but not sufficient for the successful application of the Self Managed Learning approach. These alone would not make an SML approach, and there are many development methods and techniques that are not in keeping with Self Managed Learning. In a recent research study conducted by the Industrial Society (1998), 38 per cent of organizations say they do 'self managed learning' but few, if any, are using the term in the way we do. This illustrates the problem of language in this field. The problem bears examining before looking closely at what goes into the design of an SML programme.

THE PROBLEM OF LANGUAGE

When Ian Cunningham came up with the term 'Self Managed Learning' in 1978 he checked the literature extensively to see if anyone had used it before and found no previous usage. Throughout the early 1980s we were also the only people using the term. (The 'we' referred to here is a group of us at that time working in higher education.) As time wore on others started to apply the label to their work, as shown in the Industrial Society survey.

We are clear that most of these organizations are using the term in quite a different way from the way we use it. But as we never tried to register the words they are perfectly entitled to call any development approach 'self managed learning'. A simple distinction will be made here, then, between 'weak' self managed learning and 'strong' Self Managed Learning (SML). The capitalized version is the version described here and relates to a very precise structured approach to learning. The weak (lower case) version describes any kind of approach that gives responsibility to learners. One reviewer of the Industrial Society report rightly raised the issue of what these 38 per cent of organizations were actually doing. The reviewer was critical of organizations that appeared to be abdicating responsibilities to their people by saying 'It's over to you – we aren't going to support your learning – you have to be self managed.'

This way of thinking is linked to other aberrations such as the use of the term 'empowerment' to justify letting people sink or swim. The best advocates of empowerment don't do this, of course. They recognize that moving away from so-called command and control methods requires new ways of working and new structures to replace the old. It isn't simply a matter of removing all the glue that holds the organization together and then wondering why the place falls apart.

So one problem with the weak versions of self managed learning is that the label is used to cover any vague self development type activity. This might entail giving people distance learning packages, offering a learning resource centre or having a discussion about learning at an appraisal interview and then sending the person off to 'self manage' their learning. In other cases people are put through a so-called 'development centre' or through 360-degree feedback, helped to write a personal development plan and then left to get on with it (which seems to be what some people consider 'self managed learning'). These weak versions of self managed learning tend to be characterized by laissez faire approaches with poor support for the learner over time. Our research has shown that the pay-off from such approaches is low and individuals can be quite critical of this sloppy approach to development.

It's a poor parent that throws a non-swimming child in the deep end without support – and it's a poor organization that does the equivalent to its people regarding their own learning. Equally, a good parent would not criticize their child if he or she needed rescuing when they did not have sufficient support. So managers who criticize their people for not delivering on personal development plans for which there is inadequate support are behaving unjustly and shortsightedly.

STRUCTURE, CONTROL AND RESPONSIBILITY

Paradoxically, even though proponents of the weak version of self managed learning would see themselves as providing an alternative to taught training courses, the two approaches are actually two faces of the same coin. This coin is the point of view that confuses 'structure' with 'control'. Learning has to be either highly structured and controlled or, in order for learners to be able to take control over their own learning, wholly unstructured, which leads to the 'sloppiness' identified by critics. In SML it is clear that 'structure' and 'control' are two separate variables.

Contrary to a common misconception, the SML process is not unstructured. However, it is not structured in the same way as a taught course. Taught courses are typically highly structured and control the content and trajectory of participants' learning, as illustrated in Figure 2.4. SML is low on control, but not in the same way as in the provision of open learning materials. Many of these frequently remain unused on the shelves of company learning centres. SML programmes are structured (through time-tabled events, learning contracts and learning groups, etc.) but not controlling, so that participants have the opportunity to make their own decisions about their learning goals and methods.

Participants making their own decisions in this way brings us back to the issue of responsibility. SML is about being *responsible to* learners by providing appropriate support (structure) so that they can really take charge of, and be *responsible for*, their own development. None the less, taking charge is not easy. Many people find it a considerable challenge, particularly initially. How challenging they find it will depend on their personal approach to learning. Each person's approach will itself have been learned, and is rooted in their past experiences.

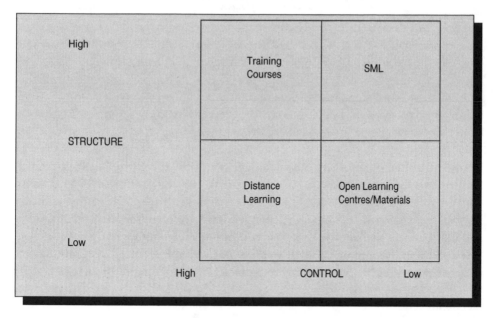

Figure 2.4   Structure and control

APPROACHES TO LEARNING

A simple model suggests that there may be four approaches to learning, and that often people go through these approaches in stages. We will take each approach in turn.

Dependent

In this mode learners may be highly passive, expecting others to teach them everything without their needing to take their own initiatives. Learners may also absorb uncritically what others tell them. This mode may be characterized by laziness and procrastination in some people. It is clearly seen by many people as resulting from experiences in education. Even recent innovations in the field of people development in organizations have not actually changed this kind of experience. For example, witness the increasing use of generic and organization-specific competency frameworks in the provision of learning opportunities and, particularly, the measurement of learning outcomes. Their use may suggest a desire on the part of many organizations to be better able to engage learners' interests by offering programmes with greater relevance. However, to the extent that learners are expected to match or restrict their learning to the framework concerned, the context for learning is no different from that associated with a traditional taught curriculum; and so often going hand in hand with the taught curriculum is the 'hidden curriculum' of dependency.

Counterdependent

This mode is associated with rebelliousness, a rejection of anything from the teacher, anti-authority behaviours and high levels of criticism of anyone in a teaching role. Counterdependence is also associated with learners playing down the need to learn, not listening to others and often a tendency to passive–aggressive behavioural patterns. It is illustrated by the teenager who says 'I'm not influenced by my parents; I just do the opposite of what they say!'

We would guess that most trainers and developers will recognize both patterns of behaviour. Often individuals can flip between these so that they oscillate between dependence and counterdependence. One reason for this is that neither pattern shows any autonomy or independence in learning. Both are reactions to authority and can be seen as patterns that many in organizations have not grown out of. They will find them more difficult to grow out of if the learning programmes to which they continue to be exposed are high on both structure and control.

Independent

In this mode learners are prepared to learn for themselves. They take initiatives, actively seek learning experiences, enjoy the pressure to perform well and welcome feedback on their work. This mode is one that organizations say they increasingly need and it is associated with a more entrepreneurial and empowered style of working.

The danger is that an overemphasis on independence can lead to a selfish self-centredness. Therefore this mode needs balancing with the next one.

Interdependent

Interdependent learners are keen to learn from others, to support others in their learning, to share their own learning and to collaborate in teams. They listen to others, question others to find out new ideas and information and they enjoy engaging in dialogue with a wide range of people. They characterize the best of a learning organization approach.

In reality the last two modes are also a balanced pair like the first two (see Figure 2.5). Independence and interdependence at best go together. The person who can stand on their own feet and look after themselves is also going to find it easier to be open and sharing with others (since they don't see others as a threat or challenge). Organizations need people who can balance independence and interdependence.

This now leads back to the role of SML. As Figure 2.4 indicated, in its absence, a lot of what is provided for learning in well intentioned and well resourced organizations may actually be reinforcing the very patterns that the organization would

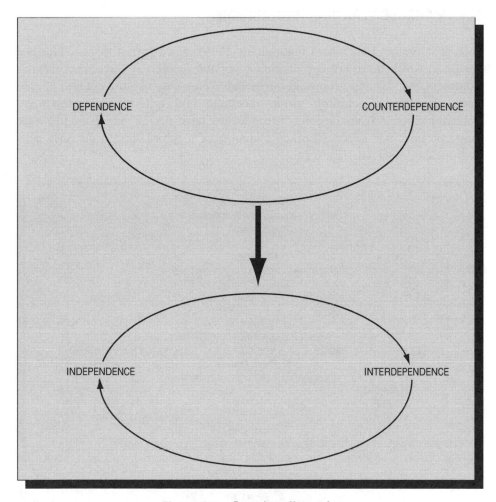

Figure 2.5   Becoming self managing

like to change. A commitment to people's development can in some cases merely continue the hidden dependency/counterdependency cycle. SML programmes ideally encourage the balanced approach described here. By challenging people to come up with their own learning needs SML promotes independence. But the person has to negotiate their learning requirements with others and engage in processes to support other people's learning, hence providing the interdependent balance.

This approach is not always smooth and easy. People can flip back into dependent and counterdependent modes. Hence SML programmes need to be carefully designed and have a support structure that can tackle these issues.

SELF MANAGED LEARNING PROGRAMMES

SML programmes have what Cunningham (1999) calls a 'robust' design. This is a design in which there are certain 'non-negotiables', such as Strategic Learning Contracts and learning groups, and negotiable elements like the content of contracts, location of learning group meetings and criteria for assessment. Robustness comes from the ability to modify the basic design to respond to a wide range of customer needs. The key elements of a robust design for SML programmes are shown in Figure 2.6.

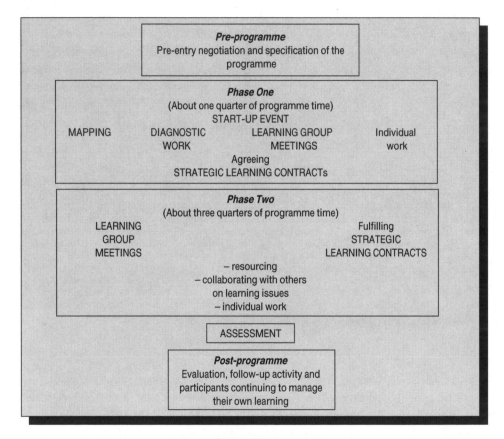

Figure 2.6   SML robust design

The design shown in Figure 2.6 is not intended to represent all the possibilities for SML programmes. Rather it shows one design that can be modified to suit a wide range of possibilities. This range is illustrated in the case studies in the chapters that follow. In preparation for these studies we have so far looked at two of the key elements highlighted in capitals in the diagram, the Strategic Learning

Contract and the learning group. We will shortly look at the remainder – the start-up event, mapping, diagnostic activities and assessment. However, before doing so we will make some remarks about the two-phase nature of the design and pre- and post-programme activities.

The essence of the design is a first phase which uses a start-up event and learning group meetings to assist the learner to produce an agreed Strategic Learning Contract. The learner will also be doing individual work such as writing the contract. This is an iterative process in which drafts are prepared and then checked out in the learning group and with relevant others outside (e.g. manager, mentor). In phase two the contract is put into practice using live work experience and regular learning group meetings. This leads to an end point assessment. The diagram also points to the importance of pre- and post-programme activities. The organizational case studies in forthcoming chapters provide examples of a range of pre-programme activities and issues specific to the organizations concerned. As far as post-programme activities are concerned, all of the case studies are derived from post-programme evaluation studies.

START-UP EVENT

In a typical programme within an organization, two days will be allocated to a start-up event. Activities within this can include:

- explaining the principles of SML
- explaining the structures of the programme
- locating the programme in the organization's strategies
- introducing participants to each other and to staff
- agreeing ground rules for working.

Much of this would be expected in any significant management development programme. The key difference is the need to get people into the SML process. Also, in a start-up event, typically there is the need to form learning groups, and to assist learners to begin mapping the context of their learning, including undertaking diagnostic activities. We will look at the processes of mapping next.

MAPPING

One important source of support to learners in deciding where they are now and where they want to get to is the assistance that can be given to them to 'map' the context of their learning. By analogy, a map is one way of knowing where we are, finding our way around and making decisions about the journey we are going to take. However, just as we do not typically confuse a map with the real territory it is intended to represent, so any information or knowledge provided to assist learners on an SML programme is not provided as objective truth. Information and knowledge is provided to help learners make choices but, as the metaphor suggests, not in a teaching or training mode.

Information about the learner's organizational context can be provided in the form of strategic directions, mission and vision statements, organization charts, job descriptions, person specifications or work protocols. Knowledge can be input based, in the form of models and theories about people, functions, aspects of managing or organizations more generally, or output/outcome based, in the form of generic or tailored lists of competences. Clearly it's important that learners are helped to distinguish between what they know they know and what they know they don't know. It's also valuable for them to find out about what they don't know that they don't know! However, on SML programmes the temptation to turn this into a curriculum is avoided.

As was apparent in the example of time management used as an illustration in discussing question 3 of the Strategic Learning Contract, the key in mapping is in understanding the needs of the learner before responding with information or ideas. For example, learners can be helped to map their existing knowledge and see what concepts and theories they currently work with. Similarly, questionnaires can be used to ask learners about their knowledge of standard techniques and methods in the management, or in other fields, in which their interests lie.

This 'questioning' approach to mapping is echoed strongly in effective behaviour on the part of the members and the adviser in the learning group. Assisting others in their learning is based primarily around questioning. An important function of the adviser is to be a role model in this regard. Group members should be able to see and experience their adviser assisting them in this way, particularly in group meetings early on in the programme when they are still struggling to make best sense of their learning territory and are coming to grips with the SML approach.

DIAGNOSTIC ACTIVITIES

To balance the mapping process, learners also need to acquire knowledge about themselves, their strengths and weaknesses, values, interests and so on. Often there is considerable diagnostic data of this kind available but it may be in a poor state of analysis. It can include the feedback or views of others, whether family and friends, people they work with or feedback provided from appraisals, assessment centres or psychometric instruments. The trouble is that the data may conflict, may be missing key dimensions or be poorly presented. Learning groups can be of enormous help to individuals in assisting them to sift and sort data, especially where the individual feels it is not possible for them to test data in the organization. Also, where this is the case or where there is an apparent absence of data of this kind, exercises drawn from the training world or normally used in assessment or development centres can be designed or adapted for the purposes of generating up-to-the-minute data.

ASSESSMENT

In SML programmes, assessment is about assessing learning. Each learner assesses if they have achieved the objectives set out in their Strategic Learning Contract. This process begins with a self assessment, which is then checked with others – fellow learning group members, the learning group adviser and, where appropriate, those external to the learning group (e.g. mentor, manager). The rigorous, multi-level assessment of SML qualification programmes is described in Chapter 8 and the potentially less complex process used in non-qualification programmes (and which may not be referred to as 'assessment') in Chapter 12. Assessment is important in SML and participants frequently find it an unexpectedly rewarding if difficult process. They are often challenged to make more explicit the evidence for changes they have made. In the process, they become clearer, themselves, about their development, usually finding that they have learned more than is in their contract. Like so much in SML, it is also important that assessment is collaborative in the way indicated above, so that an approach that balances independence and interdependence is encouraged.

SUMMARY

In this chapter we have provided an introduction to what SML is and to how it works. By way of a summary of some of the features and elements we have outlined, but from a different perspective, we can return to the 'Seven S's'.

STRATEGIC

SML demands that people take a strategic stance in relation to their own learning. Strategy here means thinking long term and with 'the big picture' in mind. Too often learning is driven by short-term tactical demands – an exam to pass, a new computer system to learn about. There's nothing wrong with such tactical learning – it's just that on its own it is too limited for the complexities and challenges we face in modern organizational life. The Strategic Learning Contract is a key mechanism for encouraging and enabling this strategic approach.

SYLLABUS-FREE

There is no required curriculum or syllabus in SML – the learning is driven by the real needs of individuals and their organizations. Mapping, diagnostic activities and membership of a learning group provide individuals with assistance to help them to make their choices of what to learn, but such help avoids authoritarian control and the hidden curriculum of dependence.

SELF MANAGED

People have to take responsibility for their own learning – but this is not a selfish activity. Self managing includes necessary and valuable interactions with others – within the learning group, in the community of the SML programme and in the wider organization. This provides a process in which both independence and inter-dependence can be encouraged.

SHARED

The learning is located in a context. SML requires learners to connect with others and especially to integrate their learning with organizational needs. This, in part, comes via the Strategic Learning Contract, as a means for each person to specify what they want to learn – and to share this with others.

SUPPORTED

Learners are supported in meeting the goals they set themselves in their Strategic Learning Contracts. One important support structure is the learning group.

STRUCTURED

SML provides a rigorous structure in order to help learning – but the structure is content-free. That is, learners decide for themselves how to use the structure. SML is not a 'free for all'; it operates within the real constraints of organizational life and requires self managing learners to work within resource and policy limits.

STRETCHING

SML is not an easy option. Some people think that managing your own learning via SML must be a laid back way to learn. It isn't. The requirement to set goals and meet them is a tough-minded approach to learning – and having to meet regularly with colleagues to discuss progress means that learners have to keep to their agreed plans (or consciously change them).

Part II
Putting it into Practice

INTRODUCTION TO PART II

This part of the book covers a range of practical examples of the use of Self Managed Learning. They are not meant to be totally representative of the applications of SML approaches. However, between them they provide a rich array of material on different kinds of usage. We have made no attempt to keep the length of these chapters uniform. Some topics have required more space than others. (However, the length of the chapter is no indication of its importance.)

Chapter 3 opens this part with a brief chapter that reviews a few cases of SML application. It essentially provides a bridge between Chapter 2 and the rest of Part II – the hors-d'oeuvres for the main meals to come.

Chapter 4 examines the use of SML for the development of senior managers via a summary of an evaluation study carried out on a consortium SML programme.

Chapter 5 moves on to a precise case of a specific organization. The chapter shows how Sainsbury's responded to pressures to change the way its personnel function operated. This chapter is written by the two directors (Judith Evans and Nigel Broome) who led and managed the process of change.

Chapter 6 shows how a local authority used SML as part of its response to the changes in local government. The author, Marcia Fellows, was one of the senior managers in Arun District Council responsible for working alongside the Chief Executive to foster the required changes.

Chapter 7 looks at the case of PPP healthcare, an organization that has undergone radical change. The chapter is written by two of the current HR managers (Rosie Serpis and Mark Aspinall) and the previous manager of the training and development function (Rob Shorrick). The chapter draws mainly on an evaluation study carried out by Rosie Serpis for her Masters degree.

Chapter 8 analyses the issues involved in providing SML qualification courses. It especially focuses on the tensions in working with the university world.

Chapter 9 describes two programmes in Finland. Tuula Lillia, who wrote the chapter, is a consultant working in Finland and she draws on her own experiences, as well as of the two organizations, in showing how SML can be used successfully in the Finnish context. This chapter is included to show that SML is an approach that can translate across cultures. There are SML programmes in other countries but Finland was chosen because it seems quite a different culture from that of the UK and the USA (where most SML activity has occurred in the past). Ian Cunningham provides an introduction to this chapter in order to elaborate on the cultural issues.

Chapter 10 shows how Ericsson used SML to operationalize an organizational strategy of moving towards lifelong learning. The author, Rob Lines, is a line manager in Ericsson and this chapter demonstrates how SML can be initiated via the 'line' rather than through the HR function.

Chapter 11 concludes Part II by showing how SML is the optimal way for achieving real Continuing Professional Development.

The next part of the book (Part III) provides a more detailed elaboration of SML methods used in the programmes described in this part.

3 Self Managed Learning – cases of action

Ben Bennett

INTRODUCTION

My main aim in this short chapter is to introduce Part II by fleshing out some of the ideas discussed in Chapter 2 in four brief case studies. These have been chosen to complement the much longer ones in the chapters that follow. The latter are each presented in relation to a particular theme. The cases here are not intended for that purpose, although each does point up some interesting aspects of SML in different situations and together they illustrate the value of learning in different organizational settings. In this context, they touch on some of the points made in Chapter 1 about the importance of conversation and dialogue in learning. They also illustrate the impact that the different work, or other, roles of participants can have on learning, the value that individuals and organizations can gain from learning and the way that the robust SML programme design introduced in Chapter 2 can be modified to meet an organization's particular needs.

CABLE & WIRELESS

Cable & Wireless was experiencing difficulties in fully deploying the abilities of all its staff as quickly as it needed to in new business situations. These difficulties were attributed to some of the consequences of the decentralization that had taken place in the organization in the late 1980s. These consequences included a lessening of opportunities for individuals to move between businesses in order to enhance their capabilities and careers. For the minority of staff who were clearly ambitious and good at networking, the changed circumstances provided potential advantages. On the other hand, those who were used to having their careers guided from above were left without the concept of taking charge of their own development. It was for this problem that SML was seen as the solution.

The programme was a variation on the robust design outlined in Chapter 2 and, when reported on in 1995, had benefited some 200 people in Sweden, Ireland and the United States, with another 21 learning groups about to be set up in the Caribbean. Some aspects of the programme, its operation and benefits are similar to those that will be covered in greater detail in the cases that follow in Part II. For example, Webster (1995) reports that, at the time of writing, most of those involved had gained additional capabilities related directly to their needs and covering all aspects of business management and modern office methods. Another feature, and a benefit common to many in-house SML programmes, was the development of a network of learners who were using each other, their managers and colleagues to capitalize on resources in the organization which had previously remained underused or unshared.

A feature of the programme that makes it somewhat different from those discussed in the remainder of Part II was the fact that many of the participants were performing work roles that were comparatively junior in hierarchical terms, for example people in secretarial and technician roles. This is not in the least surprising, given that SML should not be the prerogative of those in management roles alone. It is genuinely appropriate for all levels and, as evidenced by the international nature of the participant group in Cable & Wireless, not restricted to the traditional consumer of management education and development – the white, middle-class male.

There were some in Cable & Wireless who were reluctant to get involved, however. By and large, according to Webster, these were more senior managers. It appears that the greater the involvement of junior staff, the greater the reluctance to participate of those who were more senior. There are a number of real issues associated with the development of senior managers that can be addressed particularly effectively with SML. What these problems are, and the way in which SML can be a powerful solution, will be examined in some detail in the next chapter. What this case illustrates perhaps is the point that reluctance on the part of individuals (and organizations) to get involved in SML is not usually based on a rational weighing up of the evidence of its effectiveness. Other criteria come into play. These can often have social or cultural roots, typically related to status, power and politics.

CHIEF EXECUTIVES PROGRAMME

This case is different from the majority of those covered in Part II. It is not confined to one organization but was provided for people at the top of a number of them. It is also about an action learning rather than an SML programme. Action learning is one of the approaches to learning and development on which SML draws. The key feature of action learning is the learning group (typically called a learning set) which, as in SML, is a small group with an adviser which meets regularly to provide the context for the kinds of learning conversations introduced in Chapter 1. Given that action learning programmes do not require participants to develop and use Strategic Learning Contracts or participate in the other elements of the SML robust design outlined in Chapter 2, why include a case of this kind in this chapter?

The answer to this question has three parts. Firstly, as noted above, like SML action learning capitalizes on conversation and dialogue rather than the traditional inputs, discussion and debate that are typical of much manager development. Secondly, the fact that SML and action learning share this important characteristic means that the experiences of the chief executives in the programme concerned should tell us some things of significance about learning and development that are applicable in an SML context, and for people at the top of organizations in particular. The experiences of the chief executives concerned should signal some of the sorts of issues that will be covered in greater depth in the next chapter. The third part of the answer is also to do with the fact that, when compared with traditional alternatives, action learning and SML both depend upon and enable participants to engage in dialogue. Action learning achieves this by focusing participants' attention on the real problems they currently face in their day-to-day work. The issue here is that, compared with SML, in a number of ways this focus in action learning is much more limited than it needs to be.

The programme concerned was the Action Learning for Chief Executives (ALCE) programme at Ashridge Management College. It was extensively evaluated (Cunningham 1996; 1986) and it is this evaluation study from which I will draw here. ALCE groups met for a day at a time, about once a month, for six months or more. For our purposes, the three quotes from participants below show the value of conversation over other means to support learning and point to some issues about development at senior levels in organizations. I will follow the quotes with a brief commentary on some of the comments the participants have made.

> The big thing about it, I think, from the point of view of somebody who is Chief Executive of a company, is that in a group like that [the learning group] you are actually able to talk and talk honestly about your problems and feelings. I think it is virtually impossible to do that with anybody else. You can't do it with people you know in the company because you're always defensive or you are always maintaining your position in relation to ... directors and ... board members. You are not as honest to them I think as within a group of people outside.

> The group gives you this support group that you can use ... and I think that if you are at the head of a substantial patch in any business it's a good thing to have. A place to go to ... the fact that you could honestly feel you had helped other people with things you may or may not have said. And also that feeling of privilege that other people talk to you as an individual or as part of the group about their problems and allowed you into their problems and to express your views and to question their views. This helped me greatly.

45

I think one of the important things about that group … is it actually does most chief executives good I would think. Certainly I felt it did me good to be in a situation where you weren't God. You know, you were facing problems with people who would actually disagree with you and you had to accept that they had every right to a different view. Whereas there is a danger in a line management situation, that you assume when people disagree with you it's because they are wrong. I don't mean it like that but you can always solve it by rank if you're not careful.

It is clear from these comments that the value to the chief executives of the conversations in their learning groups was partly a function of the emotional and other support gained from group membership. The evidence suggests that where this support is valued by members of learning groups generally, it is likely to be of particular significance to those in senior positions. As the first chief executive above points out, everyday conversations at or near the top of organizations can be characterized by desires to maintain a position in an obviously competitive situation. I am reminded, in this context, of the metaphor of 'castles and battlefields'. The learning group is the castle – a place to go to recover from the trials and injuries of battle. Where we might reflect upon the desirability of an alternative metaphor to that of warfare, as was pointed out in Chapter 1 with regard to strategy, this remains the root metaphor for many people for much of their organizational and commercial life.

Interestingly, the third quote suggests that the value of the conversation in the learning group itself was a function of being challenged or confronted as well as supported; that the battle is not just restricted to the battlefield when it comes to learning. However, this is not the 'battle' of debate but the combination of support and confrontation inherent in the notion of dialogue explored in Chapter 1. In the evaluation study, this environment in the learning group is called 'supportive confronting' (Cunningham 1996: 320).

From the perspective of senior people in organizations this is a particularly important issue given that, as the third quote highlights, it's so easy to sweep challenging questions aside in other circumstances when you feel you have the necessary rank to be able to do so.

The issue that remains to be discussed is that the focus of action learning is more limited than it needs to be. The evaluation study showed that most participants benefited from the chief executives programme. There were specific organizational pay-offs for some and opportunities for self analysis and personal re-appraisal for many. However, for some people the focus in action learning on the problems they currently faced in their day-to-day work wasn't enough. For example:

I think I would very much like to learn more how to actually deal with those problems identified; how to solve them as well as realizing I've got them. I'm not sure I actually found out that at the end of the day. If you like I'm still struggling with the problem.

The basic notion of working on problems before working on solutions is valid enough but if solutions are not eventually addressed the programme is missing something. Although this might seem to justify adding a taught element to such a programme, the evaluation study provided no support for such a position. Of the chief executives interviewed, none wanted such a move. What seemed to be needed was the freedom for participants to access learning resources as they chose. In order to do this they needed assistance in knowing what was available. As shown in Chapter 2, from an SML perspective this does not mean teaching people but, through the mapping process and the Strategic Learning Contract, helping them to find their own ways of meeting their own needs. With a Strategic Learning Contract the participant above would have had the opportunity to clarify current problems as part of answering question 2 ('Where am I now?') and, through answering the remaining questions, would have been helped to find and work on the solution. Also he or she would have had the opportunity to 'learn more how to actually deal with those problems identified'.

As demonstrated in the longer case studies in the chapters that follow, SML locates learning clearly in the foreground (as distinct from action). A final point about SML in this context is linked to another aspect of the limited focus of action learning. As covered in Chapter 2, SML is concerned with participants' longer term, bigger picture, strategic learning, rather than the inevitably more limited and tactical learning associated with the focus on current problems characteristic of action learning.

ELECTED MEMBERS IN REIGATE AND BANSTEAD

The contrast between dialogue and debate is also illustrated in the third case. It complements the much longer case on local government in Chapter 6. In the case discussed here the participants in an SML programme were elected members of a council, and from different party groups. This case is reported by Urwin (1996). The rationale for the programme (created by Ian Cunningham and Brian Urwin) was to provide a context for local councillors to be able to take responsibility for their own development in the changing local authority scene. As one participant, Councillor Liz Pinn, put it:

> The new councillor, with time at a premium, must maximise the effectiveness of that time. Long unproductive meetings are not acceptable. Councillors must live in the real world, in touch with customers. The credibility of the council will be enhanced if its members are perceived to be fully part of the community, sharing the same pressures as everyone else.

She went on to comment on the value of SML in the following terms:

Presenting our learning contracts to each other was an odd experience. Having time and permission to talk about our own situation, hopes, aspirations and difficulties was very therapeutic.

Comments, suggestions, ideas and support from colleagues [in the learning group] enabled each individual to identify their learning needs. The next step was to consider how we would meet those needs and solve those problems. We discussed a range of ideas, from acquiring basic IT expertise to honing our chairmanship skills.

By the end of the programme we had grasped how important it is to review regularly, not only the goals that have been achieved, but how well or badly the process went.

Having started with no notion of the concept of Self Managed Learning, I am now firmly convinced of its value. Appreciating the scale of the councillor's role, and feeling entitled to seek help to do it with maximum effectiveness has made me optimistic about my ability to rise to the challenges of the future.

Councillor John Barton commented in similar terms:

We learnt a great deal from each other ... Scrutiny of our role as councillors and our relationships with colleagues, officers and the community led to the next stage of our learning strategy ...

As someone who was greatly influenced by George Orwell when I was forming my political views, I came to these sessions, and their 'management speak', with a high degree of scepticism. However, I have found the experience interesting and stimulating. There were so many issues raised in an atmosphere of tolerance and interest from my fellow group members, that I feel more confident in facing the changing scene in local government.

Finally in this section here are some comments from Councillor Julie Kulka:

Before the [second] meeting I had to draw up my learning contract. At the last minute I was still staring at the computer screen not knowing where to start. Then I realised that of the five questions the most important for me was 'Where do I want to get to?' Once I had established this and filled in my ambitions, the rest followed.

My contract was the first one discussed. This had the advantage that there was nothing to compare it with, so it could not be perceived by the others as totally wrong. I was able to explain how I approached it and although I had difficulty discussing some of the shortcomings, I was pleased to get constructive comment.

Listening to the next person's contract was fascinating, as they had approached the task in a very different way. In subsequent sessions I found the other contracts very interesting. Once this exercise was over, I felt I knew a lot more about what influences and drives my fellow members and I felt a kinship with them over shared needs.

The whole project has been of benefit to me. I now have clear goals in mind with short, medium and long-term achievable targets. I know the importance of disciplining myself and referring regularly to the work I have done, to make sure I am on track.

SHELL UK MATERIALS SERVICES

The fourth and last case in this short selection is the 10-month SML programme provided for Shell UK Materials Services (SUKMS). This was an SML programme leading to a qualification, a BTEC Certificate, so it is also discussed in Chapter 8. The reason for discussing aspects of the programme here is to cite some examples of features additional to those in the robust SML programme design introduced in the last chapter.

The additional features included:

- mentors for programme participants;
- group projects during phase two;
- a handbook for participants to provide basic data, guidance notes on resources and an explanation of the programme;
- access to a 'learning community' when learning groups came together to work on common issues.

The operation of the learning community, and how and why project work was included, will be discussed in Chapter 8. The interesting feature I will look at here is the way the mentoring scheme for participants was fully integrated into the SML programme design. This is an innovative example of one of a range of sources of support for SML discussed in Chapter 14.

The SML programme in SUKMS was designed for younger graduate members of staff. Therefore the mentoring scheme was included to provide an additional source of support to participants in planning their career development, integrated with their design and implementation of their Strategic Learning Contracts. It had a number of creative features and these are outlined below.

Firstly, participants chose their own mentors prior to the start-up event from amongst a group of committed senior managers. Then, during the event, mentor and mentee workshops were provided which looked at the respective roles and contributions of each in developing effective mentoring relationships. The start-up event also included the first meetings of the mentor/mentee pairs, preceded by the necessary preparation for these. The preparation phase included the use of specially designed mentoring checklists which both parties completed and took with them to their first meetings. The checklists outlined the range of roles and activities required for effective mentoring. Mentors were able to conduct some self-assessment with regard to their mentoring abilities and to identify those things that they were prepared to offer their mentees. Mentees had the opportunity to specify the kinds of things that they wanted their mentors to provide. In this way each mentoring relationship got off to a productive start, with clarity and agreement about mutual expectations as well as a planned schedule of meetings.

CONCLUSIONS

I have presented four short cases in this chapter. Some of the issues that they highlight will be covered again in greater detail in the chapters that follow. What the cases show is the way seemingly disparate groups (secretaries in Cable & Wireless, Chief Executives, local councillors and purchasing managers) can all benefit from the environment of the learning group, how features additional to the robust design introduced in Chapter 2 can be integral to SML programmes (Shell), and how SML builds on and extends the scope of action learning.

Senior manager development – the evaluation of a consortium programme

4

Ben Bennett

INTRODUCTION

This chapter has two aims. One is to highlight some of the distinctive issues associated with the development of senior managers in medium to large-sized organizations. The other is to show how a well-designed SML programme, supported by a consortium of organizations, is a powerful way of tackling them. I will draw from an evaluation study of a programme of this kind designed and run by Strategic Developments International (SDI) for the Management Development Consortium (MDC). Specifically the issues will be discussed with illustrations drawn from the outcomes of the study. These illustrations will both highlight the issues and demonstrate how a consortium SML approach provides the means to address them successfully.

The issues explored will include:

- the transition from specialist to generalist
- the transition from operational management to managing strategically
- the need for expanded horizons and new perspectives
- managing change
- mutual assistance in learning
- some individual and organizational outcomes of senior manager development.

I will first provide brief details of the SML programme concerned and the evaluation study that was undertaken. This will lead to an exploration of some of the individual and organizational benefits gained by participants that have a direct bearing on the sorts of issues noted above. I will discuss these in the light of specific features of SML, notably the role and dynamics of the learning group, and an exploration of the consortium model of development. The value, to senior managers in particular, of working with others from different organizations and sectors will be assessed. In doing so I will examine the need to balance the independence and self reliance characteristic of the senior manager's leadership role with the interdependence required both for good learning and for organizational effectiveness.

THE DEVELOPMENT ALLIANCE PROGRAMME

MDC commissioned SDI to design and run an SML programme for senior managers in member organizations. Each programme group was composed of senior managers from different member organizations. The programme, called the Development Alliance Programme (DAP), was a variant of the robust design outlined in Chapter 2. It required a total of nine day's attendance over nine months and the flow through the programme is outlined below.

Pre-work   Participants were asked to prepare information about themselves and their companies to present to their learning groups. In the case of the former this could include information drawn from appraisal reports, assessment or development centres, psychometric instruments, feedback received from colleagues or others and so on.

Phase One   Three day residential – hotel based. Participants were expected to learn about the programme and to form, and work in, their learning groups, primarily to assist each other in developing first drafts of Strategic Learning Contracts. To support this, diagnostic activities were provided to generate data to complement that which participants had brought with them.

Phase Two   Two learning group meetings of one day, each with a learning group adviser, and in different consortium companies.

Mid-point   One day for learning groups to come together, or to continue with separate company meetings as above if they wished.

Phase Three   Two learning group meetings of one day each as in Phase Two.

Phase Four   Final day – presentations on learning within learning groups.
(end-point)

EVALUATION APPROACH AND METHODS

The primary purpose of the study was to enable consortium members to evaluate this method of developing senior managers by providing a systematic account of the experiences and learning of those involved. In addition it was intended that the account should explain or elucidate key features of the programme to others who were not currently involved but who were interested and/or might be involved in the future. It was also seen as a potential contributor to the growing wisdom about designing and running consortium and other SML programmes.

My role was only to evaluate the programme. The approach I took was to attempt to do it with those actively involved rather than to impose it on them. For example, I conducted open-ended, lightly structured interviews with individual members of the two learning groups that made up one programme. I talked openly about myself and my motives for doing the research. Where appropriate I shared ideas and conclusions I was reaching with the person I was interviewing so as to check my understanding of what they were saying and to provide them with the opportunity to respond to my ideas and to express their views. My questions were guided by the need to find out what benefits were perceived to have been gained from participation in the programme, and to ascertain the relationship between these and the main elements and processes in the programme.

Each interview took between forty-five minutes to one hour to complete and, with permission, was recorded on audiotape. All the interviews were transcribed for the purposes of analysis. I drew heavily from these transcripts in drawing up my report to MDC. This was circulated in draft form to those interviewed and to programme staff to give them the opportunity to check that the picture of the programme presented made sense to them and to tell me if they felt it needed changing in any way. No changes to the report were suggested.

THE DEVELOPMENT OF SENIOR MANAGERS

Like all SML programmes, DAP offered potential benefits to participants and their organizations through their involvement in a significant development programme which was intended to integrate learning with real business needs. It was designed to offer the greatest potential benefit to those in senior positions who:

- wanted to build on success;
- were committed to their own development – and prepared to take responsibility for it;
- were open to new ideas and prepared to take the initiative; and
- were capable of further career enhancement.

Not surprisingly, participants were also expected to be in positions of substantial responsibility and, like many senior managers in medium to large-sized organizations, able to draw on significant organizational experience gained through several years in more junior positions. However, the programme was designed on the premise that several years of organizational experience alone is not necessarily sufficient for effectiveness at senior levels. For example, the results of the evaluation study showed that the programme was of value to participants in contributing to their achievement of one or more of the following:

- making the transition from specialist to generalist
- making the transition from operational management to managing strategically
- gaining expanded horizons and new perspectives.

I will deal with each of these elements in turn.

FROM SPECIALIST TO GENERALIST

Years of organizational experience alone may be insufficient for effectiveness at senior levels particularly if it has been restricted to specialist or functional roles. As one participant commented,

> I've learned that for me there is no point in being a specialist in a particularly small part of the company. To be a generalist is the way forward and to be flexible and adjust quickly to change. I think I've realized that over the course of the months.

Another participant encapsulated this element in the notion of the need to develop as an 'all-round' manager.

> I suppose developing as the more all-round manager in my case. Being very good at certain parts of your job isn't enough. You have to be very good at change — throwing away the way you've done it for the last two years and starting a new way. That's the way to achieve survival and progress. I now raise my head above all the work to see that.

As illustrated above, participants were concerned about the processes of managing generally and, in particular, about the process of managing change. Change as an issue came up frequently in my conversations with them and I will be returning to it again later.

FROM OPERATIONAL MANAGEMENT TO MANAGING STRATEGICALLY

Compared with their junior colleagues we might reasonably expect those in more senior positions to have a more significant involvement at strategic levels in the organization. Years of organizational managerial experience can make an important contribution to their effectiveness in this sphere too. Again, however, such experience is insufficient on its own, particularly if it has been restricted to operational management. What is demonstrated in the quote below is how thinking and acting more strategically were intimately bound up with the participant's experience of managing their own development. This in turn involved working with a longer term vision while unlearning habits rooted in the past.

> You certainly can't [think about the long term] when you're doing 60 hours a week, thinking everything is the right way round because you're immersed in it. So, I'm stand-

ing back, asking other people for their points of view – planning my way of working over the much longer term. It took a long time to get rid of that feeling that I had to produce something now that was measurable. At the end of six months I thought, 'I haven't really produced much that is really measurable.' I mean there's been a lot of change going on and I've achieved a lot of sub-goals. The difference now is I don't get so caught up in the nitty gritty of what I have to do and allow that to cloud my vision of the direction I'm heading towards, which it can so easily do. It's a difficult thing to do but now I'm finding ways to balance it.

The mechanism that had prompted and enabled this individual to begin to break old patterns, particularly in the face of the evident difficulty experienced in doing so, was the Strategic Learning Contract. Another participant commented on the difficulties and struggles involved, and how the recognition of them was itself part of their own development:

I gave a great deal of thought to the process of development in an organization, and my own role in my personal development, and that's probably the first time I'd given any thought to that ... One of the most important contributions was finding out that everyone was having difficulties. So people really were struggling with it. Talking to others made me realize it was a very important thing to start to do. It reaffirmed that I was going to be responsible for this myself and that in the future it was going to be more and more my responsibility not less and less.

These quotes are testimony to the need for the learning process to match the desired outcomes of development. In the case of senior managers, the SML approach is a particularly appropriate match given that the desired outcomes in today's organizations include increased self responsibility, leadership in the sphere of learning and development and enhanced capabilities to work strategically rather than just tactically and operationally. An important point to reinforce is that outcomes like these and their achievement can be related as much to the individual's participation in the process of SML as to their inclusion in the substance of their Strategic Learning Contract.

THE NEED FOR EXPANDED HORIZONS AND NEW PERSPECTIVES

An important element of taking a more strategic approach is looking to the bigger picture as well as the longer term. Doing this effectively can prove difficult if the senior manager's experience has been gained in only one organization or sector. This is particularly likely to be the case in those organizations that have invested a lot in developing people to fit what is seen and valued as a strong culture that can be linked historically with business success. As one of the participants remarked,

We are quite a specialized company; we do things in a particular way and tend to develop people to fit the business ... It's probably true in all organizations: you fit the culture, you process people.

All cultures are based on shared and unquestioned assumptions. However, the present and the future are demanding that what is taken for granted is questioned and that senior managers take a lead in doing this. This implies that the development opportunities offered to them should provide them with new vantage points on their own experience; in the way of the common experience of travellers who come to understand their own culture better at a distance and by contrasting it with those in foreign lands.

Well-established ways of doing things in any organization inevitably limit or constrain thinking, so one of the benefits of interacting with others from different organizations or sectors is associated with the generation of new ideas or alternatives. This is shown in the next two quotes.

> For me I think the benefit and probably the enjoyment, has been the fact that I've interacted with a group of people who are not part of this organization. They are of similar status but from different companies ... It enabled me, I think, in the periods between the learning group meetings when issues came up to say, 'I'll log that and I'll raise that at the next meeting. I'll get the group thinking on it.' I've not had that before. I think that was the biggest benefit to me. The power of group thinking but outside the organization.

> It allowed me to build in experience of people outside my organization. There tend to be tried and tested ways of doing things in any company. By working with people at a similar level from other industries – again it generated alternatives that perhaps I wouldn't have got from people working in my own organization.

In DAP the learning group was also of value because, at another level, it highlighted the similarities between members and their situations rather than the differences. The quote below illustrates this.

> The whole thing seems to me to be based on change ... It was really good to go into and work with people in different industries. We're blinkered in our industry – no other industry could possibly have the problems that we do – and it was a real eye-opener to see that it doesn't matter what industry you are in, they all seem to be going through this period of dramatic change. There are differences but also similarities that I would never have realized.

Here, the participant has articulated a frequently cited theme in the evaluation evidence – the significance to participants of managing or leading change. I will deal with this issue next.

MANAGING CHANGE

The relationship between organizational change and the role and development of senior managers can take various forms. Some of these are illustrated in the quotes from DAP participants below. Each quote is followed by a brief commentary intended to point up the features of the person's experience and learning salient to this theme.

> In a way I came on the programme at the right time, because a month before we had gone through a major change with my staff – bringing two groups of people together who had never worked together before and totally changing the format … But being on the programme and being with the learning group helped with all that. As far as I'm concerned that was one of the most difficult things I've had to deal with in my career so far. And, yeah, things may get more difficult; but as far as dealing with people is concerned, it couldn't get much more difficult than that … when you're having to change your work, change the people you're working with, build up new relationships and deal with completely new sorts of work. There was a lot happening in a very short space of time. So, having done all that, I know it's going to happen again in the future. So the timing was quite good actually.

Here the participant's learning was inextricably involved in managing change in a specific set of circumstances and time-scales. Membership of the learning group was clearly of value and was a timely source of support. The comment below shows another, and frequently cited, aspect of learning associated with managing change. This is the relationship between successful change management and feelings of confidence.

> There's no question it was a confidence builder; undoubtedly. Generally speaking, I feel more self worth. It made me realize I was capable of doing what previously I had been wary and frightened of. It made me terribly relaxed about changes. We will be going through some really dramatic changes over the next couple of years. I have no idea at the moment how they are going to affect me. A year ago I would have been worried sick about it but now, let it happen. I'm ready for it. I think I can say with confidence that the programme really did help me there.

For the participant above, their growth in confidence was rooted in judgements of self worth which were based less, apparently, on learning new skills than on the re-evaluation of their current capabilities. Further, they have reported moving from being 'worried sick' about uncertainty to being 'relaxed' about it. This suggests a development in their way of construing the process of managing change; from the notion of needing to be able to predict the future, and worrying when faced with its inevitable unpredictability, to the notion of being prepared or ready for it, whatever it may bring. This process of reflection and re-evaluation is attributable to several months involvement in the SML process. The significance of sharing this process with others from different organizations is shown in the following quote. Part of the senior manager's evaluation or re-evaluation of their situation and capabilities can valuably include the benchmarking that comes from comparing and contrasting oneself with others who are 'of similar status but from different companies'.

> At one stage in the programme, when things were even more unsure than they are now, when I was thinking, 'How much longer am I going to stay in this organization?', I felt, 'You're a senior manager now. Do you have to stay in this sector? Could you manage outside this industry?' I firmly believe I could. Obviously I wouldn't have the background skills of the industry, but I would be able to manage. I realized that I was not in a tiny little corner. I do love my job and I intend to stay here but I have no fears now about

what might happen. If it happens, it happens. I'd rather be in here with the changes than out there making rather more dramatic ones. So all of that did come out of it. In bits – it doesn't all happen at once.

In both this and the preceding sections, evidence has been presented about the value of mutual assistance in learning, the power of the SML learning group and, with the latter in mind, the added value that stemmed from the fact that each group comprised people from different organizations in MDC. I will say more about MDC and the rationale for a consortium approach to senior manager development next. Having done so, I will return to a further examination of the ways in which others can assist the senior manager in their learning.

THE CONSORTIUM APPROACH

The consortium model offers a way for organizations from different sectors to come together to pursue their common interest in providing opportunities for their senior people to engage in a range of development activities. In particular, it has the potential to provide opportunities for both representatives of member organizations and their senior managers to overcome the potential narrowness of view associated with organizational or sector-specific experience. Of course, an organization does not have to be a member of a consortium to find open or public development programmes in which senior managers can be exposed to views and perspectives different from their own. However, as part of a consortium, the organization can benefit potentially from both the advantages of openness and the economic and other powers that come from the collective commissioning of services. Thus programmes can be open, like a wholly public programme, and, at the same time, tailored to the needs of consortium members.

The participants in the DAP that was the subject of my evaluation study were from the following MDC organizations:

Amersham International	EMI Music Services (UK)
Barclays Bank	Ladbroke Group
CT Bowring & Co	Norwich Union Insurance Group

The other members of MDC at the time of the study were:

Abbey National	IBM UK
BP Chemicals	Kodak
BP Oil UK	The Prudential Assurance Co
British Airways	RTZ Pillar
Electrolux	W H Smith

MDC invited SDI to design and run a development programme for senior managers from member organizations. The published aims of DAP included providing opportunities for participants explicitly to gain the kinds of expanded horizons, new perspectives and insights into other organizations illustrated above. One mechanism that contributed to enabling this to happen was the deceptively simple device, noted in the earlier description of the programme, of holding each learning group meeting in the company location of a different group member on each occasion. As one participant commented,

> You can visualize the environment people work in but it's never the same as the real thing ... In any company, you get a certain culture or flavour the moment you visit it ... you get a feeling when you walk in a building, you can almost taste it, and it does validate sometimes what people are saying about their company culture.

Of course, visiting the locations of different consortium organizations alone would not have been sufficient to achieve the programme's aims in this area. To have what people are saying about their company culture validated (or not) in this way is of benefit to the extent that it helps group members to assist each other in their learning. The process of mutual assistance is all about each member learning from being posed questions that are informed by the different organizational experiences of their questioners and, by the same token, gaining from having to learn about and from their questioners in order to be in a position to assist them.

MUTUAL ASSISTANCE IN LEARNING

Many managers at senior levels in organizations need no reminding of the fact that they, either alone or with but a small number of people, carry the biggest burdens on behalf of others in the organization. They may feel a strong need to demonstrate their self reliance and independence. This is invariably a feature of hierarchies, of course, and compensated for through the provision of significantly higher material and other rewards than those received by their more numerous junior colleagues.

However, this is not sufficient when it comes to encouraging and enabling development. We know from research that the rate and quality of an individual's personal development can be increased significantly with the assistance of others. It's not a matter of downplaying self reliance but more of recognizing the importance of balancing independence with interdependence – and the need for learning how to achieve both is becoming ever more important at all levels in organizations. For some senior managers the others referred to above can include individuals who are supposed to have a formal role in their development, such as a coach or mentor. However, merely having someone in that kind of role does not necessarily mean that the managers will receive the support that they need. The quote below shows how, for one DAP participant, getting that support required them to approach their sponsor in new ways. They included this in their Strategic Learning Contract as a necessary step towards achieving their learning goals. In the event the process of gaining additional support was closely linked with, and contributed to, other aspects of their development.

> I already had a very good relationship with my sponsor. I had to talk quite regularly with him and, because of the type of programme that it was and because of what it was all about, I was able to talk to him in a way that I hadn't been able to talk to him before. That is, really probing him, 'What do you see as my future?' 'What's going on?' So, it was sort of double-edged one could say. It gave me the nerve to ask about the things I hadn't had to ask about before and, as part of the programme itself in the way it was structured and what you had to do, I had to develop the confidence to do that.

Of course, some senior managers work in organizations in which there is not the same formal recognition of the sort of developmental role indicated above. Further, they might even be working in a highly individualistic macho culture in which it is not the done thing to admit to mistakes or to request help. Even if their organizational culture is not so extreme, many at a senior level experience their aloneness as 'loneliness'. Undertaking development with others can be important, if only because these others become their fellow 'comrades in adversity'.

DAP participants valued their learning group membership highly. It was the feature of the programme about which they provided the greatest amount of information. For one person the learning group was a major contributor to what they termed 'the uniqueness of the experience':

> It was probably the uniqueness of the experience. It was quite a change for me personally to be in an environment where I could do some soul searching, to be quite open and frank in what I suppose could be deemed a safe environment ... to gain from others who had gone through similar experiences. It is difficult to really analyse yourself and I realized I didn't know myself as well as I thought I did. When you take your normal environment away and put yourself down in the cold light of day then it's quite an eye-opening experience. To suddenly think, 'What am I doing; where am I going? Do I really have things mapped out?' I always tended to think that I had goals and plans but when I came to write them down, I realized I didn't have them. I just thought I did. To practise writing down goals and then to break them down ... this was a good experience. Then to share all this with others is what I call unique. In quite a short period of time I was developing relationships with a number of other people in whom I wanted to show an interest and for them to show an interest in me; in order for all to best benefit from the experience. I mean that, very broadly, was the experience – and seeing other people's environments and customs and practices was of interest – but perhaps the big experience of putting the whole thing together was the greatest area of learning.

It is instructive to consider why such sharing with others can be experienced as unique. Some of these reasons are explored below. Each 'reason' is represented by one or more quotes from DAP participants. In effect, each quote illustrates both particular aspects of the 'uniqueness' of an effective learning group and thus, by implication, indicates the organizational barriers to the everyday achievement of the aspect concerned. I have categorized the quotes under the following headings:

- the preparedness or readiness to assist
- the preparedness to be open
- the impact of organizational politics.

I will deal with each category in turn.

THE PREPAREDNESS OR READINESS TO ASSIST

The availability to senior managers of the kinds of 'comrades' noted above within their own organization may be limited in a number of ways. For example, there may be insufficient numbers of people at the same level or with sufficient time. This was highlighted by one of the DAP members in reflecting on the learning group experience.

> When you really sit down and talk to people who are in the same situation, you can develop that confidence to be more assertive about things and say, 'I'll resolve this once and for all.' I think there was quite a lot of that went on. I don't believe we would have done that in any other circumstances. Very few of us, I suggest, have people in our work environments or partners who are prepared to listen for that length of time and to advise actively even if they are able. It was great for that reason. The safe environment, with other people of similar intelligence who had said they would guide you if you were prepared to say what your problems were.

THE PREPAREDNESS OR READINESS TO BE OPEN

In some cases the manager's organizational culture does not encourage the amount or kind of sharing of information needed to make the most of learning opportunities. It is probably rare for anyone, in their normal working environment, to develop the same degree of openness that is experienced, and valued, in a learning group. As one DAP participant put it:

> I feel probably it was the most open from the point of view of what people were prepared to say. It quickly became one of the most open discussion groups that I have participated in, which, you know, was I think of significant value to the progress people made and the contributions that particular individuals made.

THE IMPACT OF ORGANIZATIONAL POLITICS

In reflecting and reporting on their DAP experiences, participants frequently cited aspects of learning group membership that contrasted sharply with features of their organizational situations as senior managers. By implication these features, particularly organizational politics and competitive peer relationships, had impacted negatively on the possibilities for mutual assistance in learning and development. As the quotes below indicate, consortium learning groups provide members with mutual support and challenge because members do not feel themselves under pressure to grind or wield political or other kinds of axes.

> One of the biggest benefits is that you're in a group that is non-political. When you're in groups at work there's often a political undercurrent. The learning group is made up of people with similar aims but without a competitive element, which helps. It brings a lot of openness.

> How the learning groups worked allowed me to say things that normally I wouldn't be able to say in the workplace, but importantly about work situations. So from that point of view I was able to express myself in the way that I wanted without the politics.

> You do need to feel you can speak your real mind and your real thoughts and talk about people in your company – how they affect you. It's very personal, it's very private. We were saying things to each other that we wouldn't say to others in normal circumstances ... Somebody asked, 'Why do it this way?' I think it's a confidentiality thing. An absence of competitiveness.

> I was able to discuss anything I wanted in a non-political environment. The ability to talk to other people without any feeling of defensiveness. I could take on board suggestions or leave them, depending on what I chose to do with them. Even when comments are critical, they are not really critical because you do have the option of walking away from them if you want to – it's more bouncing ideas off each other.

On reading the quotes above, one might feel that if all learning groups do is to provide a safe haven from the normal difficulties of organizational life at a senior level, then they are not necessarily equipping participants to deal any more effectively with these. This is not in fact the case. The learning group is not always a comfortable place to be. The openness that is experienced is associated with challenge as well as support. Through the very process of highlighting these differences, the learning group also provides the context in which members are able to identify and address the features of their organizational life that impact on their effectiveness and learning, along with the other elements of their Strategic Learning Contracts.

Some examples of the ways in which these issues were addressed by DAP participants will be covered next, together with some other individual and organizational outcomes with which they were associated.

SOME INDIVIDUAL AND ORGANIZATIONAL OUTCOMES OF SENIOR MANAGER DEVELOPMENT

What follows is a sample of quotes from DAP participants, with commentaries from me, showing a range of outcomes related to the discussion so far. Following these examples I will draw together some points about what the DAP study is telling us more generally about the content and process of senior managers' learning. One of these points will also lead on to discussion of one more, and the final, piece of evidence from the study to be presented in this chapter.

APPLYING LEARNING GROUP PROCESSES IN THE ORGANIZATION

One DAP participant used what they learned from the process in the learning group to attempt to change the established climate or culture in their organization.

> Well, one of the things I've liked particularly about the learning group is the value to be gained from peer review and group thinking. What I've done is to try to bring that into the management group of which I'm a member.

Another focused their learning of this kind on improving the effectiveness of an established organizational process in which they were involved.

> I've been better able to look to the people who report to me and consider how well they are doing. I have been able to have quite frank discussions with them during appraisal interviews to help them sort things out, and I intend to continue by opening up a bit more about myself.

ADDRESSING SPECIFIC ISSUES

For others the learning group experience prompted or triggered them to address specific 'political' and other issues, by heightening the existence or importance of them. For example:

> One of the benefits [of the programme] was that, at the time, I was in a conflict within myself about how I felt things were going at work – probably a lot to do with politics – and one of the things the programme helped me to see was that this conflict existed and it needed me to resolve it; that it was no good jogging along thinking somebody else was going to solve it – life's not like that. That was probably the greatest benefit I gained.

> There are particular things that I have implemented that are part of my Strategic Learning Contract. For example, I've changed the way I take on work and problems – the way I field the amount of work I do or the number and kinds of issues or causes that I take up with other people.

INFLUENCING OTHERS

For some participants learning how to learn effectively in their organizational context was linked closely with an area we might conveniently label as 'influencing others'. This is an area that, not untypically, is of particular concern to managers whose overall effectiveness depends on their abilities to negotiate with and persuade senior peers, or to have a greater impact on those at the very top of the organization. The three quotes below illustrate this theme.

I have highlighted a need in myself to be able to negotiate better, not necessarily doing business deals but in the day-to-day negotiations of life.

I have added things to it [the Strategic Learning Contract] since the end of the programme including certain persuasion techniques, part of my efforts in empowerment. We have now come to the time when we're heavily into planning for next year and I'm revisiting the relevant parts of my original Strategic Learning Contract as a form of feedback in relation to communicating and negotiating upwards ... I think, following observations I have made, that my negotiation skills upwards have improved and I've produced better results.

It [the programme] has enabled me to become more confident about what I want within the organization, and I'm confident in my dealings with the people above me, which had not been the case before.

MANAGING DIFFERENTLY

The outcomes of the programme included ones which can be categorized very broadly as 'managing differently'. The two quotes below give examples of some of these. The first quote is concerned with the individual learning about their general style of management. It includes some changes that they made to it over time coupled with their development of the means to measure their progress. The second quote illustrates an individual's learning over an even broader front. The learning included gains in knowledge and understanding associated with new areas of work, new work relationships and membership of a new team. It was linked closely to significant changes in their role and responsibilities and achieved at a faster pace than they might typically have anticipated.

Undoubtedly everything changes a bit. I suppose the difference is in the way I manage. That's probably another thing I've learned. My style was very consultative and I have written into the contract that I want to learn to be a little more directive. I tended to want to be the democrat and took everyone's opinion into account to come up with the best solution. The net result was that we probably only came up with the best compromise. So being a bit more directive, I guess that's evolved, and I've developed ways of measuring my way of managing.

At the time of joining the programme I was making a transition from being responsible for one business area to being part of a much larger business area ... I had to gain knowledge about the new area very quickly and build relationships with those in the other parts of the business. Also understanding more about what they were involved in and becoming an effective member of the new team were, I felt, much accelerated in terms of my learning approach.

The examples discussed illustrate that the outcomes of DAP included one or a combination of the following.

● Addressing specific issues, problems or relationships for the first time or in new and different ways.

- The application or development of particular techniques.
- More holistic personal learning, including greater knowledge or awareness of oneself and one's impact managerially, increased self confidence, heightened responsiveness or proactivity in the face of change and so on.

From these examples and categories, one generalization that can be made quite reasonably is that the development needs of senior managers are never likely to be reducible to lists of competences or discrete subject areas with universal validity. This is not to say that theories and models of managing are of no value. They can inform the way the individual addresses issues, problems or relationships, underpin the understanding of techniques, and in other ways make a contribution to personal learning. However, they should be the servant of the learner not the master. If the assumption had been made that it was feasible to prescribe what participants on the DAP were expected or required to learn, there would then have been the temptation, as there so often is, to 'teach' or to 'train' them. Adopting a teaching or training mode would have conflicted with the principle introduced in the section on the senior manager's role in managing strategically. That is, that the development process itself should match the demands of that role.

GAINING A BETTER BALANCE

As the quotes and discussion so far demonstrate, more often than not DAP participants provided evidence of their learning which included aspects of all the three outcome categories outlined in the section above. However, one aspect which I have not looked at in any detail but which it would be valuable to consider in the context of senior manager development is another example of an important element of the third category (more holistic personal learning). This is to do with gaining a better balance between various facets of work and life.

As indicated in Part I of this book, many people in today's organizations are experiencing ever-increasing pressures and demands. The option of 'living in order to work' rather than 'working in order to live' is one that many senior managers in particular find that they have adopted (along with all the 'costs' to themselves, their partners or families) without necessarily consciously and purposively having chosen to do so. SML provides the means for individuals to make more reasoned choices with regard to this issue, as part of agreeing and pursuing their career and life goals. For example, the quotes below give illustrations of the range and depth of one participant's learning in this area.

THE SHORT TERM AND THE LONG TERM

I put a short paragraph in my Strategic Learning Contract about wanting to be there in front, very much a part of the changes going on in this organization, making that point very strongly to my sponsor and to anybody else. And because I have achieved and been seen to have achieved the shorter term goals in my Strategic Learning Contract, whoever is involved should be able to say that I'm certainly capable of accepting change.

TIME

Maybe a year ago I was just coming in and going through the motions. I was working very hard at everything but was it getting me anywhere? Now, selectively, I work hard on the right areas. I think very much about what other people's expectations are of me in the organization and at home and I balance my time so that it is spent on the things that matter.

PRIORITIES

It's learning to be a better manager of my life by prioritizing those things that are important and learning to put other things to one side even if they're the things I'm comfortable with and happy doing: which was one of my goals and one of the things I'm getting better at. It doesn't have an end point. I can feel the quality of my life improving, or I think I can, while I do this . . . so I've changed in that way.

WORK AND HOME

It gave me a good opportunity to find ways of making my home and work life operate in harmony rather than in conflict, although I hadn't been aware that they were in conflict because I hadn't thought deeply enough about it. One of the reasons why I think I identified it was that on day one, in the Life Lines exercise, I saw how closely home and work were linked. They tended to run in parallel even if they were going up and down all over the place. I decided I needed to balance the two – which is very important in an environment like this where we have an operation working 24 hours a day seven days a week. The organization benefits because I'm goal setting and planning more effectively, not just work but home life as well, becoming an all-round individual who's moving in the right direction.

What is particularly interesting about this participant's experience is that gaining a better balance was just that, a matter of balance, and not a 'forced' either/or choice between work and other important aspects of their life.

SUMMARY

SML combined with a consortium approach is a powerful approach to the development of senior managers. I have shown how the needs of senior managers and the contexts in which they work can be clarified by drawing from an evaluation study of a programme of this kind. Examples of the variety and depth of senior managers' learning have been provided and these have been explored in relation to both the processes of the learning group and the advantages to be gained from working in this mode with others from different organizations and sectors. Drawing from my discussion of the evaluation evidence I have commented critically on the temptation to teach senior managers how to manage effectively and shown how this is neither necessary nor desirable. Finally, I have touched on a significant example of holistic personal learning which illustrates one manager's solution to the increasing pressures and demands on people working at senior levels in organizations.

Developing the personnel function using Self Managed Learning – organizational change in a major retail company

5

Nigel Broome and Judith Evans

INTRODUCTION

This chapter is about changes in Sainsbury's. We have both been directors responsible for personnel for five years and at the time when the changes we will describe here were happening Judith was Director, Corporate Personnel and Nigel was Personnel Director – Retail Operations. Since then we have moved to new roles – Judith as Human Resources Director at Homebase and Nigel as Director, Human Resources – Operations in J. Sainsbury.

The changes in the role and culture of Personnel were initiated by a number of factors. One was the increasingly competitive retail environment within which the company has been operating. Sainsbury's had had a remarkable history of successful growth and profitability over nearly 130 years but by the early 1990s it was apparent that we needed some radical changes to respond to our competitors. These included reducing the cost base, which was achieved through a business process re-engineering exercise which reduced costs considerably and transformed business processes to be more customer facing. As a company we also needed to move away from a rather over-directive style of management which had inhibited creativity and innovation.

A key dimension of the changes needed affected the personnel function. With over 120,000 employees Personnel/HR was (and is) a vitally important activity in the company. However, by the early 1990s it was apparent that the function had not responded adequately to the needs of the business in a number of areas. When we surveyed managers around the business they raised a number of important points about the changes they wanted to see. Their requests to Personnel included:

- better support for them
- a more coaching role from Personnel – and help in coaching their staff
- greater visibility – communicate better what's on offer

- use the customer's language – not personnel jargon
- challenge bad practice (appropriately)
- work as an integrated function delivering the needs of the customer (in this case our internal customers mainly).

Alongside these specific issues for Personnel the company embarked on a business process re-engineering project which affected Personnel (along with other parts of the business). The project was labelled 'Genesis' and Figure 5.1 summarizes some of the changes initiated through the Genesis process.

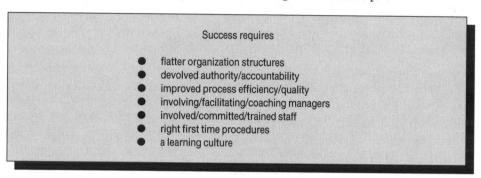

Success requires

- flatter organization structures
- devolved authority/accountability
- improved process efficiency/quality
- involving/facilitating/coaching managers
- involved/committed/trained staff
- right first time procedures
- a learning culture

Figure 5.1 The 'Genesis' requirements

Line managers were required to be more actively involved in the people aspects of their role. The transformation required in human resource management was described as shown in Figure 5.2. The role of Personnel, or HR as it was relabelled in keeping with trends elsewhere, was to facilitate this transformation. The shift in ways of working in HR to achieve this transformation was significant, as we will explain later.

From	Defining tasks	*To*	Agreeing targets
From	Directing action	*To*	Facilitating achievements
From	Following up	*To*	Coaching and counselling
From	Holding accountable	*To*	Motivating and rewarding
From	Reporting results	*To*	Representing the group
From	Management	*To*	Leadership

Figure 5.2 Adapting human resource approaches

Since we embarked on the work we have seen significant shifts within the personnel/HR function. People now do respond better to the requirements outlined in the figures. Personnel professionals are more inclined to take responsibility for their own development, to assess their needs better and to network and support each other, and our customers in the business (line managers and staff) are more positive about our contribution to their work. We will show some specific evaluation evidence later to support these assertions.

CHANGES IN PERSONNEL/HR

The personnel function in Sainsbury's also had to respond to what was happening in the 'people' area in organizations in general. One report that we used to generate discussion on these issues was that published by the Institute of Personnel and Development in 1995, entitled *People Make the Difference*. Figure 5.3 provides some extracted highlights from the report.

Organisational requirements

- 'step' change and continuous improvement of products, processes and services
- quicker response times
- lower costs and sustainable profits
- flexibility from people and technology
- investing in people

Affects on people

- decentralisation and devolvement of decision making
- slimmer and flatter management structures
- total quality and lean organisational initiatives
- developing a flexible workforce
- project based and cross functionl initiatives and team working
- empowered rather than command structures

Issues for people

- greater self-management and responsibility for individuals and teams
- commitment to personal development
- ownership by everyone of their own development
- create capacity to take advantage of as yet unforeseen opportunities and provide a defence against as yet unforeseen threats

Figure 5.3   Extract from *People Make the Difference* (IPD 1995)

We also used the two diagrams in Figure 5.4 to exemplify a desire to shift from a situation where personnel professionals were strong on organizational understanding, for example who to go to for what, and had a traditional HR mindset (Figure 5.4a) to a situation of greater business understanding, for example of commercial pressures and priorities, and more of a consultancy mindset (Figure 5.4b) In raising these issues we wanted to help people to see that the changes we needed to make were part of a wider trend and not some fad that the directors (us!) had dreamed up.

STARTING THE PROCESS

The Genesis re-organization resulted in a significant restructuring of the personnel function. About 20 per cent of the posts were removed and many people found

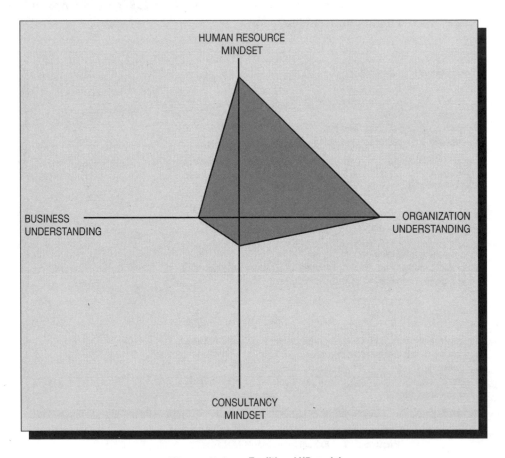

Figure 5.4a   Traditional HR model

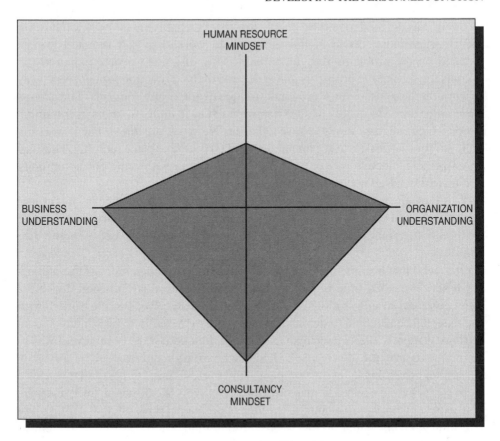

Figure 5.4b   New HR model

themselves in new and unfamiliar roles. We knew that this restructuring was only part of the needed change. More importantly we needed to create a quite different style of personnel operation along the lines we have outlined above.

We knew that we could not initiate these radical changes on our own. One key resource was to bring in Richard Boot and Ian Cunningham as consultants to help us. They had both already done work for the company and understood well the organizational context of the project. With their help we kicked off the process of exploring and creating the new role for Personnel. One important event was a large-scale 'Open Exploration' event. This was designed on similar principles to open space/large group process events. It had some significant differences from such events, as the programme was designed to specifically address the issues we faced, using ideas that Ian and Richard had used successfully in other contexts.

We invited around one hundred people to a one-day event held in a large open space. John Adshead, the Main Board member to whom we reported, came along to open it and spelled out some of the company imperatives. The rest of the morning was devoted to getting people to express what issues they saw following the re-organization. Most of the time people worked in self selected groups focused on the problems they identified. In the afternoon people explored the options for solving the problems and at the end of the day action groups went away to work on the issues. This was a totally unique event for the company. The groups were empowered to make changes happen such as in improvements in communications. One suggestion was to have follow-up 'Network' meetings. These were initially set up quarterly, but by popular demand (!) now take place monthly. They are an extremely effective way of rapidly communicating within the HR community and up to a hundred people attend each session.

A follow-up meeting (also one-day) was held some weeks later and groups reported back on action as well as planning new work to carry out. A crude 'swingometer' indicated to all that a shift had taken place between the two events.

One need that became obvious was that the senior management of the personnel function needed time to pull together some of these strands and develop a more coherent strategy for the next stages of the change process. We worked with the external consultants to design a two-day off-site meeting to be attended by all our direct reports (the senior managers in the function). Part of the event was to introduce them to the idea of a Self Managed Learning programme to be run for all personnel professionals in the company. However, in order to make that work we were clear that we needed to map out more effectively the direction for Personnel. One aspect of this was to elaborate the idea of personnel professionals acting more like internal consultants and less like bureaucratic administrators of personnel rules and procedures.

Another piece in the jigsaw was the agreement to nine measures of effectiveness, labelled 'How will we know?' These are reproduced as Figure 5.5. The production of these measures was the focus of a team building event for Senior Managers who would be leading the function into the new way of working. The measures were later used to judge how effective the Self Managed Learning programme had been. The advantage of having this material up front was that it gave everyone a clear steer as to how we needed to operate.

Following the senior manager meeting we then refined the plans for a Self Managed Learning programme with Ian Cunningham and Richard Boot. We had originally asked them to come up with ideas for a consultancy skills programme based on our thinking about the need for people to have a more consultancy orientation to their work. They convinced us that we needed to think of a longer term development process that would lead to fundamental shifts in people's way of working (as opposed to a short course on consultancy skills). They came up with a design, which was subsequently implemented more or less as they had proposed.

HOW WILL WE KNOW?

These nine points were developed and agreed by the senior personnel team. They describe in simple terms the role for the function once the programme is complete.

1. Managers and personnel professionals working in partnership to solve business problems.
2. Personnel professionals understand the business.
3. Personnel professionals have the confidence to challenge line managers, and the professional competence to address issues.
4. Personnel professionals are engaged in their own development.
5. Personnel professionals use their network to enhance their solutions.
6. Line managers are more actively involved in training, selection, coaching, managing absence, etc.
7. Personnel professionals are brought in earlier and are involved in longer term issues.
8. The function and personnel professionals in it are more respected, valued by line, and seen as a One-Stop-Shop.
9. Personnel professionals are involved in facilitating outcomes. Support staff are involved in administration.

Figure 5.5 **Measures of effectiveness**

The principles of the programme are covered in other chapters in this book. Suffice it to say here that we used Strategic Learning Contracts and learning groups as the core of the process. We also made certain that the programme was supported by an opening workshop to map out the issues and a handbook covering a range of background matters plus advice on writing Strategic Learning Contracts and on how to make learning groups work effectively.

When we started the programme we were still thinking of a consultancy mode of working. We ran two large-scale workshops (of about eighty people at a time) to map out this new mode of working. The workshops raised many issues and one of them was a discomfort with the concept of 'consultancy'. In the end we dropped the title though we still kept to the principles outlined earlier for the new role for Personnel. It seemed as though we could achieve the needed changes without having to enter into a controversial debate about the nature of internal consultancy.

The two-day mapping workshops also proved tricky because we were challenging staff to think and work in new ways. Many found them uncomfortable and the events proved quite unpopular with many people attending them. In retrospect it was probably necessary to have these relatively messy events as they clearly signalled a change in the way we were going about development issues. The Genesis changes had indicated, for instance, that training needed to move away from a standardized instructional mode to a more customer responsive style using coaching, learner-centred workshops, etc. However, people were still trying to get to grips with this mode of working when we launched the programme for Personnel professionals.

THE PERSONNEL DEVELOPMENT PROGRAMME

We labelled the programme the 'Personnel Development Programme'. It was shortened to PDP in much in-house literature, but given the potential confusion with the more common use of the acronym (to denote 'Personal Development Plans') we will just refer to it here as 'the programme'.

At an early stage we had to consider how to roll out a programme for nearly seven hundred personnel professionals that was cost-effective, long-lasting, thorough and in keeping with the nine points in Figure 5.5. The external consultants proposed a design that would require the development of a range of people inside the function to act as 'learning group advisers'. They started at the top with some work with the senior management team and ourselves. They then spread this down to other levels in the organization. The design of these workshops followed that outlined in Cunningham (1999). Eventually we developed almost one hundred people to play this role. We ourselves took on the role, each of us working with a learning group of people who reported through the other, that is Nigel worked with a group of people who reported to senior managers in Judith's team and Judith worked with managers who reported to senior managers in Nigel's team.

One way we found of showing how the Self Managed Learning programme linked to the management structure is shown in Figure 5.6. Here we wanted to show how the left-hand 'strand' (the management strand) was linked to the development process (shown in the centre and on the right). The needs of the business (shown top left) fed into the Mapping Workshop as this latter event mapped out the needed changes in the role of Personnel. The left-hand side also shows the role of managers in feeding in initial data to the development process and then agreeing Strategic Learning Contracts. It is worth noting here that one of the Genesis changes was that Personnel Managers at the Regional and District level switched to reporting to line managers. Hence a District Personnel Manager would need to discuss his or her Strategic Learning Contract with the District Manager (the latter, being a line manager and not a Personnel Manager, was not directly involved in the programme as a participant).

Figure 5.6 shows that after the Mapping Workshop people attended a Development Workshop. These were two-day off-site events with typically 15 to 18 people attending, allowing for the formation of three learning groups from each workshop. The logistics of getting everyone through these workshops was clearly complex. We started with a cohort of 164 people who either were in head office corporate Personnel roles or were the most senior people in the field (at Regional and District level). Hence we had to run ten Development Workshops for this population. And we had to have in place learning group advisers to work with all the groups.

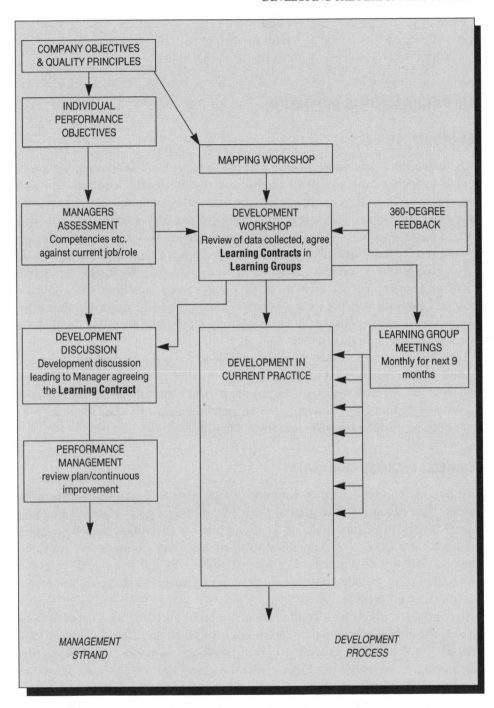

Figure 5.6   Linking the programme to the management structure

Parallel to this process we created three other learning groups: two for the senior managers and a mini group for the two of us. This modelling from the top was crucial, and was beneficial for us (more on that later).

THE PROGRAMME IN OPERATION

360-DEGREE FEEDBACK

In between the Mapping Workshop and the Development Workshop we asked people to gather evidence about themselves via 360-degree feedback. As with most parts of the design and operation, the external consultants worked with our own staff to devise an effective way of carrying this out. The most novel feature was that, in keeping with Self Managed Learning principles, people devised their own 360-degree feedback questionnaires. They were given a handbook on how to do 360-degree feedback and they had a briefing at the Mapping Workshop on what to do. From a purist point of view many of these self created questionnaires would not look very sophisticated, but what we sacrificed in purity we gained in commitment. People had to take seriously the feedback they received as they had created the questions and chosen their raters.

We were aware that the 360-degree feedback was only one part of the diagnostic evidence each person used to create their Strategic Learning Contract. Also the results of this exercise were seen only by the person's learning group and were not recorded elsewhere, for example on their personnel records. The feedback was used only for learning purposes and raters knew this.

STRATEGIC LEARNING CONTRACTS

The contracts were agreed in learning groups and were supposed also to be agreed with managers. The groups were, by and large, quite rigorous in doing this. However, in a later evaluation we found that not all managers took seriously their role in relation to the person's Strategic Learning Contract. We provided guidance on writing Strategic Learning Contracts in the handbook everyone received and we included in that some criteria by which to judge an acceptable contract (see Figure 5.7).

In our own contracts we identified about five areas each that we wanted to work on over the nine-month period. In Judith's case this included a goal of shifting time towards developing strategy and away from day-to-day demands. Judith found that she learned some useful techniques from the group she was advising as well as through working with her personal assistant. Nigel's Strategic Learning Contract helped him to tackle areas such as conceptual thinking, influencing styles and a number of personal values – all with some success.

Criterion	Tick off if met by the contract
1. Demonstrates developing a 'quality' approach.	☐
2. Shows a contribution to the function in terms of the mission and priorities for action.	☐
3. Shows that what is to be learned is in keeping with the direction of the business.	☐
4. Shows contribution to the nine points 'How Will We Know'.	☐
5. Is owned by the person – they show that they are genuinely committed to the contract.	☐
6. Has clear, meaningful goals.	☐
7. Is feasible in terms of time and resources.	☐
8. Is 'stretching' – it will require real learning from the person.	☐
9. Acknowledges where the person is – uses feedback received.	☐

Figure 5.7   Criteria for development contracts

LEARNING GROUPS

The learning groups were crucial to the success of the programme.

In the learning group in which we were advisers, the initial assessments were very frank and honest, and it was easy for people to identify the areas they wanted to develop. The early learning came from sharing experiences and ideas with each other. What Bill found difficult, Susan found easy. The procedure Susan was trying to design, Kate had a manual for.

But there were bigger issues that people were struggling with: 'Why am I here?' 'What am I supposed to be doing?', 'What do I really want out of life?' There was some deeper self analysis and struggling with personal choices: 'Do I want to move location to further my career, or do I want to stay here and spend more time with my family?'

Everyone has discovered more about themselves; what they want out of life, what their strengths and limitations are and who they can call on for support. Discussing where they stand has given people greater confidence to tackle situations, to learn new skills and to take on the full remit of their new roles. So Self Managed Learning has given us much more than a traditional training course. As well as people with more skills, it has given us more confident and able individuals who have the courage to tackle the many tough issues brought about by a changing organization.

Some points that are important to raise here include the following:

1. The learning was strategic for the individual and for the organization. People have commented that Self Managed Learning has helped them become more strategic in their careers through exploring some fundamental questions in depth and over time.
2. The development was holistic. Exploring some of the issues outlined above isn't usually part of a business school curriculum but there is no doubt that it is important in working in changing environments.
3. The programme was not an individualistic programme; it was designed to produce real business benefits as well as pay-off for individuals (it was provided for all professional personnel staff at all levels). Learning groups ensured that learning was shared.

One benefit for us as a result of our mini learning group was that our otherwise good working relationship became an excellent one. This was important given the way that our jobs interrelated. We have different skills and capabilities and we looked to each other for feedback and advice. This excellent working relationship has become even more important now that we have new roles and Judith is based at a different location in her role as HR Director of Homebase. We have found it easy to resolve issues that otherwise might have been a bit 'sticky'.

EVALUATION

We arranged for one of the personnel managers to lead a team to undertake an evaluation of the first cohort of the programme. We were aware that others had yet to go through it but we wanted immediate feedback as to whether we were moving in the right direction on the 'nine points' for evaluating the change process (see Figure 5.5). The evaluation team conducted the following survey methods:

- Questionnaires distributed to the 164 participants on their views of the process (response rate 29 per cent)
- Interviews with line managers
- Focus groups of both line managers and selected participants
- Feedback from a representative sample of learning groups.

This multi-dimensional methodology allowed us to cross-check different perceptions. The research also very specifically looked at the 'nine points' and gained information on a before and after basis, examining how the personnel function had changed since the beginning of the programme. This enabled us to assess not only what people had learnt through the programme, but also what had been applied, and whether that was seen by line managers to have added value.

Figure 5.8 provides a summary of the evidence on changes related to the 'nine points'. The changes from before the programme and after one year were plotted on a 9-point scale but rounded to the nearest 0.5. The scores come from the views of line managers and participants and what was remarkable was the level of agreement between the two groups. If anything line managers were often able to identify larger changes than could the personnel managers themselves.

	Start	End
1. Personnel professionals engaged in their own development.	5	8.5
2. Personnel professionals have the confidence to challenge line managers, and the professional competence to address issues.	5	8
3. Personnel professionals use their network to enhance their solutions.	5	7.5
4. The function and personnel professionals in it are more respected, valued by line and seen as a One-Stop-Shop.	4.5	7
5. Line managers are more actively involved in training, selection, coaching, managing absence, etc.	4	6.5
6. Managers and personnel professionals working in partnership to solve business problems.	5	7
7. Personnel professionals understand the business.	5	7
8. Personnel professionals are brought in earlier and involved in longer term issues.	4.5	6.5
9. Personnel professionals are involved in facilitating outcomes; support staff are involved in administration.	4	5.5

Figure 5.8   Changes in the personnel function (on a 9-point scale)

We will elaborate a little here on each of these headings.

1. Personnel professionals are engaged in their own development

This change was, to some extent, self evidently happening. People commented in the survey as follows:

> It's integral to the process – if you have achieved your contract then you are doing this.

> The programme has made this more meaningful.

> I now have the confidence to put myself into new situations and nominate myself for things.

Line managers confirmed that they had seen a shift in this direction and there is no doubt that two years on we can still see this happening.

2. Personnel professionals have the confidence to challenge line managers and the professional competence to address issues

Some comments here from the survey included:

I feel more comfortable in upward challenging.

I have improved my influencing skills.

And from a line manager

They are showing greater ability to do this in a range of circumstances.

3. Personnel professionals use their network to enhance their solutions

A major advantage of conducting a programme that involved every personnel manager was the cultural shift towards more sharing and support and better communications across the function. Some comments included:

It has improved through using the learning group.

It has increased options and awareness. The group meetings refocused me once a month.

Since the programme I have used my group to network on project issues and general queries.

4. The function and personnel professionals in it are more respected, valued by line and seen as a One-Stop-Shop

Participants and line managers had seen a change in this as reflected in such comments as:

Store managers now contact me!

As line managers have grown accustomed to the One-Stop-Shop concept, respect and value has increased.

5. Line managers are more involved in training, selection, coaching, managing absence, etc.

This was an important shift for the function. We needed to move away from being involved in all the day-to-day staff issues and instead support line managers in their role with their staff. Some people commented that this was slow progress and that, at the time, they had seen little shifts in this direction. Others were more optimistic with comments like:

All managers now conduct their own interviews – and develop staff very effectively.

100 per cent managers involved in managing absence – 50 per cent involved in selection.

6. Managers and personnel professionals working in partnership to solve business problems

Line managers commented on improvements here including reference to specific changes such as personnel managers being more involved in review meetings against business goals. Others felt that they already had a good partnership prior to the programme.

7. Personnel professionals understand the business

Participants were able to quote evidence such as:

> I am now accepted as an equal [by the District Manager].

> This is growing with my role as a result of the programme.

8. Personnel professionals are brought in earlier and involved in longer term issues

There were some mixed comments on this category. Some people said it had never been a problem, others had seen only small changes. However, the general trend was in the right direction and we have seen improvements in this area since.

9. Personnel professionals are involved in facilitating outcomes. Support staff are involved in administration

This point was motivated by concerns that personnel professionals had been too much sucked into administrative tasks and had therefore paid less attention to the real needs of line managers (and were operating less strategically). As the development programme had not specifically focused on this issue we saw less movement on this factor. However, a number of participants commented that they had become aware of delegation issues and were working on them.

EVALUATIONS OF THE SPECIFICS OF THE PROGRAMME

In the above evaluation we have deliberately focused on the strategic changes we were looking for. In these terms the programme was an outstanding success. It was also highly cost-effective. For instance, the consultancy fee cost averaged out at less than £30 per head. We were aware though of some specific comments that came out of the evaluation and we will refer to just a few here.

We have already said that the main criticism that came from the evaluation of participants' views was the variable quality of the support from managers. As this was the first time they had been confronted with people eager to pursue their own development through the use of Strategic Learning Contracts it is perhaps not surprising that this was an issue. However, we believe that this aspect has improved since the programme as managers have come to recognize the value of having more motivated people reporting to them.

We were also not surprised to learn from the evaluation that 57 per cent of respondents said that they found creating and implementing a Strategic Learning Contract difficult. Again this was the first time that people had been asked to seriously consider their own development and take charge of it themselves. Yet, despite the turbulence that required 49 per cent of participants to revise their contracts due to changing circumstances, we were pleased to see that 96 per cent of respondents said that they had achieved most or all of what was in their contracts.

Approximately 81 per cent of people said that their learning group had been effective in providing them with support and challenge. We also know that a number of people (possibly as high as 10 per cent) were uncomfortable with the Genesis changes and were re-evaluating their positions in the company, for example thinking about whether to leave. Nearly all these people chose to stay because their group provided them with a safe, confidential environment within which to explore career options. And they could also see from their Strategic Learning Contracts a way forward for themselves. However, it is true that a small number of people found the notion of a changed role for Personnel (and the SML process itself) too much to take and they did leave the company. We feel that one value of the programme was that it did help these few people to make such a choice and move out of the organization in a civilized way.

CONCLUSIONS

The value of the programme has been enormous to the company in times of change and turbulence in our markets. The principles of Self Managed Learning, such as using real work as a basis of learning, have underpinned a major change management programme for directors. Without the success of the Personnel Development Programme we would not have been able to pursue that and other new projects. We have also incorporated the thinking coming out of the programme into our strategic business planning, so the principles again live on in these new modes.

It is easy to take for granted the function we have now as having always been there, but the Personnel Development Programme was a key stepping stone in helping personnel/HR people take responsibility for their own development. The function and the individuals within it are much stronger as a result. They both need to be, in order to help the organization meet the needs of an increasingly competitive environment.

6 Responding to change in local government – Self Managed Learning in Arun District Council

Marcia Fellows

INTRODUCTION

Public sector organizations the world over are having to cope with great change. Expectations from the public are changing, producing pressures to deliver more for less cost. In the UK local authorities have been experiencing particular demands, not just from members of their communities but also from central government. The concept of 'best value' is one such example. Local authorities are under pressure to demonstrate that their services are being delivered in the most cost-effective way.

Another change is the notion of working more in partnership with other agencies in order to achieve better results for the community – and to use resources in the most efficient way. The resources that are available are also increasingly allocated through competition, which affects how a local authority works on a day-to-day basis.

Increased legislation affects local authorities – and such legislation comes as much from Brussels as it does from the UK government. And 'Green' policies specifically affect local authorities, which are at the sharp end when it comes to environmental issues.

All of these trends demand local authorities to:

- learn more from each other
- be more strategic
- keep abreast of changes
- manage knowledge more effectively
- make better use of reducing resources
- be more flexible and more creative.

This chapter shows how one district council in southern England has responded to some of these pressures and changes. I will say something first about the background to introducing Self Managed Learning into this local authority and then I will discuss some of the practical outcomes of our work. As we have evaluated the use of SML I will be able to quote from some of this evidence. Much of the evaluation evidence focuses on individual pay-off. If you ask people for their views they tend to start with themselves, which can also tend to underestimate the pay-off to the organization. However, as a general statement I can say that SML has contributed greatly to this local authority's ability to respond to some of the changes mentioned above. Some of the tactical decisions made in the authority proved to be faulty (as I shall explain) but the general strategic direction for the development of people working there has proved valid.

SELF MANAGED LEARNING IN ARUN DISTRICT COUNCIL

I discovered Self Managed Learning when I undertook an MBA through the Self Managed Learning route. This programme was offered by Roffey Park Management College and the award of an MBA made by the University of Sussex. The SML approach had been introduced to the college by Ian Cunningham, who was Chief Executive when I studied there.

I found SML to be a most powerful personal experience providing a framework for growth and development. I wanted to share this strategic approach to personal learning and development with others in my work place – Arun District Council – a district local authority on the Sussex coast employing 600 permanent staff and providing a wide range of public services.

Arun District Council has always been committed to training, development and, more recently, learning. The authority was created in 1974 and immediately budgeted for training and development. Surprisingly this was not a typical action in local government. Initially training was very much led by the Training Officer with a mixture of work based training, in-house programmes, including a wide-ranging manager development programme, and substantial support for qualification courses and professional skills.

In 1983 a new Chief Executive identified training and development as a significant part of his approach to strategic planning and managing change. The leadership for a corporate training strategy shifted to him, management development initiatives being created around goals for cultural change. The Council became very performance-oriented and people management responsibilities were shifted to line managers, with clear policy directives and standards being determined by the corporate centre.

A business planning ethic was adopted by the Council and appraisal and training rigorously linked to performance action plans and performance related pay. In 1990 the CEO left, the culture shifted towards a service orientation and training plans became more individual than corporately driven. I then became responsible for HR including training and development.

In 1992 the opportunity to reconsider our training strategy and provision arose and I was able to recruit a trainer, Peter Taylor, who believes in the philosophy of encouraging people to own their own learning. Peter and I then introduced SML into the in-house programme.

INTRODUCING SML TO ARUN DISTRICT COUNCIL – STAGE 1: A VOLUNTARY BASIS

We 'marketed' the concept of Self Managed Learning to all employees. Through our annual in-house training programme we invited staff interested in their own personal development to join a learning group of five participants all drawn from Arun. There were no rules about who should or should not join; there was no selection process.

We held introductory sessions to explain the process and the following framework was adopted:

- learning groups: minimum 4, maximum 5 participants
- meetings: every 4/6 weeks
- programme: minimum six meetings
- adviser: either Peter or myself
- venues: away from normal workplace
- group meeting dates: fixed and committed with only emergency exceptions
- 'push' start for members of groups (based on the Strategic Learning Contract)
- ground rules: to include total confidentiality to encourage openness and trust.

At the same time I was introducing SML principles into the way I worked with my management team of six managers. This challenge and support atmosphere for departmental management team meetings took us from effective to super effective. It was a way of working together to realize both shared and differing goals: a healthy environment of using different styles, perceptions, knowledge and views to mutual and individual advantage.

Meanwhile Peter and I drafted the corporate appraisal scheme into one that emphasized each individual's ownership of their personal action and development. We called it PALS – Personal Appraisal and Learning Scheme.

Peter also continually developed in-house courses that emphasized individual responsibility for learning and introduced employees to techniques that helped them learn to learn and address the core people skills competencies.

THE PROGRAMME IN PRACTICE

The first two learning groups were an enormous success. Participants were highly motivated and acclaimed SML as a most powerful tool for personal development. Their managers reported positive changes in behaviour that benefited both individuals and their service. The programme for voluntary groups continues to this day and more are planned for the future. It is part of the in-house programme.

I believe the key to SML's success is linked strongly to the following factors:

- The ground rules – for example people kept total confidentiality – it was never to my knowledge broken.
- The process encourages task-oriented people to develop and use reflective skills.
- The mixture of challenge and support created within the group dynamics.
- The focus provided through the Strategic Learning Contract – using the five questions and determining criteria for success.

As a learning group adviser my personal experience has been that all groups are different. The framework is tight and provides a discipline to the approach to learning but, of course, the *people* vary and therefore so does the content.

The process means that participants are practising – experimenting – with strategic thinking and management all the time but in an entirely *safe* learning environment.

EVALUATION OF THE VOLUNTARY PROGRAMME

Since 1992 Arun has run 10 voluntary learning groups with 43 participants. I have evaluated the voluntary SML programme in a number of ways, namely:

- a written questionnaire sent to 40 participants
- a discussion with groups as a whole and with individuals
- an in-depth analysis with the most recent voluntary group.

In discussion with individuals the SML process usually produces a common experience of progress. Participants report the following positive effects:

1. They feel more in charge.
2. They see things in different ways.
3. They become more open.
4. They grow in confidence.
5. Their horizons are widened.
6. The experience can be life-changing.
7. It brings a wisdom.
8. They adopt a strategic approach.
9. They manage change more positively.

The points above are based on a general analysis of the programme from the evaluation study. They are in keeping with other evaluations, including those in this book. In order to give some more specific reactions to the SML process some direct quotes from individuals are given below. They show how various features of SML have been valued.

Unique self development process with the learning group providing encouragement, challenge, help and support.

Discovering how I learnt; refreshing, innovative, experimental.

Education is now recognized as a lifelong experience and I believe the SML method goes a long way to achieving this aim.

Not a panacea but a great approach to learning.

Changed my life and outlook.

The feeling of self achievement in realizing your own Strategic Learning Contract is very rewarding.

Open discussion, enjoyable atmosphere, opportunity to try out things in the group, without fear.

Real benefits of building bridges, improved networking, breaking down barriers leading to improved communication and understanding.

We learnt self discipline [and] the importance of preparation.

It gave us freedom to try ideas (especially in talking and presenting).

Gave us access, in the workplace, to an unusual forum of confidentiality and trust.

Help in ways of improving skills, for example organizing yourself.

Help in managing yourself/stress. Taking a step back/right perspective/balance.

Understanding the importance of the personal side of development has been increased.

SML FOR MANAGERS AT ARUN DISTRICT COUNCIL – STAGE 2

In 1995–96 the overall success of the SML groups was, to me, obvious. I was concerned, however, that few managers were volunteering for the groups or indeed taking their own management/personal development as seriously as one would hope.

I do believe that management responsibility starts with showing that you can manage yourself and this was an approach not so apparent in many of our managers, many of whom had been in their jobs for 10 or more years. Most managers supported their staff who were in the learning groups, but in many cases managers lacked the maturity and commitment to tackle their own development.

At this time the CEO (the fourth one, appointed in 1992) discussed with me his plans for a management review. After significant change from 1983 to 1990 we had had a period of stability and indeed since his appointment in 1992 this had been a main aim.

The Council was moved to meet the political goals of becoming more consultative and more community focused. The CEO saw a need to 'get the organization fitter for the year 2000+'. He had sounded out a number of service managers on the conventional option of employing consultants to conduct a management review but their response was, 'why pay for consultants when we have the knowledge and ability in house to conduct the review?' The CEO espoused a very consultative approach and favoured involving managers and staff in the review. He did not wish to create an elite review team. Out of our discussions, coupled with a mutual concern that managers were less than serious about their development and learning came an unfortunate corruption of SML.

At the time it seemed to me an opportunity to extend what I saw as the virtues of SML to all of Arun's managers. Out of 600 employees, 50 people were identified as managers. The criterion for this was first, second and third tier in the hierarchy. This definition had flaws and some fairly junior people, in terms of responsibility, were included, whilst others with perceived greater responsibilities were excluded.

The Chief Executive then embarked upon a tell and sell approach with the managers. He approached the 50 managers on the basis of 'This is my proposal – will you sign up to it? The alternative is consultants.' Managers were reluctant but prepared to agree, or perhaps more disinclined to be seen to dissent.

We chose 10 learning group advisers and Ian Cunningham and Ben Bennett ran a two-day workshop for them to equip them to take on the role. Given that we had had some experience of SML by then we did not have to start from scratch in developing people as group advisers.

The 10 learning groups of five managers each were chosen randomly but with one very simple proviso – you could not be in the same group as your boss. Learning group advisers were also members of a group (but not the one they advised). This double role became a significant learning point.

Each group discussed and agreed a management review task. These were confirmed at a plenary session of all 50 managers. Topics were explained to the groups as follows:

> The Working Groups are asked to consider what issues they feel should be addressed during the Management Review process.
>
> It is suggested that these may be subject topics, but they are open to change. Are there any other topics more important?
>
> 1. What is the future communication strategy for the Authority?
> 2. How should we be developing client and contractor roles?

3. How does the manager's professional role fit with their other roles?
4. What is the role of the Directors' Management Team? How should it work, how does it fit with other Management Teams?
5. How should policy be developing within the Council, what are the processes, what is the role of managers and officers?
6. What do we need to do in future to address the skills needed for consultation, participation, marketing and lobbying?
7. How will we be using market research and target setting in the future, both corporately and for which services?
8. What future is there for a stand-alone Chief Executive?
9. Is management development working, how can it be improved; should we better address succession planning and exit strategies?
10. How can we find the right balance between performance, quality and customer care?

This allocation of a 'team task' was also a learning point as during the next few months group advisers tried to structure meetings to accommodate 1) personal time for individual Strategic Learning Contracts and 2) the team task. In groups where individuals were reluctant to identify and discuss their Strategic Learning Contracts they had the opportunity to put their time and effort into the task and ignore their own self development.

At the time I set out my thoughts and learning so far for the 'Centre for SML' newsletter. (The Centre for SML provides a network for organizations involved in SML and its newsletter is one mode of communication for network members.)

Thoughts and learning so far:

Chief Executive commitment has been essential – it seems to have come from 'gut feeling' that SML will work, rather than from a deep understanding.

I'm still learning about SML and will always be doing so.

If my organization had the money, I'd use experienced learning group advisers. I do worry that in-house individual advisers can develop their own agendas and may have more difficulty than a professional in influencing learning.

Some of our learning groups balance the review task and their Strategic Learning Contracts extremely well – probably a lot to do with the skill of the adviser. However, some appear to lose sight of the need to be disciplined about the Strategic Learning Contract and some individuals are not convinced that it's for them.

Learning groups in-house have broken down departmental barriers and helped focus on the whole organization. (This is especially difficult when your organization does so many very different things.)

The structure of learning group meetings is significant in developing learning.

Creating a decision-making forum of 50 people has been a lot more productive than people would ever believe! We threw out the hierarchy and the 'people in power', i.e. Directors, and the 50 participants decided on their own learning group membership (out of a hat!) and the task topics and their allocation.

I may be speaking too soon, but so far doing it is a lot easier than getting people to start the process! However, time will tell as to whether an improvised introduction of SML blights the approach.

We completed the management review tasks. This work identified a number of issues to be considered. We took stock of SML and management development. For managers the Chief Executive reiterated these principles.

Arun expects every employee to address his or her development. The Council's commitment is reflected in its Human Resources strategy and the resources made available for training and development and learning. This approach is an integral part of the sort of organization that we want Arun to be.

This approach is reflected in PALS (the Council's Personal Appraisal and Learning System). The system is currently being reviewed to strengthen the links between organizational and individual expectations.

The Strategic Learning Contract encourages each individual to negotiate a plan that is relevant to his/her needs and with his/her manager's assistance to ensure that it is appropriate for the role he/she has at Arun.

For managers the value of belonging to a learning group is that the group provides a discipline and support from his/her peers. There is also added organizational value in working in groups drawn from all departments in Arun.

Individual Strategic Learning Contracts will vary to reflect roles and the person. Some may link very much to self development and future applications, some may concentrate on developing personal managerial skills and some may have strong links to CPD (Continuous Professional Development).

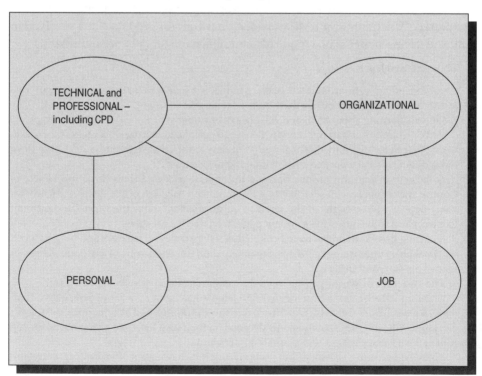

Figure 6.1   Learning contracts

This last point is illustrated in Figure 6.1

There was a recognition that the first introduction of SML for managers as the 'compulsory management development programme' could have been 'done better'! The Chief Executive still insisted on the approach, even though group advisers expressed concern.

We had learnt that the compulsory element and the lack of linkage to organizational strategy gave some managers the opportunity to dismiss the approach as irrelevant, many especially cited organizational change and the ongoing review as a reason for not investing in their own development and learning. So we decided that future learning groups would be devoted to developing Strategic Learning Contracts and group advisers would have their own learning group to aid their development. It was determined that the managers should 'channel energy into self development and fully test the SML' approach.

The learning groups were re-formed and then ran from May to December 1997. This was in parallel with a restructuring proposal led by the Chief Executive. The managers were generally unhappy with the proposals and not convinced of the need for change. It became a struggle to adhere to the consultative approach and it is my perception that we shifted away from the natural, and almost promised, participative approach to the review and returned to a more authoritarian style. This chapter, however, concentrates upon SML, but the background, as ever, is important. The negative comments that accrued to this compulsory SML programme were in large part due to the confusion and lowered morale created in the Authority.

EVALUATION OF THE COMPULSORY SML PROGRAMME

This review was conducted in learning group discussions. I met with each group in turn and I was able to gain a good impression of how the programme had gone. Despite the problems, it did seem that most managers had benefited significantly. However, some had been distracted by the management review.

Here are some direct quotes from this evaluation study, to exemplify the responses heard.

> Experience in the learning groups has been good and has helped set up new working relationships, enabling learning from others in a 'safe' environment.

> SML is an excellent vehicle for personal learning and skill development linked with the CPD.

> The process has a unique value, a useful tool for management and personal development.

> SML should be optional for all staff and left to individual choice.

> Distraction of the Management Review seriously damaged SML when 'forced' onto managers.

Management Review has blighted openness and trust although the group did offer support during difficult times.

Input has been constrained by fear and lack of understanding.

Managers are comfortable with tasks more than with revealing themselves.

Benefit of building bridges, improved networking, breaking down barriers leading to improved communication and understanding.

Lack of clarity in organization's overall purpose.

Concern that the principles and discipline of SML have not been linked by the learning groups and the process being ignored has led to a mixed experience

PULLING TOGETHER THE EXPERIENCE

The SML programme at Arun has been reviewed and evaluated in a number of ways:

- discussion/review in the learning groups, both voluntary and managers' programmes.
- review by group advisers
- specific evaluation by open questionnaire to participants in voluntary groups (20 responses received)
- one-to-one discussion
- discussion at managers' conference.

The conclusions drawn from our experience and review of five years experience are as follows. There is a significant, widely held view that SML is a powerful tool for self development. The proof is in the acknowledged change in individuals felt by them and perceived by others. However, the 'compulsory' programme for SML brought about a negative approach by many participants and this lack of motivation and therefore commitment to SML detracted from the process and its value to participants.

Specifically SML has contributed to people's personal development, in their view, through:

- increasing confidence
- sharing
- understanding others
- providing challenge and support in a positive way
- bringing clarity and focus
- inspiring new ways to learn
- providing an open/trusting environment.

SML continues to be offered on a voluntary basis, while the future of management development for Arun District Council is under review.

A PERSONAL VIEW

Firstly I declare an interest, a belief in SML – it worked for me. I was among the very first 15 experienced managers who undertook an MBA through SML. For me the SML route opened up an opportunity to take an MBA that provided a rigour in testing my capabilities as a manager rather than just my knowledge. The discipline provided focus, challenge and support.

I personally benefited and grew as a result of the process:

- I learnt how to learn ('give a man a fish you give him a meal, teach him to fish he is fed for life').
- I learnt how to use challenge and the perceptions of others in a constructive way.
- I realized my own capabilities and potential more fully.
- Already confident, I recognized my attributes and determined to pursue my own path.
- I gained significant knowledge, indeed wisdom.

In comparison to previous education and training experience these qualities stay with you for the rest of your life.

The SML experience is not without difficulties and for me there was a danger of spending too much time pondering 'the meaning of life'. I think this is helpful but too much of it can detract from the value of stretching your intellect.

The key to SML's potency in my view is twofold. Firstly, there are the five questions:

- Where have I been?
- Where am I now?
- Where do I want to get to?
- How will I get there?
- How will I know when I am there?

The discipline of these five questions being continuously applied and challenged is essential to the value of forming an effective Strategic Learning Contract. Secondly, there is the challenge and support role of the learning group. The fact that the group is made up of human beings of course also means that the dynamics will vary and in my experience can affect its level of impact.

Since 1992 my commitment and belief in the value of SML has been cemented by the experiences of others, mainly at Arun. Something is always gained. For some their attitudes and capabilities have been much improved; others say it has changed their lives. The most disappointing experience has been that SML has not been seen as a totally positive experience for all the managers at Arun. I believe that this raises serious questions about how SML can be influenced by the organizational context.

Like anything there is a direct correlation between what you put in and what you get out. Participants who don't truly participate will obtain limited value from being a member of a learning group. But why is it that some people do not fully participate? Making people join is not a good start – compulsion creates resistance and is not the ethos of SML. SML offers a powerful personal development approach for individuals. This could also apply to teams and/or organizations but it needs to be purposefully managed. I would like to think that an SML style of leadership creates a motivation of 'If I'm going to succeed around here I need to join up and participate in this way of working.'

7 Organizational change through Self Managed Learning – the case of PPP healthcare

Rosie Serpis, Mark Aspinall and Rob Shorrick

INTRODUCTION

This chapter is based on the use of Self Managed Learning as part of a major change process in PPP healthcare. The emphasis of the chapter is on the way SML has both fostered change and made it easier for the organization to respond to change.

The PPP healthcare group is a healthcare and financial services organization. It includes not just a private medical insurance company but other organizations such as Denplan (a leading private dental plan provider) and it has a part interest in a number of private hospitals. It was founded in 1940 and was, until recently, called 'Private Patients Plan'. In 1994 a new CEO, Peter Owen, initiated changes, some of which we will comment on in this chapter. In December 1997 PPP healthcare was bought by Guardian Royal Exchange, which, in turn, was taken over by AXA.

This chapter is based a great deal around research conducted by Rosie Serpis, HR Manager within PPP healthcare, for her Masters degree in Employment Strategy (Serpis 1998). The research was conducted mainly on the senior managers in PPP healthcare, who had gone through a Self Managed Learning programme entitled Personal Development for Business (PDfB, for short). The research showed the value of Self Managed Learning as a strategic development approach which has supported and enabled the management of significant change in the company.

BACKGROUND TO USING SML

The extent and speed of organizational change is ever-increasing as technological advances create new and exciting opportunities to evolve the way in which businesses operate. Many trade in a global market and established 'brand leaders' are facing fierce competition from new, innovative market entrants. The 'excellence' (Peters and Waterman 1982) models of the 1980s, and striving to achieve such excellence, have influenced the way in which senior executives look to develop and manage their organizations. A frequently reported phrase on the lips of many CEOs is 'the status quo is no longer an option: change is a way of life around here!'

Whilst most, if not all, employees within an organization are likely to be affected by such change, the group who bear the accountability for its implementation and who can influence dramatically the way in which that change is introduced and received by the majority of employees is the senior management team. The successful implementation of change is one of the biggest challenges that senior managers face. Strategies that can support and enable the change process to be faster and more effective will provide significant competitive advantage to those organizations that can identify and use them to their full advantage. It is our belief that SML, as an approach for management development, is one such strategy.

PPP healthcare has undergone significant change. And this process of change is continuing unabated. SML, through the PDfB initiative, was specifically chosen as a management development strategy to facilitate that change. At the time the research was conducted, it had been in use within PPP healthcare for the previous eighteen months.

Our decision to use SML came out of a critical study we undertook in looking at alternative development approaches. The decision was not taken lightly. Rob Shorrick joined PPP healthcare as Manager for Group Development and Training during the early days of Peter Owen becoming CEO. Rob Shorrick had had experience of SML through working with Ian Cunningham while with his previous employer and was already convinced of its value. We also looked at the evidence of use in other organizations (which has now been conveniently published collectively in Cunningham 1999) and this confirmed our choice. We will not go into the details of how SML works because this is covered in other chapters, but we will show how it was used in PPP healthcare and we will draw on the evidence from Rosie Serpis's research. However, we feel it is important to explore some key reasons for choosing SML before moving on.

LEARNING AND CHANGE – AND SML

Looking at practical ways in which managing change can be improved, Ian Cunningham cites the major interest that is currently being shown towards developing learning organizations that can learn and change continually, transforming themselves as a result of that learning. Like Revans (1982), he believes that change is impossible without learning and goes on to identify one of the key challenges in this area.

The difficulty has been that senior managers have often assumed that it is others that need to learn but not themselves. Yet it is arguable that unless someone can manage their own change (i.e. learning) can they manage others? ... We believed passionately [referencing the motivation behind the birth of SML] that unless managers took an active role in managing their own learning and development they would not become effective change managers ... By having to manage their own learning they [senior managers] had to really take a strategic look at their own lives and face the need for sometimes significant personal change.

(Cunningham 1995: 7–8)

A second article by Ian Cunningham, 'A Strategic Approach to Learning' (1993), is short and to the point. Linking to the view of Revans outlined earlier, he sees a key, strategic connection between learning and successful change:

A lot of people are talking these days about 'learning organisations'. This shift from arid paper-driven strategic planning toward a more human and developmental view of strategic change makes good sense, because, if organisations want to change strategic direction, people have to learn new ways of operating. If there's no significant learning, there's no significant strategic change.

We know a major problem is that top managers often think they are making meaningful change when they do things such as re-shuffling the organisation chart or changing logos. This kind of tinkering may require only trivial learning for employees.

Strategic learning is different ... learning new ways of operating, including learning how to make change happen in this new, more difficult world.

(Cunningham 1993: 3)

The article goes on to give an insight that is particularly relevant and, from our perspective, typifies an approach that is frequently taken in reaction to impending change. The key is in Ian Cunningham's use of the word 'prescription' with its associated connection to medicine which sometimes can reach a lasting cure but, on other occasions, may only act to suppress the symptoms that are causing the problem:

Often it is assumed that what is needed is 'strategic thinking'. This is too narrow a prescription. Thinking is not enough. To make strategic change happen requires courage, emotional maturity, intuitive ability and a whole lot of characteristics that can't be subsumed under the label 'thinking' ... Developing strategic leaders is not about stuffing people with knowledge, skills, competences or whatever. Rather it requires a holistic approach that recognises the heart and the guts as well as the head.

(Cunningham 1993: 3)

As do Hamlin and Davis (1996), Ian Cunningham, in the concluding paragraph of the article, reflects on the challenge and demands that managing change brings to senior managers and CEOs in particular:

Learning to manage change needs both the developing of the ability to deal with the big picture (the environment, the market, the total organisation) and the little picture (me and my close associates and my family). A constant theme from my research on CEOs has been their emphasis on the emotional, physical and moral demands placed on CEOs. If we are to take the idea of a 'learning organisation' seriously, then learning to meet these demands must be at the core of the changes being made.

SETTING UP THE PROGRAMME

The management team at the time of the launch of PDfB comprised 150 managers with an approximate male to female ratio of 5:2 and a wide age range of late twenties to late fifties with the majority in the 35–45 band. The managers held a variety of positions from technical specialist/professional with limited people management responsibilities to line managers responsible for large numbers of staff.

The PDfB programme was offered to this population. The catalyst for this major change to the development and training strategy was the arrival of Peter Owen as CEO (in August 1994) and Denis Walker as HR Director. Building on his experience in British Airways during the 1980s, Owen instigated a dramatic culture change programme, repositioning the organization from 'medical insurance to healthcare'. The organization became informal yet dynamic, fast moving and energized. People-focused (both internal and external) corporate values were developed which mirrored the corporate brand, 'There to support you'. Peter Owen places great significance on the role of the HR team in driving, enabling and supporting change. Denis Walker, who had worked with Peter Owen in the past, took over the direction of HR in January 1995. Following Denis Walker's appointment Rob Shorrick was recruited as Group Development and Training Manager and given the challenge of recommending a development strategy for the new organization.

Rob Shorrick's approach was far removed from the standardized training experiences of the past:

> We introduced the concept of a strategy for learning. I didn't want anything we were doing to be seen as a training course, it was important for the activities to be seen as: linked/coherent; part of the business planning process; clear drivers of the HR strategy; not one-off exercises but part of the longer term strategic process ... The necessity was to mirror the business need for cultural and strategic change. It had to appear radical, but in essence it also had to be safe.
>
> (Shorrick, in Serpis 1998)

From talking to the key stakeholders, the directors and senior managers, Rob was clear that they did not want a standard 'sheep-dip' management development programme at a business school. They wanted more choice to meet their individual needs and the needs of the business, in terms of both time and content. Above all, the strategy had to add, and be perceived to add, value to the business. The choice of SML, therefore, was not just to introduce something radical but to introduce something that was different and challenging whilst allowing people to make their own development choices in terms of style, content and timing.

The approach designed encompasses performance management (managing the present through a Performance and Development Review (P&DR) process) and 'collaborative career planning' (managing the future through a process called

'Blueprint'). Managing the gap between the present and the future is where PDfB fits into what is an integrated HRD strategy. The whole approach is illustrated in Figure 7.1 as 'three elements of the whole'.

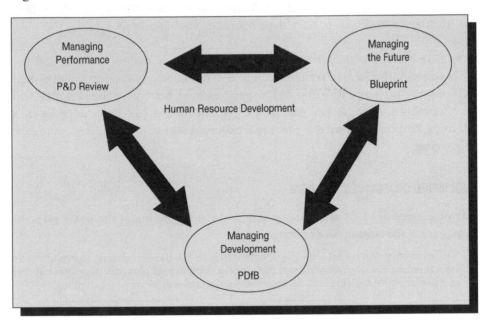

Figure 7.1   PPP healthcare HRD strategy: 'three elements of the whole'

SML was introduced within PPP healthcare in September 1996 when the first learning groups were formed. The programme was run under the guidance of Ian Cunningham. It starts with a half-day introductory briefing session at which participants are introduced to the PDfB concept and given some diagnostic exercises to help them identify their learning styles and development needs. A key part of this is a 360-degree feedback process which is used to provide information on the managers' development needs from the perspective of their immediate managers, peers and direct reports, all of whom are asked by the manager to complete a questionnaire on their perception of the manager's performance. The process is directly linked to PPP healthcare's generic management competencies and the outputs from it are discussed by HRD staff with the manager before he or she starts PDfB.

The main introduction to PDfB takes place over a three-day residential workshop. Here people form learning groups (usually three groups of five or six managers each supported by a learning group adviser), identify their desired learning outcomes (using the five questions (see Chapter 2) to assist the planning process) and gather the ideas and solutions that will form their Strategic

Learning Contracts. Following the initial workshop, the learning groups meet on average every six weeks for a period of some nine months. At the end of the formal part of the programme they then meet informally with managers from five or six other learning groups, and with Peter Owen, Denis Walker and the MD of the healthcare business, to have their learning outcomes 'endorsed' by the business.

As part of the changes made to support the implementation of PDfB and the HRD strategy, the former Training Centre was completely gutted and refurbished to Denis Walker's and Rob Shorrick's specifications, becoming the Learning and Development Centre. A key part of the refurbishment was the equipping of a Learning Resource Centre that provided resources and an environment conducive to learning.

PUBLISHED OBJECTIVES FOR PDfB

The objectives of PDfB are strongly stated at the beginning of the notes given to managers at the start-up workshop:

> The workshop you are attending is designed to give you the opportunity to explore your own learning needs, to learn about the current thinking on personal development and organisational learning and to develop your understanding of strategic thinking.

The workshop notes take this further:

> To promote continuous development;
> To link personal development to the needs of the business;
> To encourage individual ownership of personal development;
> To facilitate cross functional support and networking;
> To promote a cost effective approach to development and training throughout PPP healthcare.

The notes also contain extracts from Ian Cunningham's writings on SML, which are not compulsory readings for those on the workshop. The notes do, however, provide a clear overview of PDfB:

> Linked to the needs of the organisation;
> Demanding - not a soft option;
> Not 'unstructured' – has a **different** structure, responding to the natural pattern of adult learning and is tried and tested;
> Equips people to learn for the rest of their lives;
> Is an ethical requirement for any manager or professional person.

THE PROGRAMME IN OPERATION

At the time of the research study some 120 senior managers had taken part in PDfB. There were 23 internal learning groups meeting regularly and two directors participating in 'inter-company learning' by belonging to an external learning group working with directors from other organizations.

In one area of the organization, Customer Service, which employs some 750 people, SML has been trialed at all levels within the function. One hundred employees are currently involved in a pilot study; early evaluations show the study is a real success.

Some senior directors are actively supporting the process: two have taken on the role of learning group adviser and several are actively involved in endorsing PDfB by acting as mentors. There are, however, a few managers who are refusing to, or finding it hard to, engage in SML.

Since Rob Shorrick left PPP healthcare in September 1997, the guardianship of PDfB has transferred to Mark Aspinall. Mark Aspinall was recruited by Rob Shorrick in 1996 and was attracted to join PPP healthcare because he saw PDfB as innovative and fully reflective of his personal philosophy of learning and development.

EVALUATING THE SML PROCESS

The research study by Rosie Serpis, HR Manager within PPP healthcare, that underpins this chapter used the following methods:

- in-depth interviews with senior managers
- focus groups with selected participants
- interviews with key influencers including the CEO, the HR Director and HRD managers
- documentary evidence
- a questionnaire-based survey of senior managers.

A starting point for the research by Rosie Serpis were the views of key players in the running of the programme.

The CEO, Peter Owen, gave the most relevant and revelatory information for the research theme of 'organisational change'. He describes his philosophy of management, its impact on line managers and the role that HR should play as follows:

> As far as possible, responsibility and accountability is devolved down the business. Easy words to say ... two of the necessary controls (used positively) are a strong HR function and a strong finance function, because you need to have confidence that people can make individual decisions that aren't going to be destructive across the group... I see HR as the holder of Group principles; as coach to the managers and as confidant to the managers ... people need somebody they can talk to in confidence ... I'm very struck by the way the more positive managers in the organisation see the HR team as people who are the springboards for personal as well as business advice.

Asked to give his views on the role that development plays within the organization and his impressions of PDfB, Peter Owen makes the following observations:

> Looking at development and training, as to how the organisation develops ... we're trying to take the whole organisation forward. I'm interested in the extension of PDfB to all levels. Development is clearly not just the preserve of the managers. I like to see it as a holistic thing.
>
> ... I was a little bit sceptical about it [PDfB] at the start and I wondered whether it was going to be sufficiently motivating for a wide enough audience, in other words, I thought one of the dangers of it was that you'd be preaching to the converted: that the people who were already thinking that way would embrace it and ... really the ones who would get most out of it might be the ones who wouldn't actually be drawn to it. But I think that the evidence so far is that there have been a number of sceptics who have taken part in it, that it has been flexible enough for people to derive different take-outs from it, that there has been some sort of business rigour to it rather than it being a chat show for people. I think that we do have [within PDfB] a paradigm that could be taken up throughout the whole organisation. There seems to be a demand for it as 'a way of doing things around here'. It has been successful.

Reflecting on the time and manner in which PDfB was introduced, one senior director and Policy Group member, one of the few who has been actively involved in PDfB, gave the following insights:

> There was a recognition in '95 that our people are important and that soft skills and personal development were two new facets that had to be incorporated in the way the organisation went forward. And for a number of us, whilst that was welcomed, it was relatively new.
>
> PDfB, P&DR and Blueprint have been a very stimulating suite of programmes. I sometimes think that if we'd had Denis [Walker] directing his energies at the business in say marketing or sales rather than HR, we might have done a lot better. But I have to say that in getting that done [the HRD strategy] Denis himself and his team had to act in a very directive way, curiously. A lot of that stuff was pushed through by the HR people rather than through the management ... they had so much on and really didn't know about these things in many cases ... I don't criticise Denis and his team, their achievements have been enormous, and to say that they were done through the management team is true in one sense, but they were definitely led by HR in a very strong way.
>
> I applaud what's happened but I have to say that, on occasions, I had worries that we were doing HR development at the expense of time we should have been giving to the business ... Much as I recognise the achievements and agree with a lot of it, I think the time we put into that relative to some of the issues we were facing as a business was out of balance. It was necessary to change the culture, but it had a price that had to be paid. In the long term it will be to the good of the business but there were short term costs.

VIEWS OF PARTICIPANTS ON THE SML PROCESS

The research also garnered the views of participants in the process. Looking at their remarks on PDfB in general, the following are representative of the range of opinions and comments made:

I was expecting nothing. [Referencing the start-up workshop] Just another 'time waster' [referencing previous MD programmes], if you like. So I wasn't looking forward to it ... I felt that PDfB was a much more useful tool and certainly had a better approach. This is the only one [MD programme] that seemed to get down to its intended and clear focus and that was that it's up to the individuals in an organisation to determine, with assistance and other people, what their learning needs are. What was enjoyable about that was that it made you really contemplate your own situation, your own life ... It's sensible and pragmatic focusing on your learning needs.

One manager, who had left PPP healthcare, made some very positive comments:

I was very impressed by the company's willingness to invest in and undertake such an innovative concept. Particularly since it was stressed at the outset of PDfB that whilst there would naturally be aspects that related to work it was not confined to that ... it was looking at the individual and encouraging them to take responsibility for their own career management. I thought that was very encouraging and quite a departure from the usual training and development philosophies that I've been involved in.

Support from some was so strong it verged on the evangelical:

It's excellent! I think the changes made have been revolutionary and leading edge. I've spoken about it to a number of people [externally], some from a leading edge consultancy firm who are very innovative and keen to find new approaches and ideas to development and a number of them have said they haven't got anything like it and are quite envious of how leading edge we've become in that area.

The emphasis that is now being put, quite rightly, on the fact that the individual must take responsibility for their own learning, it was something that as soon as it was explained to me the logic and rationale was obvious, and yet beforehand I'd never really thought about learning in a business context. I'd just thought that the Training Department and one's manager were the people one should bow to in this area. And the thing that I immediately found fascinating was the fact that there are so many opportunities to learn in the world, in the environment around us. One's learning subconsciously all the time. How much more you can do when you actually decide to take control of that yourself, be proactive about it and be open-minded about all the different options and solutions that are there ... I've been encouraged to become far more systematic about my learning and to link it explicitly to my personal objectives.

Another manager commented on the discussions they had with managerial/professional friends outside PPP healthcare:

I'm impressed by the whole PDfB process and how it's taken seriously and not necessarily through the traditional training routes ... we have more control over our own destiny.

Just talking to managers from other companies ... they're a lot more rigid and less flexible, using the traditional routes ... we can do more in-house ... we don't seem to have to buy in much ... the in-house route is more personalised, immediate and helpful.

An invitation to attend the programme shortly after joining PPP healthcare proved invaluable to one manager:

Shortly after I arrived at PPP healthcare, I was asked if I'd like to go on PDfB. It was actually one of the best things that happened to me ... It was fairly leading edge. I'm not sure the buy-in was there from all parts of the company, whilst I actually think the majority of people who went on the programme understood and appreciated what it was trying to do ... some who didn't attend were saying, 'The business comes first, training will have to be put on hold.' It could have been explained to people more strongly that it wasn't training, it was developing you in many more senses than just picking up knowledge ... It was well structured and had a very good, sound base as well as a positive focus.

The few negative comments related to the programme seemed to come from those who felt that they had been compelled to attend. For example, one unhappy participant (a newcomer to PPP healthcare) commented:

I fully appreciate that when you join a new organisation it is important to go back to basics and relearn and retest your learning in the context of your new environment, I fully support and endorse that ... But it's the fact it was imposed on me.

The comments made at the focus groups showed that many learning groups initially experienced cynicism with the SML processes. Unlike the person quoted above, though, the general consensus from focus groups was that, other than for one or two individuals, this cynicism was short-lived and usually abated by the third or fourth meeting. Some also talked about initial concerns that there was a 'hidden agenda' within the programme. These concerns were also soon resolved for most people. In total, from the questionnaire-based survey, 74.6 per cent of participants rated the programme as effective.

THE LEARNING GROUP

Reviewing the comments that were made about the learning group, the following are representative of the range of feelings given:

Development is very important. I don't think we can afford to stagnate at all, I think it should be an intrinsic part of our working life ... It was a lot more difficult before [PDfB] as it wasn't such an easily accessible route: I didn't have a plan or a Strategic Learning Contract.
The Learning Group gives me time to think about my development with people who can give me an objective view, if I want that. The good thing about the Learning Group is that you only share what you want to.

Some love the learning group process, placing great emphasis on its role:

A vital part of PDfB is the fact that one is in a Learning Group. That is fundamental to the process. In the past a lot of my learning has been with me as an island, or with me just talking to my boss. The relationship is not as open as the relationship [in the learning group] where there is not that formal hierarchy. Being in a relationship with peers, I can discuss openly ideas, actions. They can challenge me, build on them, suggest observations which I've not considered myself and suggest other things they've encountered themselves that they think will be of value to me.

Another comment was:

The first workshop was an eye opener for me. I liked the input from the external lecturers; it put things in context for me. The business link was very clear to me; it is very business focused all the time. I liked the involvement of the Policy Group. I've never had anything like this before in the other companies I've worked for ... it was exhilarating and exciting even though it was challenging.

To me the Learning Group has been central to my development ... my Learning Group has been absolutely brilliant and we have such a wonderful spirit in the team ... there is a good chemistry ... When it works well it gives you that buzz ... it's motivating, belonging to that group. It has been very meaningful for me as I'm in a role where I work on my own. Therefore, it's very important to me to have the Learning Group as a framework. We have the trust of each other ... a forum where you can discuss issues that are to do with your day-to-day work is so useful. It's a non-threatening environment.

Others raised concerns about the size of their learning group. The following comments are from a member of a learning group that started with only four members rather than the optimum five or six:

In a small group I do think it's difficult to get the wide diversity of experience ... and input. It's also much more noticeable if someone can't make a meeting at the last minute, as happened to us, even though it couldn't be avoided. [The absent member had been rushed to hospital.] It would have been better to have had a slightly larger group.

One director within PPP healthcare is involved in an external learning group, which has been organized by Ian Cunningham to enable senior executives to benefit from SML. She highlighted a key benefit of inter-company learning:

The external Learning Group has been perfect for me. It's been absolutely fascinating because on top of everything else I'm getting out of the Strategic Learning Contract I'm getting a better understanding of other businesses which is especially valuable ... You have all these real-life business scenarios; it's like sitting in Harvard Business School but better as there is the ability to discuss things openly, candidly in a very open environment.

Denis Walker made the following point, which was later to be taken up by Peter Owen:

The thing I feel is that this programme [PDfB] and the Learning Group in particular, is replicating real life and the situations we find ourselves in at work. It's almost organisational learning in microcosm. Organisational life *is* threatening, it *is* intrusive. You are often put into teams with people you don't particularly like and expected to get on and deliver. You have to make relationships work. Sometimes it can feel very vulnerable. However, when you've done it once it is much easier the next time – it can even become very enjoyable and rewarding.

(Walker, on PDfB as a microcosm of organizational life, in Serpis 1998)

THE STRATEGIC LEARNING CONTRACT

Commenting on the value of and feelings towards the Strategic Learning Contract one manager, who has minimal support from her line manager, gave the following insights:

I think they're very useful, particularly in the context of the Learning Group. Your colleagues keep you on track and keep you committed. I don't think it would work so well if I just sat down and wrote one [Strategic Learning Contract] completely on my own and had no one else to review it. I think the Strategic Learning Contract helps clarify your thoughts and gives you deadlines as well as a record of achievement as you look back. It's a constantly evolving thing ... it hasn't remained static.

Some found that the structure the Strategic Learning Contract gave them was most helpful:

Going through the process of writing it [the Strategic Learning Contract] forced me to think about my career in a structured way, which was very helpful ... There's been one major lesson I've learnt, and the Learning Group and Contract have been a major contributor to that, it's about thinking about myself as a marketable individual ... rather than thinking about progressing up conventional, hierarchical career lines which is how I used to think ... I think that has been much more productive for me rather than an old style development programme which is much more focused on giving me, say, claims or finance knowledge.

THE LEARNING GROUP ADVISER

The views of the participants revealed a wide divergence in the effectiveness of the learning group advisers:

We were fortunate with our Learning Group Adviser, X, he was very committed to the structure. [He was] very strong and confident. It won't happen without a Learning Group Adviser. In the early days we were not really clear on what we should be doing, the same thing had to be explained again and again. There was great rigour in our process. One of the non-negotiables, [contributing] to our success, was that everyone there regarded the meetings as sacrosanct. I think that during that whole period [the manager was in one of the first groups to be established] it was quite evident that the whole organisation too was making a commitment to the process: it was constantly referred to at management fora. It was high profile, Rob [Shorrick] was a great PR exponent for it ... everyone was fascinated by it as something new. Managers at all levels were going through it and were involved in it, including Policy Group Members.

I do worry, as we move into the second year that those ingredients are not going to be in place ... partly the novelty is no longer there; partly the passage of time; partly the fact that there is no longer the overt board level commitment or championing of it that there previously was and there is no external goal to catalyse us [referencing the endorsement event], though we shouldn't really need it. If we really had achieved Self Managed Learning, we wouldn't need it.

This was contrasted by a manager who was not impressed by the competence of his adviser:

Our Learning Group Adviser was not as enthusiastic about it as the others. There was no rigour at all in our group. The LGA was fairly 'deadpan', which didn't help what was a difficult group. I think it needed someone with more enthusiasm and drive at the beginning ... it came across as if we were to do things because we'd been told to rather than wanted to ... it was too intense ... As much as the Learning Group Adviser is only meant to be an adviser, I think it's a very important role and key to the success of the group.

One manager, for whom the process did not work terribly well, sees the approach taken by the learning group adviser as one of the main reason why things were not successful:

> It took me a long time to agree to go on it ... What made me go in the end was that I knew I wouldn't get a clobbering if I didn't fit in, if I didn't get anything out of it. So I went open-minded. The process itself [the three day start-up workshop], I was very disappointed by it. Our group didn't enjoy those three days. We regretted seeing the other groups laughing and having fun. With hindsight, I hate to say it, but I think it was up to X [LGA] leading us. I don't think X has the experience or brief to be a bit more flexible in her approach. X was very strict with us ... there was little time to talk about who we were, why we're doing it and what our interests were in life. It was 'Let's get on with the Strategic Learning Contract.' It was very qualification driven. It was very tangible skills rather than soft skills: say accountancy exams – you could put a label on that, it was very easy to measure. The more personal skills, the softer skills ... where it's harder to measure ... X shied away from those ... I actually found some of those sessions quite depressing ... 'This is the way you will do it.' I get the impression the rest of the group felt similarly ... Having thought about it since then, I'm wondering whether X was nervous about it, as if she didn't believe in herself and was scared she was not delivering a successful group ... Since then we've had one formal Learning Group meeting ... it was all so very much, 'Have you finished your Strategic Learning Contract? Why not? You said you'd finish this last time. You're not sticking to the timetable.' Anything that was put in that was slightly frivolous was treated as not acceptable ... it was the business all the time, the hard stuff.

This opinion is contrasted by a manager who sees the responsibility for making the process work as coming from within the group itself, supported by the learning group adviser:

> It's up to us. The Learning Group Adviser steered us that way but we managed it ourselves. The format works, it's just a case of sticking to it without letting it become too mechanical which could be irritating; there has to be some flexibility ... The beauty is that you get out of the process what you put in, and more.

This view of the process is expanded by one of the managers.

> I've always believed strongly in personal development ... I think PDfB increased my self-knowledge and enabled me to learn more about PPP healthcare and the people in my Learning Group. However motivated you are, it's always good to have reminders of what you've promised yourself you'll do and that was one of the biggest benefits of it. You've got to make the commitment to the time to do it otherwise it just doesn't work. I think the Learning Group in particular is excellent because, if you like, they are like a little alarm clock along the way to remind you of what you've promised yourself to do.
>
> There's no pressure on you to do things ... it's a bargain with yourself, like New Year's resolutions, but they have to last. Taking the time to get together with your Learning Group is a great prompt. It helps to talk things through and make changes in your contract. Again, like New Year's resolutions, in the heat of the moment you might make ones that you know you're not going to keep and then you start to think, well, are they appropriate for me? When you talk them through with the group, they can give you insights into you as they know you so well. The Learning Group Adviser really makes that happen as they have the best interests of the group at heart.

The divergence of approach and competency amongst the learning group advisers was commented upon specifically by one manager during the 'final reflections' part of the interview and consequently was not prompted in any way:

> I think we've got quite a diversity of advisers and I'm not sure some of them take it as seriously as others. I think we've probably got both ends of the spectrum, to be honest. Some take it far too seriously and apply far too rigid controls and some take it as a bit of a social gathering once a month for a general chat rather than anything else. So maybe we need to get some standardised approach to that role. I became aware of this from the experiences of people in other learning groups, both colleagues that I've spoken to about it, and those who report to me.

THE VIEWS OF LEARNING GROUP ADVISERS

Many of the learning group advisers talked about being 'petrified' and 'frightened' when they started with their first groups: 'The fear factor came from so many people relying on me.' They felt they did not have anything to benchmark themselves against as most of them had not been in a learning group themselves. Many wanted feedback on how they were doing in the role. Several thought that mentors for learning group advisers would be very helpful. They also wanted to get together more frequently as a group so that they could learn from and support each other more.

When asked what they saw as the benefits for themselves, the answers were very positive: 'I see it as helping to change the culture'; 'I get a great buzz – it's rewarding, motivating and part of my development, it's increased my self-awareness'; 'I certainly don't see it as a soft option – it's challenging.'

Since the research we have put more energy into supporting learning group advisers, for instance by organizing half-day get-togethers to review progress. Also now that the programme is in its second year we can choose advisers from people who have had experience of being a learning group member. This makes a big difference to the effectiveness of the adviser.

VIEWS FROM THE QUESTIONNAIRE-BASED SURVEY

The responses to the questionnaire-based survey showed that fewer than 30 per cent of PDfB participants had had any effective review of their Strategic Learning Contracts with their line managers. Those who had taken no part in PDfB showed an even more dismal picture, however, so the use of Strategic Learning Contracts had had some impact although not as much as would be desirable.

These results are supported by comments made in the free text section of the questionnaire:

> Since joining PPP healthcare I have felt that I needed to drive my development – never

experienced any blocking but on the other hand little structure/encouragement was offered.

(Non PDfB manager with three years service)

Whereas I understand that responsibility for training and development is up to the individual, I feel that we need more stimulus from that department as to what's available – otherwise it's difficult to get agreement to things – development for self and subordinates always seem to come second to business objectives.

(PDfB Manager with three years service)

As one manager commented in an interview:

Some directors and senior managers just aren't interested in people things – they just focus on technical things. I'm not criticising here, it just happens.

EVALUATING THE BUSINESS IMPACT OF SML

Peter Owen as the key strategic informant was asked for his views of the business impact and benefits of PDfB. His reply was instantly forthcoming and detailed: 'I think there are six':

1. 'The obvious networking benefit of people finding out what's going on elsewhere.'
2. 'This may not be an obvious one, but I think it's apparent from where I sit, I think there's been a huge increase in self-confidence in the managers who take part in it. It may be a bit unconscious for them ... but I think it's quite important.'
3. 'As a way of, a method of, working. So not just the networking benefits of simply knowing what's going on in other parts of the business, but of understanding that where we ultimately want to get to is that you don't need a dictat coming down from the Policy Group, that, actually, managers see that we need to do this, to get together and get things done ... there's no sitting back as a spectator and waiting to be told ... They [managers] see from that the power of just getting on and doing things.'
4. 'Another important benefit is the challenging side of it. This sort of process also gives people confidence in understanding that, in terms of our values, they have the right to be heard as managers, to say what they think, openly and not subversively.'
5. 'In terms of an organisation that is in an environment where change is going to be a constant bedfellow, then, clearly, this type of working is also conducive to that fresh approach all the time.'
6. 'There is the hard learning bit, what it enables people to do through the Strategic Learning Contract ... where they need to learn new skills or gain a new qualification.'

He concluded:

> These are the things I see and applaud from it and I don't really see any negatives: the talking shop is a potential negative, but I haven't seen any evidence.

One of the brilliant things about PDfB is that it is highly cost-effective. We have worked out that the cost per person is about £1000 per annum. When you compare that with the very tangible benefits that people are saying they are getting out of it it represents good value for money.

ADDITIONAL VIEWS FROM MANAGERS

One of the managers interviewed was a Policy Group member and consequently had managers reporting to him who had been involved in PDfB. He was asked to give his views on the impact of PDfB on those managers:

> With my own people I see people taking an interest in themselves in a structured way ... they've been challenged in a number of ways about things I think they'd never have wanted to admit to themselves ... I think their learning allowed them to accept that ... They've all had weaknesses highlighted in a way that I think would have been difficult as a straight manager to do. They need to see it for themselves rather than be told ... If I have a criticism, it's that I don't think the follow through of corrective action or training has been as powerful as it could be ... it's been better at diagnosis than cure. I'm not saying there haven't been examples of cure, but diagnosis has been better and that's because it's Self Managed Learning ... whilst the Learning Group has worked to some extent, I think there needs to be additional strong ownership by someone other than the person themselves to make sure things happen. Probably this should be the line manager. So if you like, bringing the line manager into that loop hasn't been as good as it could have been.

Most of the managers interviewed found the question of benefits from PDfB quite easy to answer. One manager described PDfB as 'gold time' enabling her to equip herself to be better in her role. The following are a representative sample of quotations:

> I think it helps people to identify development needs, probably more clearly than through the P&DR as that tends to generate what the boss thinks rather than a detailed discussion about you and your needs. It's good to get to know people which is as much a benefit as all the other things. You get a much better network.

Some emphasized the benefit of 'holistic' learning:

> On the personal side ... the more you enrich your own mind, the more you develop yourself as a whole, is all to the company's benefit as well as your own. Developing creativity helps the brain to work better and that naturally comes back to the organization ... For great learning to work, it needs a mixture, a balance of work related learning and personal development; that combination brings great benefits to the business.

One of the most enthusiastic of the managers gave the following broader view of the benefits of PDfB:

> The business and the Learning Group have definitely benefited … I find it very stimulating … when you're stimulated you have better energy levels. It's a great environment to discuss things that normally don't get discussed, but really do need to be discussed.
>
> Really PDfB must help retention; it's such a selling point for the company … I'm very pleased to be working for a company that's doing this … on the leading edge. So many people are motivated by development … it gives you so many more skills in your tool bag and that way there's more value in what you can give to the company. We've all had lots of fun. The cross-functional bit was brilliant!

The final theme of the interview structure ('A final reflection – any other thoughts or comments') proved to be invaluable in this particular interview. Some 10 minutes after the comments above had been made, the discussion appeared to reach its natural conclusion. When the 'final reflection' question was asked it yielded the following nugget of pure gold:

> The other important benefit is to do with knowledge creation. One of the most wonderful things about this process is that through the Learning Groups and discussions, you're creating corporate knowledge. And, because you make things explicit, things happen. If you share the knowledge and ideas you have, or if people talk about things they want to do, things happen. Organisational knowledge is created when tacit knowledge becomes explicit – when it is shared and articulated through socialisation within the Learning Group.
>
> It's about creating concepts and making people plan and take action – action is very important. The more people are talking to each other, communicating, the sharper the company will be. There's more action. If people keep all their brilliant ideas and thoughts to themselves, nothing will happen. This is a very focused way of getting ideas and knowledge shared. Corporate knowledge is created. Knowledge kept to yourself is useless, if you share it other people get excited by it and add to it – that's really brilliant – it makes things happen!

Almost without knowing it, the manager had proved her point: had she not agreed to be part of the research, to talk about her feelings, this highly perceptive insight would not have been shared.

SUPPORT FROM LINE MANAGERS

We commented earlier, in relation to support for Strategic Learning Contracts, that the response of people's managers was often less than ideal: the line managers were not acknowledging the achievements in terms of learning and development that their direct reports had made. This naturally led both to frustration and to some extent sadness from some of the PDfB participants. We also gained further evidence for this from the general questions asked in interviews. However, these criticisms need to be balanced with comments such as the following:

> X is very supportive, it goes back to recruitment as well. He's the type of manager who recruits somebody he expects to be able to do the job. He gives you all the support and framework and then lets you get on with it. We did have P&DRs – development and my Strategic Learning Contract were discussed which was very helpful as my Strategic Learning Contract changed quite substantially over the period.

This view is supported by another manager who reports to the managing director of one of the associated and fairly recently launched businesses. The managing director has taken part in PDfB and is a member of a learning group:

> I get 100% support and commitment from my manager. He takes an active interest in it, which has been really encouraging. I would expect that of him though as I know he puts great effort into his own personal development and is very interested in the idea of the Learning Company – that's what he wants to achieve here.

SML AND CHANGE

Reflecting on the impact that PDfB had on change, one manager made the following comments:

> It's got to be a positive ... generally human nature in the short term is resistant to change ... Therefore, the more people can understand and talk around the issues associated with it and the implications of change ... that in itself will help ... It makes people more aware that change can happen ... simply talking about being and doing things differently gets you in the right mindset.
>
> [The learning group] is a practical environment in which to prioritise the order of development ... and having those ideas supported, challenged or alternatives introduced will help the individual prioritise how best to manage their own change process. MD will remain a priority ... in a changing organisation you need someone or something to manage that change physically and lead people through it and the learning necessary to achieve the required change ... You cannot afford to neglect what is essentially one of the most important parts of it.

This is supported even more strongly by another view:

> If we hadn't had PDfB, I'd have had a totally different perspective on the change process. Because the kind of processes we've had to go through are quite painful at times. Before PDfB I had quite a different perspective on change ... I can now see the reasons for it better. You're looking at yourself in relation to the business strategy. You can see that the company is going to keep changing – it becomes part of your life. I think it's about self-awareness and an awareness of the business.

This view was supported by a senior manager who had a particular interest in managing change, as her role within PPP healthcare was one that often identified areas of the business where change was essential:

> I think it [PDfB] actually helps people to deal with change because, in a way, your Learning Group becomes like a supportive family, a team in itself. It provides an anchor that you can come back to, a safe environment where there is great trust. You can talk through with those people what's happening in a free and frank way. It enables people to talk things through, get things off their chests and get a different view on things as well as see what's happening to their colleagues ... The influence your peer group has on you is very strong. If you're with negative people, no matter how positive you are, they always drag you down; you never pull them up. So you need to be with positive thinking people some of the time to combat that. The Learning Group serves some of that function. Actually, I think that aspect of it can be quite helpful in times of great change, you can boost one another up. Equally importantly, people can also [within the

learning group] focus on the learning they're going to require for whatever new challenge they're being given ... You see people change from doing it [PDfB] – measurable change. You can see that they are better equipped not only to do the job that they are doing but also to move forward in their career.

One of the directors involved in PDfB tackled this area from a broader perspective:

Change has lots of problems associated with it. Mainly because it makes people feel insecure, it pulls them out of their comfort zones ... it's emotion laden. If at the same time you're giving people quite a lot of company time in which to think about their development within a process which isn't simply bought off the shelf, it's not a sheep-dip approach – there's support and stepping stones to help them ... then, I think you're saying to people, 'We do value you.' They gain a certain degree of security: you're developing them and helping them gain the skills they need to accommodate the change ... That gives them more confidence to do their job, increases their loyalty to the company and makes them feel more positive about the change. They don't feel they're being pulled out of one element they feel safe in, only to be chucked into another and left to sink or swim.

One point that came over strongly from the PDfB focus groups was that many saw the learning groups as a 'forum, a solid foundation to support change through the integration [with Guardian Royal Exchange] period as well as beyond'. Many managers said they valued greatly being able to speak in a forum that was totally confidential, particularly if the relationship with the boss was not 'as good as it could be'.

CONCLUSIONS

'How effective is Self Managed Learning as a management development strategy for an organization in change?'

This was the research question that Rosie Serpis's case study set out to answer. We have given an overview of her work together with our thoughts as a team in this chapter. We are very fortunate at PPP healthcare because in Peter Owen and Denis Walker learning and development has champions at the highest levels. We believe that endorsement at this level is essential if SML is to deliver its full potential to any business. The time was also right for SML within PPP healthcare: effective management of change was what so many of us were spending our energies doing. PPP healthcare's approach to people management was delivered through an integrated HRM and HRD strategy, which was, and still is, closely linked to the business strategy. As Denis Walker (in Serpis 1998) put it: 'HR should be a proactive business leading part of the organisation ensuring capability to meet changing business needs.'

Our research has shown that SML, through PDfB, has proved to be highly effective as a development strategy with only a handful of managers expressing dissatisfaction with the initiative. This is despite initial scepticism from both Peter Owen and participating managers. The published objectives for PDfB discussed earlier in this chapter remain as valid today as they did when they were written. Areas for improvement have been identified from the research – in the main they relate to the competence and confidence of the learning group advisers. Crucially our case study has identified the lack of interest by line managers not involved personally in PDfB in actively supporting and being involved in the development of their direct reports. This involvement is critical to ensure the strategic link between personal development and the business which, after all, is what PDfB is all about: Personal Development *for* Business.

Having said that, benefits from PDfB have been considerable and varied. Some, for example new product developments, fresh approaches to market research and a radical, new way of creating and documenting the strategy for Customer Service, have very clear measurable benefits for the business; others are less measurable. One of the most striking of these, and perhaps least expected, is the increase in confidence shown by, and highly visible to Peter Owen, of those managers taking part in PDfB. Arguably, the most important benefit, the one that has clearly had a 'strategic impact', however, is that PDfB has become a paradigm for organizational culture change and is seen as a highly effective way of working collaboratively and inclusively.

In overview, development within PPP healthcare has changed beyond all recognition over the last four years. SML and PDfB have taken development and learning within PPP healthcare to exciting levels. It is now business focused, strategically linked to HR, flexible, able to meet the changing needs of individuals, teams and the organization, and fun and innovative.

Our main conclusion is quite simply that SML has been proven to be a highly cost-effective way of promoting and supporting change in PPP healthcare. The evidence we gathered from Rosie Serpis's research has been confirmed in day-to-day interactions in the business. The use of SML has been an agent for key strategic change in PPP healthcare, although not everyone has found such widespread change comfortable. SML challenges people to take charge of their own development and to integrate their learning with the needs of the business. Decision-making on priorities and learning approaches has been handed over to the individual – in other words, we have given them choice. And with this choice has come responsibility. One of our key aims was to create a set of capabilities that did not just relate to the job that people were in but was effectively a lifelong skill, once acquired: the macro rather than the micro approach. Not everyone has found this easy. But it is difficult to see how we could have made the necessary major changes in the business without using an SML approach. Above all, for us, SML actively supports and enables the PPP healthcare corporate value, which in itself embodies change: 'We grow by learning.'

8 Self Managed Learning and qualification programmes

Graham Dawes

The relationship between Self Managed Learning and the academic world is an interesting one. When Ian Cunningham first articulated Self Managed Learning as an approach (Cunningham 1978) he was working within an academic context, North East London Polytechnic (now the University of East London), and the first SML programme began there in 1979. Yet, as an approach to learning, SML presents an implicit challenge to much of what goes on in academic education. Therefore, we might expect the relationship between the two to be somewhat troubled, even while each provides a contrast to highlight the qualities of the other.

This chapter will explore the relationship between SML and academia by describing three SML programmes which have been established within academic contexts. Their features and their fate will be considered and facets of their history will be drawn upon to illustrate those aspects that have the greatest bearing on the viability of SML within the academic world. The examples discussed here have all been located in the UK. However, our experiences of universities in other countries suggest that the issues explored in this chapter have general applicability. Also those using the qualifications discussed in this chapter have come from a variety of countries.

A first acquaintance with SML is likely to highlight its unconventionality as an educational approach (i.e. that it is different in kind from the educational experiences most of us have had). This might lead to the expectation that it would find more acceptance within the organizational world, where the (avowed) criterion is 'does it work?', than within academia, where the (avowed) criterion is the upholding of academic standards. Indeed, the first concern of many academics on hearing of SML is precisely that they cannot see how academic standards can be upheld on a programme where nothing is taught, as such, where the 'students' make up their own programmes of study, and where qualifications are awarded through a process very far from the typical, unilateral, staff-led assessment their world accepts as a norm.

THE POLITICS OF LEARNING

However much it may seem so to those wishing to influence its direction, academia is not one unitary and monolithic entity. There are factions and fashions in academia as there are anywhere else. In the academic world, as in the political world, the pendulum swings between conservative approaches and liberal (or even radical) approaches. Essentially, as in the political field, these orientations are founded on different conceptions of the person, so it is not surprising that they will lead to differing ideas on how people learn and what type of programme will assist them in doing so. The late 1960s and early 1970s was a time of considerable challenge to, and debate about, what had been held to be the 'tried and true' educational methods. Some of these challenges came from within the education field, some from outside it, but a common proposal was that the learner should be at the centre of the educational process and no longer the teacher or tutor.

This position stemmed from the idea that students should be seen as 'autonomous agents'. This was a philosophical idea carried forward from the ideological upheavals of the late 1960s. It was tricky to accommodate this idea within current educational practice where it was assumed that learners 'didn't know' while teachers or tutors 'did know'. The logic that followed, therefore, was that it was the job of tutors to fill learners with the knowledge they lacked. The underlying metaphor for the educational process was one in which the learner arrived as an empty vessel, gradually to be filled with knowledge by succeeding ranks of teachers. Because learners 'didn't know' it would be meaningless to consider their opinion of what they needed to know.

Of course, when learners were seen as autonomous agents it no longer seemed quite so appropriate to ignore their preferences, their thoughts, feelings and desires, while imposing upon them both *what* they must learn and *how* they must learn it. Such an imposition now forfeited its easy justification.

THE HIDDEN CURRICULUM

Another of those 'dangerous ideas' that disturbed the status quo became known as the 'hidden curriculum'. This is of particular relevance to Self Managed Learning in that it alone is sufficient to justify the importance of SML and similar approaches. It is also emblematic of the rather awkward and difficult to answer challenges being made against the norms of educational practice at that time. Not only of that time, either, since this is a challenge that has not been adequately answered by the majority of academics.

It was assumed as an essential educational equation that what was taught equalled what was learnt. In practice, of course, it was obvious that students didn't always learn what they were supposed to, though it was less often observed that they might learn other things that weren't intended. The answer given to the observation that the equation did not reflect real life was that either the students were lazy, shiftless or incapable, or that educational methods simply needed to improve in order to make the equation work.

Such misguided optimism found no support from educational research which showed that people learn things from the manner in which they are taught. It was called the 'hidden curriculum' because no learning was intended or even recognized to occur due to the influence of the method of learning itself. The attention of teachers and educationalists had been firmly on the content to be taught and learnt, not on any effects that might result from how this was done.

Disconcertingly, the standard educational methods, those familiar from school and university, appeared to be teaching dependence. This was not what was intended. Nor was it that dependence was learnt *instead* of the particular subject content intended. What the research showed was that whatever subject matter may or may not be learnt, the way in which it was being taught encouraged dependence. This was a disturbing notion. It hardly demonstrated the staunchly avowed intent of education to produce self reliant citizens.

These findings were not seriously challenged by subsequent research, yet nor were their implications integrated into the norms of educational practice. Perhaps these implications were just too challenging. Or it may have been that the issue itself was too intellectually challenging to be understood by most educators.

ORDERS OF LEARNING

The issue of the hidden curriculum was difficult to understand without the concept of 'orders of learning', which did not enjoy much currency in the education field. Though we are, here, talking of a time some twenty years ago, this is still a concept that awaits incorporation into the practice of most of those engaged in the promotion of learning, whether in academic or organizational contexts.

In the case of the hidden curriculum, if learning the intended subject matter is labelled 'first order learning' then the unintended learning of dependence is 'second order learning'. Both orders of learning happen at the same time, but they work in different ways. First order learning was thought to work in a rational, logical and linear manner while second order learning, since it wasn't intended, appeared to be arational, alogical and, more than anything else, systemic. The first was a conscious mind way of learning, the second seemed to bypass consciousness and lodge itself in the unconscious mind. Recognition of this latter point could well have brought greater understanding of the workings of the hidden curriculum in that it suggests a link to childhood learning. We know, and often lament, that children learn more from what adults do than from what they say. Psychologists call this process 'modelling'. The child models the adult's behaviour unconsciously.

A parallel process was operating in the educational context. Learners were dependent on the teacher for the knowledge the teacher parcelled out. They were also dependent on the teacher, through the marking of tests and examination, for knowing whether or not they had learnt what they were supposed to learn. Most of the time the learner was in a passive position, able only to be receptive to the teacher's presentation of the subject. There was little room for becoming actively engaged in learning; even opportunities for discovery, exploration and experiment were substantially curtailed.

It has been pointed out, somewhat sardonically, that the kind of obedience and lack of initiative being developed by the hidden curriculum may have been in tune with the times in which compulsory schooling began. Then the call was for a very different kind of workforce. Today the requirements are quite different and yet, despite various educational reforms, the hidden curriculum still pervades most educational practice.

THE SCHOOL FOR INDEPENDENT STUDY

Within the context of educational questioning and challenge that was the early 1970s, a group of tutors at North East London Polytechnic presented the Council for National Academic Awards (CNAA) (the body that validated non-university qualifications) with a proposal for an Independent Study programme. This was designed to lead to the newly established qualification, the Diploma of Higher Education (considered equivalent to two of the three years of a first degree). Ian Cunningham was among those who developed this proposal.

The proposal gave lengthy arguments for each point at which it diverged from educational norms. Yet the resulting programme presented an implicit challenge to just about every other programme the CNAA validated. It had no exams, there was no predefined syllabus, there were no imposed objectives for the students, and there were no academic entry requirements. While the process was not smooth the programme was eventually validated, and it started in 1974.

Over the next four years the School for Independent Study expanded its offerings with a part-time programme and the possibility of doing an extra year, after the Diploma of Higher Education, for a Bachelor's degree. Those four years experience with the programme led Ian Cunningham to question elements of the Independent Study design, which didn't seem, in practice, to be as supportive of the learning process as was envisioned. In essence, these elements of design are what distinguish Independent Study from what was to become Self Managed

Learning (see Cunningham 1981). Two key factors were the notion that assessment should not be imposed unilaterally by tutors and, secondly, the need for small learning groups to support students more effectively. When colleagues in the School for Independent Study resisted these design changes, Ian returned to the Management Centre of the Polytechnic (from where he had been seconded to the Independent Study initiative). There he was able to set up a Personal Development Division and propose a Self Managed Learning approach for a Post-Graduate Diploma in Management.

POST-GRADUATE DIPLOMA IN MANAGEMENT (BY SELF MANAGED LEARNING)

The Post-Graduate Diploma in Management (by Self Managed Learning) was a two-year part-time programme. It followed the outline of SML given in Chapter 2. (Vignettes of this programme can be found in Cunningham 1999.) The major difference from a standard in-company programme was the use of a termly residential weekend which provided a basis for the whole community to meet. This was initially for mapping purposes to introduce people to ideas and issues that would help them to write their learning contracts. Later residentials were designed by the participants so that they could address aspects of their learning contracts.

The PG Dip, as it was known, began in 1980 and the last cohort was taken on in 1988. During that time there were roughly 200 participants. From a balance when it began, the public sector came to represent about 70 per cent of participants, with local authorities being the largest single professional area on the programme. The number of women on the programme also increased over time. The PG Dip closed, not because of lack of interest, in fact there were nearly twice as many people per intake at the end than at the beginning, but because the staff members central to running it gradually moved on and the institution was unable to take it over.

After the first year of the programme, there were always two cohorts attending the residentials. This overlap meant there was a greater range of expertise to be drawn on from programme participants in the design of each residential. The overlapping two cohorts also meant that those participants who had become interested, in their first year on the programme, in the SML mode itself might take the opportunity to be co-advisers to learning groups, with a member of staff, for one of the new groups beginning its first year. In some instances, this co-adviser role was a way in which the participant could accomplish learning goals already established in their learning contract. For others, the decision to be a co-adviser required an adjustment of learning goals (which needed to be negotiated with the person's learning group). There were also cases where being a co-adviser didn't relate to the person's learning goals and was being pursued outside their learning contract.

THE ROFFEY/SUSSEX SELF MANAGED LEARNING MBA

The Self Managed Learning approach had begun within an academic context. From there it spread into the organizational world. This was an obvious transition in that participants on the PGDip were themselves largely working in organizations. However, this did require tailoring the SML design to different requirements, for example a shorter length of programme. In 1989, with Ian Cunningham as Chief Executive, Roffey Park Management Institute launched a Self Managed Learning MBA in concert with the University of Sussex. I was one of the team that planned and organized it.

SETTING UP THE PROGRAMME

Initially, Ian had approached the University with the idea of such an MBA and met with a favourable response. However, the validation process for a new programme, together with the process of accrediting an institution, Roffey Park Management Institute, would have been expected to take two years. Yet the MBA programme was running within six months. This was due, in large part, to the efforts of the Senior Pro Vice-Chancellor who wanted it to happen.

There were also helpful factors in the wider educational context. The government had made clear that it approved of universities that were 'relevant' to the needs of business. Sussex had no business school. It had previously looked into the possibility of setting up an MBA itself, but it had quickly become apparent that the University lacked staff with sufficient experience of the field. Thus, we at Roffey Park were in a position to supply what the University needed in order to include an MBA among its offerings.

Despite these considerable advantages there remained a number of challenges. Those in universities view themselves as upholders of academic standards and feel that anyone outside academia must surely lack the rigour they bring to such matters. While those who had to run the University could see the advantages of collaboration with Roffey Park, doubts were expressed by some of those on the academic side. Given some of the elements of a Self Managed Learning programme this is not surprising.

The validation process for the programme included its passage through a number of committees. The Sussex academics on these committees were confronted by a proposal for a programme that aimed to select people who may not have a first degree, where there was no standard curriculum to be validated, and where the 'students' were to be involved in assessment. And this all leading to a Masters degree their university was expected to confer. This is where it was so important that senior people in the University had had the opportunity to get to know Ian Cunningham and felt able to trust the team at Roffey Park to do what we had undertaken to do, and to pursue it with at least as much rigour as those within the University. This link into the University at a high level and the establishment of that trust provided a context in which the validation process proceeded; it was tough and it was rigorous but less poisoned by suspicion that it might have been under other circumstances.

Although the programme, being an SML programme, was unfamiliar to those within the University, when it came to the specifics of how things would be done they found nothing that fell below their standards. Indeed, there was tacit admission that the Roffey Park selection process, by using an assessment centre type of approach, was more rigorous than their own.

Within Roffey we formed an Academic Board to oversee the MBA, and the other academic programmes that began in its wake. Though this Board had no official link to Sussex University, its existence gave some confidence to those within the University who had residual concerns about collaborating with another institution.

THE CHOICE OF EXTERNAL EXAMINERS

Another factor in setting up the programme was the choice of external examiners. On an SML qualification programme the external examiners are more involved than is the case with conventional programmes. The usual role of external examiners, when a programme has a fixed curriculum, is in evaluating whether the (unilateral) assessment process is rigorous and fair and whether standards are being maintained. Typically, unless there are any problems with the programme, this can be a fairly simple almost 'rubber stamping'. The role of an external examiner on an SML qualification programme is much more demanding.

The first demand, which shouldn't be ignored, is to understand the programme. This is no small thing. As the SML approach is unfamiliar in the context of academia it would be easy for someone looking for the typical safeguards of academic programmes to miss the rigour inherent in SML and think that the safeguards were missing. Such a perception could jeopardize the work of a whole cohort. All two-years' worth of their work would be condemned to go unrecognized if the award were withheld. This would be a disaster.

The two external examiners chosen for the Roffey/Sussex MBA brought different backgrounds to the programme. One was a professor of management learning, and therefore able to oversee the whole field in which the programme was located, the other was a professor of finance, with much experience of traditional MBAs, who could add the 'hard-nosed' perspective of his own discipline. The first of these external examiners was very familiar with the SML approach, the second, completely unfamiliar. Fortunately, he was able to grasp the aims of the programme and understood the way in which its structure was designed to achieve those aims. Although his ready understanding boded well for the programme, it could only be an understanding in the abstract. It remained for us to discover how he would react to the actuality of the programme when it was running.

Once the nature of the programme is understood, the second demand on external examiners is that, in the absence of one already validated curriculum, they need to oversee the adequacy of each individual, personally designed, curriculum of study.

THE PROCESS OF ASSESSMENT

In any SML programme the question of whether or not a particular Strategic Learning Contract is appropriate to the length and level of the programme is initially addressed within the learning group. Obviously, more will be expected of a Strategic Learning Contract for a two-year programme than for one that is a month long; similarly, more will be expected of one for a Masters degree than for a Post-Graduate Diploma. However, in line with SML principles, it is for each group to identify what is required. Each person's learning goals will be different so there is no possibility to apply an across-the-board measure for adequacy. This means the learning group must take the time and make the effort to establish its own criteria by which to evaluate each member's Strategic Learning Contract. This can be a challenging process leading to much debate about what a particular level, for instance Masters level, actually means when examining a concrete, and unique, contract.

With the group criteria established, it is for each individual to present his or her own Strategic Learning Contract to the group and make the case for its meeting those criteria, and that they should be awarded the qualification if they can demonstrate having met the learning goals in the contract. The group, including the learning group adviser, will evaluate the case presented by the individual. Typically, this involves tough questioning through which group members seek to assure themselves that the contract is well thought through and that its accomplishment would be worthy of the qualification. When consensus agreement is reached the contract is forwarded to one of the external examiners. (If the group does not agree a contract, yet there are sufficient grounds for believing an adequate contract can be reached and fulfilled, they can make a case for the individual being allowed extra time to develop it.)

The external examiners' role is to assess the assessment process of the learning group. They will examine each contract to check the adequacy of the group's assessment, referring any doubts back to the group. Either their questions will be answered, or the contract will need revising in their light. Whichever is the case, the process means that each Strategic Learning Contract has been thoroughly evaluated and it has been agreed, across a number of levels of evaluation, that it represents a programme of study befitting the qualification level. This may not be the end of the matter, though, as there is frequently a need to revise a contract. It may be in light of discoveries on the way to the learning goals or it might arise through a change of circumstances which renders the original contract less relevant. Minor changes, those deemed by the group to lie within the general outline of the original contract, need only be agreed with the group. Substantial changes require that, after agreement by the learning group, they are sent to an external examiner.

It can be seen that this is a more challenging role than that of an external examiner on a conventional programme. It is very unusual, on such programmes, for students to have anything to do with the external examiners; they rarely even have occasion to know who they are. SML qualification programmes are quite different in this regard. The external examiners do not remain faceless figures, representatives of an abstract 'They' who must be satisfied, they actually attend a group meeting to respond to the contracts they have been sent. This is, once again, an unfamiliar role for most academics who are used to unilateral assessment, a process taking place behind closed doors. In this case, they will be putting their questions, their doubts about any particular contract, to the learning group and to the individual. This means that they can be challenged in turn and will have to defend their opinion.

The role of external examiners in the final assessment at the end of the programme is much the same as has been described above. There are the same layers of assessment, beginning with the individual making a case for having demonstrated completion of the contract, the group assessing that assessment in the light of their own experience of what the person has done, and the external examiners assessing the group's assessment for rigour and avoidance of collusion. A significant difference at the time of the final assessment is that the learning group must devise and send to the external examiners its proposed process of assessment. This document will include the criteria the group is going to apply when evaluating the contracts (and which will have been developed and sharpened up since the time of contracting) and how they will concretely go about the process. They also need to state how this process will be conveyed to the external examiners. In other words, how is the external examiner going to know whether the learning group held to the proposed process or how rigorously they conducted the assessment? The group's proposal may occasion debate back and forth until the external examiners are convinced that they will be able adequately to carry out their role in the overall process.

MAPPING

This MBA programme was a fully-fledged SML programme. One element of SML design that was foregrounded in this programme was 'mapping'. The purpose of mapping is to give an overview of the territory within which learning goals might be chosen. Being an MBA, the territory was that of general management. Participants needed to have a sketch of this territory if they were to be able to make informed choices about their learning goals. Giving participants the freedom to make their own choices was not enough. Without their having an idea of what existed in the area of general management they would have insufficient basis for their choices and, in all likelihood, would opt for what already happened to be familiar to them. This is one way in which freedom of choice can confound its own purpose and lead to highly constrained goals. To avoid this, early one-week residentials contained sessions in which experts in a particular area of general management would present an overview of what was contained in their area. This was rather different from teaching participants about the area; it was about letting them know what was there and responding to their questions as they sought to identify what relevance that area might have for their own learning needs.

By 1993 the core group that had designed and operated the Roffey/Sussex MBA had left Roffey Park Management Institute and were working elsewhere. Although aware of the added difficulties of lacking an institutional base, we sought to establish another SML Masters degree programme.

THE MSc IN MANAGING CHANGE

This new venture had a different focus from that of the MBA, and was designed to enable participants to concentrate on learning to respond to, run with, and initiate those processes of change that had been falling upon organizations in succeeding waves. We found colleagues in the Business School at Sheffield Hallam University who were interested in this idea and we set up the Centre for the Study of Change, a company limited by guarantee, as the other entity in a partnership that would offer an MSc in Managing Change.

Once again this was designed as a fully-fledged SML programme, running part-time for two years. While the 'mapping' for the MBA was able to follow the content areas of general management as delineated by many years of MBAs (plus the addition of a few areas not found in other programmes), the focus on change meant that the mapping had to encompass some fairly uncharted areas like, for instance, a consideration of what might be appropriate to an as-yet-not-existing general theory of change. Admittedly, a lot had been written about the topic of change but much of it was shallow and there were no agreed criteria for the inclusion or exclusion of elements. It provided an interesting challenge and, as in all SML programmes, participants had their own challenges in finding their individual paths through the mapping to choose learning goals relevant to themselves and their particular situation.

The two university colleagues who were to work with us on the programme had no experience of SML programmes specifically, though they were, in different ways, involved in the field of organizational change. In talking through the design of the programme with them there were elements with which they had more concern than with others. Perhaps not unexpectedly, it was the workability of final assessment that aroused most doubt. (It was satisfying, some years later, to hear one of these colleagues speak at a conference about his surprise at finding that learning group members were tougher on each other than he would have been; in comparison he considered that participants on the University's conventionally designed and unilaterally assessed MBA had an easy time of it.)

The planning meetings between us and our Sheffield Hallam partners tended to encompass both what needed to be done in order to get the programme up and running and discussions about the Self Managed Learning approach and its viability as a programme design. One of our number spent some time with them on learning group adviser development work so that they would be ready to take that role when the programme began.

As we proceeded, cracks began to appear in the relationship. This resulted in the core team from the Centre for the Study of Change moving on (though the programme continued). Below I will indicate some of the bases for tensions with academia.

WORKING WITH UNIVERSITIES AND INSTITUTIONS

Having sketched the history of three SML qualification programmes, it is time to draw out the lessons learnt from these experiences of working with universities and institutions. The three cases were all with higher education institutions but many of the same considerations apply to professional institutions. Many such institutions, overseeing professional qualifications of various types, are pursuing a Continuing Professional Development (CPD) route. Often, involvement in CPD is made mandatory for their members. While CPD is one of those things that can be counted a 'good idea', its real value varies considerably in practice. All too often it degenerates into a cynical exercise in bureaucratic box-ticking. However, allying CPD with an SML framework (as can be seen from Chapter 11) offers a way to fulfil the intended promise of the CPD concept.

In as much as this section deals with various challenges to the SML design (and attempts to compromise it), points made here have relevance to all SML programmes whatever the context in which they take place. In addition, though the programmes mentioned have all been drawn from the UK, the issues raised here appear to reflect those with universities globally (judging by our experience of different continents).

GETTING THE RELATIONSHIP RIGHT

The nature of the relationship between the parties involved, in the above three programmes, can be seen to have influenced what was possible. Often, what was accomplished through those relationships exceeded anything that could have been expected. Therefore, developing a good relationship can be counted as the primary prerequisite. That this is not always possible in practice must be recognized, but only serves to confirm its value.

The importance of trust can be seen by considering its alternatives. These are either to proceed on a swampy foundation of uncertainty or to attempt some sort of legalistic agreement. The legalistic route is unlikely to work for not only is it impossible to legislate for all the eventualities, it must be borne in mind that the university always has the more powerful position due to its ability to withdraw the qualification.

The best situation, therefore, is one where the university has something at stake, some advantage of its own which is tied to the existence of the programme. This was the case with Sussex University. Whether you are in a position to know of any advantage to the university depends on how the negotiations are conducted. In an open negotiation, where cards are laid upon the table, the advantages to each will be plain. However, this is not usually the way in which negotiations are conducted within universities, and it is a mode likely to be unfamiliar to those who have spent years in environments as political as universities appear to be.

Not only are you looking for a rare individual, you are also looking for one who has a role senior enough to shepherd the SML programme through the university's validation process. Even when the direct relationship is not with someone at this level, it is worth meeting with those at a higher level and endeavouring to gain their assent to what is planned.

It is likely to be of more benefit if the university staff have their focus on the advantages to them, rather than having a particular interest in the programme itself. It is much easier if one is left to get on with it, and simply link in to the university at those points that guarantee to them the validity of the programme. Paradoxically, it can be a disadvantage if there are SML enthusiasts within the university, for they can make unnecessary enemies in their efforts to promote the approach. Depending on their own political affiliations within the university, their support can be a definite liability. It is important to retain focus on the programme itself and not to get side-tracked into fighting on issues of educational ideology which are likely to ruffle feathers all over the university.

Part of the paradox here is that if universities were the kinds of places they often remain in public mythology – places of rational debate over practices and principles, animated by the highest ideals – then the point would not need to be made. Beneath the façade of rational debate lie many clashing agendas which can give rise to a politics all the more vicious for its being cloaked in the rhetoric of rationality. A university environment is not always kind to those with good intentions.

Despite the difficulties in forming fruitful relationships with universities, they are more open to considering working with outsiders than they would have been in the past. Still reeling from the attacks of the Thatcher years they are much more eager to contemplate anything that can show a financial advantage to themselves. In the past, any outsider was suspected of having 'sold out' to commercial over academic interests, but nowadays they see that their own academic interests can only be pursued if they manage to generate sufficient revenue. This leads to another paradox. We have often found ourselves in the position of being champions of academic standards and rigour while those from universities have been far more concerned about commercial factors.

RELEVANCE OF RESEARCH

Though the importance of relationships has been emphasized, it might be thought that universities would pay a lot of attention to research in evaluating the worth of an educational approach. This notion stems from the idea that universities are the fountainheads of rationality. That myth has already been punctured. It should no longer be surprising that research counts for less than rhetoric when it comes to decisions regarding whether a university will be home to an SML programme.

There is now a good deal of research on SML. None the less, that is not the basis on which decisions are made. Lack of research is often used to justify a choice not to do something, but the existence of research is usually far from enough to lead to its being done. Decisions tend to be made on emotional grounds, and based on advantages to the individuals or institutions involved. This should not be a surprise when we consider that awareness of the 'hidden curriculum' mentioned earlier has had minimal effect on educational practice.

EXTERNAL EXAMINERS

Universities rely on external examiners to oversee an externally run programme, just as they do with an internally run one. This means that once the programme is up and running the external examiners become the people who, in a sense, represent the university's interests, at least as far as academic requirements are concerned. We have seen that the role of external examiner for an SML programme is much more demanding, and much more involving, than for more conventional programmes. Potentially, then, eternal examiners have considerable power and influence over the programme. For this not to become problematic depends on their having understood that their role, on an SML programme, requires them to be open to discussion and challenge. This has been illustrated in terms of their

129

meeting with learning groups and needing to be open to questioning on their response to individual contracts or, later, to proposed assessment processes and their results. The very same manner is required in relation to their views on how the programme itself is run and their discussions with those who run it. This should mean that any reservations or concerns about the programme can be explored and resolved without having to involve the university (which may over-react through feeling less in touch with the programme and, therefore, less in control of it).

All that has been said of external examiners suggests that they need to be both open and sophisticated thinkers. Even when they meet these criteria, the relationship with them is not always a straightforward or easy one. This stems partly from their recognition that their role is much more significant in this than other programmes. They have more responsibility, they know this, and might easily get twitchy about things they would ignore on other programmes. While this may make for occasional difficulties, external examiners on an SML programme can be of great benefit to the programme. Through working in groups, participants will have come to see that one level of academic 'They' (the group adviser, a tutor-level role) can be questioned and challenged and with external examiners (their ultimate academic 'They') they find that the same applies. This experience can be sufficient to revise a dependent, passive or reactive response to authority in general.

When choosing an external examiner, their previous writings and pronouncements on educational matters are not an infallible guide. The times have become much more conservative. In retrospect the 1970s appear as a time of radical educational innovation. The universities have been under attack in the intervening period and, in response, many within them are exhibiting the more conservative stance of their attackers. The result is that those who previously supported or openly championed the more inventive educational modes are now more conventional in their thinking. At times it seems as if they have regressed to the days before those innovations they themselves championed, as if these had not happened. Unless you are prepared for this it can come as a nasty surprise.

SELECTION

As with an employment interview, there are two sides to selection. There is the decision as to whether the person is right for the programme, and also whether the programme is right for the person. In selection, we need to look to both sides, though the applicant may not be looking to their own side. People may want to get on a qualification programme for all sorts of reasons. It may have been recommended by their company, and they are passively following the suggestion. They may want to bump up the value of their CV by adding a qualification. They may even be attracted by the lack of requirement for a previous qualification; indeed, this may be the only programme they have a chance of getting on. These are not sufficient reasons.

Part of the selection process involves giving the applicant some sense of the kind of programme they are applying for. They will have either been to an open evening to hear about the programme or had some previous contact in which the programme was explained to them and their questions answered. The selection process provides another context in which they can have questions answered. We also have a lot of questions for them, and an unstructured interview has been a significant part of selection for the above mentioned programmes. Among other things, we want to know whether applicants are likely to be able to meet the demands of the programme. Have they any evidence of taking charge of their own learning? What evidence do they have of being able to keep at something demanding over time (the programmes discussed above were all two-year part-time programmes)? What bearing is their work and family situation likely to have on the work they will need to do for the programme? What does their partner say about it all?

As mentioned above, all three programmes provided opportunities for potential applicants to find out about the nature of the programme. This was an important first stage in that written materials about the programme could not adequately convey just how different it was likely to be from other learning experiences. This is not to imply that a live presentation is wholly effective in conveying those differences, just that it can be more effective.

Selection for the PG Dip involved the application form and an extended interview. For the Roffey/Sussex MBA, when the application form looked promising, we used an assessment centre process comprising a psychometric test, the Watson–Glaser Critical Thinking Test (scores on which were useful in persuading the University of the appropriateness of those without first degrees), a group discussion, an essay written at the time, and an interview. For the MSc with Sheffield Hallam those who passed through the application form phase had to write an essay on change which they brought along when coming for interview. They were interviewed, separately, by two members of the team on both the thinking expressed in their essay and on more general aspects of their situation and how they thought they could make use of the programme. In all cases where there were any concerns about a person's suitability for the programme, referees were contacted.

The selection process has been emphasized here, in the context of qualification programmes, in a way it usually is not in the case of in-company programmes. There are two reasons for this. These qualification programmes ran over a two-year period and we had to assure ourselves, and the institutions, that those we selected had a good chance of gaining the qualification at the end of the programme. Therefore, we had a responsibility to the institution and to the individual to accept only those who could fulfil the demanding requirements of such a pro-gramme. This is different from the case with in-company programmes which tend to be a lot shorter and in which the focus is more on the individual learning and benefiting, rather than reaching a particular standard, like that for a Masters degree. However, this is not a reason to forgo assessment on in-company pro-grammes.

ASSESSMENT

In the case of most educational programmes, assessment is something tacked on at the end, like a test in school, to make sure you have learnt what you were sup-posed to have learnt. In contrast, within an SML qualification programme, the final assessment has the potential for being a very rich source of learning; indeed, some have said it was the phase in which they learnt the most. However, it is also the eas-iest part of the programme to lose control of as it is likely to be so different from the process used in any other programme of the qualifying institution.

A great deal is lost if the final assessment becomes one of conventional (uni-lateral) assessment by tutors. Not only does the potential for learning through the assessment process vanish but the programme becomes incongruent with itself. The SML programme design is based on a view of participants as being able to take responsibility for their own learning, to create and pursue a programme of study, and to work with others, supporting and challenging them in the pursuit of their own learning goals. Having a programme that takes this perspective is in con-flict with the message of conventional assessment: that participants cannot be trusted to evaluate their own work, nor to evaluate the work of their peers. This distrust takes two forms: that they cannot be relied on not to cheat or collude and that they cannot be trusted to be able to make an effective evaluation. Very differ-ent views of the person are at stake here. For this reason, a conventional final assessment undermines the message of an SML programme.

This is not to say that the process of assessing your own and others' work is an easy one. None the less, many people engage in this as part of their everyday work. At least, the role of assessing others is one that managers take on in the appraisal process. If they appraise others they should be able to appraise themselves. Often this is not the case. A final assessment provides an opportunity to bring all these strands together. Participants are cheated of this chance by unilateral assessment.

Those on SML programmes have the possibility to build up their abilities to assess as they go through the programme. They will have taken part in an assess-ment process at the time of agreeing Strategic Learning Contracts. This assess-ment process ratchets up to a higher level when it comes to final assessment.

Culturally, we tend to be coy about assessing others, and unused to assessing ourselves (for we were taught at school to rely on others to tell us how we are doing). Participants often find it a struggle to switch from a feedback mode during the pursuit of learning goals to a judgement mode at the time of final assessment. We are usually more comfortable with feedback (though this in itself can be difficult enough at first). Giving feedback is giving your responses to what someone has done. It may indicate other things they could do, or that you think they could do more or better. It is left to them to decide whether or not to take notice of your response, and what to do about it. Your *judgement* they have to take notice of. It is much more imperative. It is also black and white. It is not saying to someone, 'You could do more', it is saying, 'This is not enough'. And they have to take notice of that.

In the making of judgements for final assessment there is the added difficulty of deciding the criteria against which to make the judgement. There is the tendency for participants to assume that there is some absolute against which to make judgement. On conventional programmes this appears to be the case as the whole process takes place behind closed doors and the implication is that a person's work is being measured against some absolute yardstick. Participants often find it challenging when they have to wrestle with defining what is appropriate to a particular qualification level. They realize that, on the one hand, there are no absolute measures and, on the other, that it isn't just a case of 'anything goes'. They are required to establish assessment criteria and to make a case for those they propose. Furthermore, they are required to assess against those criteria in a thorough and rigorous manner.

Final assessment can push everyone involved to a higher level of learning. There might have been something bothering you about someone's work, yet you've never managed to pin it down. Assessment brings the pressure to get it clear and convey that concern. Looking to your own work, you know you are going to have to make a case for it as demonstrating achievement of learning goals, and to the appropriate standard. This often brings new understanding of your own work. Recalling, for the learning group, learning points you made along the way can bring out personally important themes.

Those who have had no experience of the process often imagine that with the group having worked so closely together it would be very difficult for anyone to fail to get the qualification. But this does happen. It can happen in two ways: either the person assesses themselves as not having achieved their learning goals, and the rest of the group support their assessment, or they assess themselves as having achieved their goals at the requisite level and the rest of the group do not support their assessment. (In the latter case, there would be a good deal of discussion within the group and if consensus could not be reached (either way) the matter would be referred to the external examiners.)

There have been cases where people have been given feedback to the effect that what they have been doing is insufficient in one way or another, but they have not taken account of it. In other words, they haven't heard the message. They were then surprised to hear the judgement of the others, and the others were surprised to hear that they were surprised. More usually, the person has recognized the misgivings of the group and attempted to meet the assessment criteria, though without doing so. In such cases, the group has the option of proposing to the external examiners that the person be given an extension, if there are grounds for believing that additional time will enable them to meet the assessment criteria. This is a heavy commitment for the group which would be expressing a willingness to reconvene after the programme has finished in order to assess the person who has been given extra time.

DIFFERENCES FROM NON-QUALIFICATION SML PROGRAMMES

There are few 'necessary' differences between qualification and non-qualification SML programmes. What differences there are tend to be the result of the different contexts in which they take place. For instance, most non-qualification programmes take place within organizations. Therefore, the make up of groups is different in that participants will be from the same organization, while on an open qualification programme it is rare to have a group with any members in the same organization.

Length of programme is a significant variable and, thus far, non-qualification programmes have not been two years in length, though they could be. There are advantages to having more time on a programme. A longer programme allows more opportunity for participants to integrate the second-order learning available in SML programmes. It happens on shorter programmes but there is more time for it to happen to more people on longer programmes. The extent of personal development that is seen on the longer programmes makes them an especially rewarding experience for the group advisers.

Perhaps the most striking difference is due to the extra effort put into the assessment process. On a qualification programme it is inevitable that it is taken more seriously and, as has been mentioned, this extra involvement in assessment can be an enriching process. This is not to say there is anything stopping an equal rigour from being present in a non-qualification assessment. It is just that it is unlikely to be there to the same extent. (However, it does suggest that those wishing to get more out of an SML programme might do well to increase the emphasis on assessment.)

ACADEMIC REQUIREMENTS

The orientation toward academic requirements is significantly different on SML programmes than on conventional programmes. SML qualification programmes have been for post-experience participants and this, along with the general SML ethos, has emphasized ability over pure knowledge. Knowledge is in the service of action, and it would not be sufficient if the knowledge were purely, as it were, 'academic'.

To take the concrete example of the SML MBA programme, it was not enough to demonstrate a greater knowledge *about* managing, participants were required to demonstrate that at the end of the programme they were, in fact, better managers. It might be thought, therefore, that academic requirements came second to practical requirements. This was not the case. Rather, it was that an increased ability as a manager became an academic requirement. The Masters degree standards that were brought to bear on written work had to be reconfigured to apply to practice. This was part of the challenge of assessment, of which much has already been said.

Given this orientation, and the emphasis in SML on real learning, the benefits of any conventional academic requirements might be questioned. Where they came into play was in evaluating written work. Again, the value of doing any written work might also be questioned. And a good deal of written work was produced. Alongside the development of the Strategic Learning Contract, which took place during the first six months of the programme, participants were working on a lengthy essay in which they made a case for their personal perspective on management. They were to draw on the management literature and the models and theories they found there and relate these to their personal experience as managers. During the rest of the programme, though different modes of presenting evidence of learning were available to them, many people wrote further essays and a dissertation at the end. Though the area of focus was different, the situation was much the same with the MSc.

The value of this written work is that it illustrated the participant's ability to navigate in the conceptual world, that is to evaluate ideas and theory, and to relate them to practice. (As such it reflected the academic requirements of standard courses, though with a greater emphasis on the relation to practice.) Now, this kind of ability is not essential in the work of many managers. There were those on the programme who were clearly very effective managers, yet who found difficulty in getting to grips with this domain. So it is not tied to effective managing *per se*. But it does seem to be tied to strategic thinking, and to being an effective senior manager. Senior managers, responsible for the strategy of their organizations, have to make sense of patterns and trends in designing a future for the organization to inhabit and thrive in. This requires the ability to navigate in the conceptual world (though this is not to say that senior managers consider themselves intellectuals).

PHILOSOPHICAL ISSUES

Behind many of the difficulties in working with universities lie philosophical and ideological differences. As has been pointed out, SML is based on a philosophy of education different from that which underlies most of what goes on in universities. In itself this need not be a problem. The university could encompass differing educational approaches and tutors could allow one another a preference for different educational practices. This is not often the case, and perhaps it should not be surprising that it is not.

At the root of how such matters are handled is the issue of how ideas are held. When a group of ideas are held as absolutes then flexibility decreases and the path is open to black-and-white thinking and rigidity. When ideas are held as hypotheses or options there is likely to be more flexibility and increasing openness to possibilities. This is just as true when talking of those in organizational life as with those in universities. The issue arises more sharply in the university context where people tend to see themselves as an intellectual elite and are inclined to use the intellect as a weapon.

Many of Edward de Bono's books include a swipe at our educational heritage for its emphasis on critical thinking to the detriment of constructive thinking (see, for example, de Bono 1996). As he says, it seems to be thought sufficient to point out the flaws in an idea or argument, without it being necessary to propose anything constructive in its place. Within the universities this negative art is well-honed and is used to intimidate others (the impression is given that a particular way is how it *has* to be, when it is actually no more than a preference on the university side).

These modes of thinking, rigid and critical on the one hand, and flexible and constructive on the other, each partake of constellations of ideas with a very wide import. Around each, constellate our ideas about everything from morality and politics to how to bring up children. Brought to bear on education, with the first, we find the importance of identifying right and wrong as absolutes, and of the importance of reward and punishment and obedience. With the second, the importance of empathy and nurturance, of understanding others and assisting them.

The conventional educational approach is characteristic of the first mode of thinking (though its excesses have been muted in the current climate), while Self Managed Learning is representative of the second. With this wider perspective, we can understand why conflicts over intellectual ideas can get so heated. Because such ideas do not stand alone, but are linked to moral stances, there is a moral force driving the shrillness that can infect (supposedly) rational academic debates.

While the last section has taken us beyond the limits of the topic for this chapter it has made clearer the kinds of factors that can weigh in the relations between SML programmes and the institutions with which they are linked.

QUALIFICATIONS WITHOUT INSTITUTIONS

There is a final point to be made, though it is of a rather different order. The three programmes that have been the focus of attention here were all situated within academic institutions. Qualifications are not awarded only by academic institutions. It is quite possible for an SML programme to lead to a qualification conferred by an awarding body. Awarding bodies tend to put their attention most directly on the quality of assessment, but not to concern themselves with the learning process *per se*.

A case in point was the 10-month SML programme for Shell UK Materials Services (SUKMS). This programme led to a BTEC Certificate. It had some interesting features. The start-up included looking at business strategy for SUKMS and, as well as the formation of learning groups, two project groups were formed (mixing people from both learning groups). These projects were concerned with cost saving and were negotiated with the senior managers.

For the regular learning group meetings, the whole cohort would meet at a hotel. The day would comprise a community meeting and separate learning group and project group meetings. Also, during the period of the programme, a block of days was given over to workshops, the subjects of which were derived from analysis of Strategic Learning Contract goals. In effect, these were in the form of extended mapping sessions, on subjects such as marketing, human resources, procurement, etc.

During the final assessment sessions, the learning groups were visited by the BTEC moderator who expressed himself as being most impressed with the results of the process. Although it was an in-company programme, the assessment process had taken on the rigour of qualification programmes. In addition, the sense among participants was that benefits of the cost-saving projects had immediately covered the costs associated with running the programme.

A new initiative in the educational field could make the idea of an SML programme with qualification through an awarding body more common. The Department for Education and Employment's University for Industry (UfI) initiative is designed to encourage learning in the workforce. It comprises a number of pathways through which learners will be involved. Not all of these will lead to qualifications. Of those that do, the Negotiated Work Based Learning pathway is of greatest interest to us. If we take the phrase apart it will be readily apparent that learning that is negotiated and work based is in line with Self Managed Learning. At this point, it is impossible to tell where the current thinking within UfI will lead. But it promises to provide a way in which programmes taking place in organizations can link in to awarding bodies and educational institutions, so that learning within the work context is recognized for qualification purposes.

While the plans for the Negotiated Work Based Learning pathway have neither been finalized nor made public we have been involved, with many others, in its development and have found a number of SML-type perspectives within the early UfI documentation. Were they to be part of the UfI provision when it is fully rolled out then these perspectives would be brought right into the mainstream of education. This could have a dramatic effect on their familiarity and, thus, on both their acceptability and their adoption.

Before this can happen, though, there are many political interests to be negotiated. Even then, there is no reason to suppose awarding bodies are currently any more enlightened than universities, so many of the issues mentioned above will remain. None the less, the Negotiated Work Based Learning pathway may well, less grandiosely, enable some interesting qualification programmes to be launched within organizations.

CONCLUSIONS

Looking at the education field from the outside, it might be expected that Self Managed Learning would be embraced as a fellow contributor to the great cause of learning. However, despite being an approach to learning, and despite having been developed within a polytechnic, SML has not always had an easy relationship with academic institutions. Though there are obvious differences in practice between SML and conventional educational approaches, we have seen that at least as great a difficulty stems from different assumptions about learners and learning.

These differences, and the difficulties to which they give rise, have been explored through the medium, primarily, of three post-graduate qualification SML programmes. Some detail has been given about these programmes to elucidate the significant facets of working, from an SML perspective, with universities and institutions. Attention has also been brought to the possibility of linking with awarding bodies, and that the government's UfI initiative opening up further opportunities across the range of qualification programmes. Hopefully, by having conveyed both the benefits and the trickiness of effective qualification programmes, others will also be encouraged to work with the possibilities, and will go forward the better prepared for what they have read here.

Qualification programmes are worth engaging with, if only because the prospect of qualifications tends to encourage people to enter into longer SML programmes. And the value of that, as indicated earlier, is that it makes it all the more likely that the benefits of an SML programme will be realized for them.

9 Self Managed Learning – experiences from Finland

Tuula Lillia

An introduction from Ian Cunningham

This chapter is different from the others in that it is written by someone outside the UK. However, this does not make it the only chapter to cover international and cross-cultural issues. For instance, Ericsson, which features in Chapter 10, is an international company based in Sweden and the MBA programme described in Chapter 8 catered for participants from around Europe. Indeed it was Tuula Lillia's experience as a participant on that programme that prompted her to develop SML programmes in Finland.

One reason for including this chapter is that Finland is quite different from the UK. There is often a justifiable concern that an approach developed in one country will not transfer elsewhere, and cultural differences are important when considering learning issues. So we hope that the two brief cases that Tuula describes in this chapter will give some indication of cross-cultural usage.

Finland is different in a number of important ways. For a start it has had a unique position in Europe. During most of the post-war era it found itself having to maintain an uneasy balancing act between the Warsaw Pact countries and the West. Given its small population (5 million), its relative poverty earlier this century and its isolated position, it has nevertheless been remarkably successful. It is now one of the wealthiest countries in the world (by per capita GDP) with the second highest per capita use of the Internet after the USA and it is home to leading international companies such as Nokia.

In considering cultural differences there are a number of ways of going about such an analysis. One made popular by Hofstede (1982) is to use generalized questionnaire - based studies to compare many countries against common factors. If we take Hofstede's original (1982) categories then we can see that Finland is predicted to be quite different from the UK. For instance, Finland is much higher on Hofstede's Uncertainty Avoidance factor and much lower on Individualism than the UK. Also Finland is categorized as a Feminine culture and the UK as Masculine.

It might be predicted from these differences that UK practices would not transfer easily. For instance, SML can be seen as requiring the ability to cope with uncertainty and Finns might not welcome such ambiguity. However, it is apparent that the SML structures have provided enough certainty to enable SML to work well in Finland. Indeed it could be argued that the more individualistic and masculine UK culture might make learning groups more problematic in the UK than in Finland, in that such characteristics could militate against supportive collaboration. What, however, we find is that different SML processes challenge each culture in different ways. We believe that it is of value for British managers to be challenged to be more collaborative in making learning groups work. In reality this challenge can be met, so our experience would not support those who are highly pessimistic about working cross-culturally. The major advantage of SML is that by being content-free it allows each culture to add its own content.

For this chapter we asked Tuula to provide two cases from her experience in Finland. We have kept the 'Finnish' style of the chapter so that it can read differently from the others. There is also little background information on the programmes as the SML features have been covered elsewhere in this book.

In this chapter I will discuss the cases of two organizations that have made use of SML. I will outline the programmes provided in each of the two organizations and then present evidence from evaluations of these programmes.

CASE 1: FINLAND POST (SUOMEN POSTI)[1]

Finland Post Ltd is a 360-year-old organization with 25 500 employees. It operates postal services by supplying:

- messaging services (letter and complementary services)
- media services (delivery of newspapers and magazines and direct mail shots)
- logistics services (delivery of parcels and other goods as an inclusive service).

It has changed from a government department to a business concern, becoming an independent limited company. Simultaneously the personnel have undergone a change from being civil servants to becoming professional providers of service to customers. Competition has existed for years but will be more intense in the future. Many challenges like electronic communications and shopping will bring large changes to this field.

The organization has undertaken a culture change process. This has included discussion of Finland Post's core values and what they mean for the work unit and the employee's own contribution.

The core values of Finland Post are found in the following statements:

- We shall be successful with our customers.
- We shall be successful together.
- I am responsible for it.

A good example of performing according to these values is the key personnel development process based on Self Managed Learning.

SELF MANAGED LEARNING PROGRAMMES IN FINLAND POST (POST SML)

The key personnel development process based on Self Managed Learning was started five years ago. Since then over one hundred employees (young people with potential as senior managers or specialists) have participated in the process. Programmes have lasted on average about one year.

The goals of the development programme are:

- to ensure that the Post has the key resources for future development
- to improve organizational learning and adaptability between jobs
- to assist personal development and career selection
- to promote personal initiative, independence and entrepreneurship as well as the skill to learn on the job
- to ensure lifelong learning.

The main concern is to make people take responsibility for their own learning. Acceptance of personal responsibility for learning means in practice that the participant:

- assesses his or her own development needs
- clarifies his or her own ambitions
- decides on the learning methods to be used
- is personally responsible for assessing learning
- works with others in order to achieve objectives and makes full use of the 'support organization' (i.e. his or her own manager, tutors, mentors, etc.).

PROGRAMME STRUCTURE AND PRINCIPLES

1. Mapping

Principle: Integrating individual learning with organizational needs (a strategic approach)

The learners establish from the outset what they must learn to be able to cope with present and future tasks. They also consider overall development needs.

Some of the questions people consider in this mapping phase include the following:

- What is the current world situation and the outlook?
- What can be known about business development and its challenges?
- What are the Post's aims, visions, strategies, success factors now and in the future?
- What are the prospects for the unit in which I work, and what skills are needed by people working there?

- What sort of people are successful in working life and what are the areas of skill and ability that contribute to this?
- What is expected of me?
- What do I expect from life?

Part of the mapping process is carried out in group sessions using outside and in-house expertise, part of it is left to the responsibility of learning groups and the individual learner.

2. Strategic Learning Contract

Principle: Learning is constant – including through work

The Strategic Learning Contract permits the individual to connect personal aims with the aims of the organization. The document ensures success at work, but also takes all other aspects of life into consideration.

The contract is based on the following questions (used in most SML based programmes):

1. Where have I been?
2. Where am I now?
3. Where do I want to get to?
4. How will I get there?
5. How will I know that I have arrived?

The contract is a means for each participant to specify what they want to learn and why – and to share this with others. The traditional training schedule in Finnish companies has been a list of courses. They have their place, too, but this programme looks for learning areas within work. People are also encouraged to use a wide range of opportunities for learning, such as travel, reading, projects, secondments and learning from others around them.

3. Large group sessions

Principle: Clear structure

During the programme there are large group sessions where the learning groups can come together as a learning community. Additional information is supplied and consideration is given to the information provided by senior management and the concerns regarded as important by the whole community of learners.

The whole (large) group has five sessions, of 2–3 days each, on the following themes:

- orientation, Self Managed Learning principles and structure, and teamwork
- business management in the Post

- strategic thinking
- success with customers
- leadership.

The participants are intimately involved in the planning, execution and assessment of each of these events. The content of each event is very much driven by the interests and needs of participants. They have the opportunity to listen, ask questions and investigate the views of senior management and the various experts. They also test and develop their own thoughts together with the other participants.

The structure ensures that personal development needs are closely linked to the needs of the Post – they are not selfishly met at the expense of the organization.

4. Learning groups

Principle: Learning together

During their learning programme participants also take part in learning groups, consisting of five or six people. These groups are important both for learning skills and for the development of management and interpersonal skills.

The advantages of the learning group include:

- benefiting from difference
- improved learning efficiency and diversity
- more fun in learning
- improved teamwork skills
- learning to manage without assertion of authority
- learning to evaluate meeting processes and to make them more effective.

5. Supporters (superior, mentor, tutor, etc.)

Principle: Learners make active use of others to assist their own development

The superior is naturally the learner's most important supporter, assisting in the outlining of core development needs and the drawing up of a realistic/challenging Strategic Learning Contract. The superior also distributes information, assigns projects and points the learner in the direction of the right people to give assistance. It is the responsibility of the learner to get his or her boss to do that and to understand the whole issue of SML.

The mentor is an important source of support. The mentor is usually an older and more experienced individual either from within the Post or from outside. The mentor can be a good friend and a wise counsellor. The mentor shares experience, views and skills to allow the learner to develop as a person both professionally and individually.

143

The most important duties of the mentor are:

● to help the learner clarify personal aims
● to help the learner recognize strengths and hidden skills
● to help identification of development needs and discovery of various development methods
● to support learning by listening, asking and guiding – not by issuing instructions.

Managers interested in mentoring these young high flyers were first given a booklet on mentoring. The booklet includes not only philosophy, theory and models but also practical tools on how to work as a mentor – and as an active mentee. In this SML programme the mentee has a very active role in finding his or her mentors in the Post or outside. After reading the booklet mentors are provided with a half-day workshop in order to develop their capabilities further.

6. Assessment process

Principle: Learners assess their own progress

Assessment is an integral part of development and takes place throughout the programme. The first kind of assessment is of the programme itself, that is how it is going etc. At least half a day in each large group session is spent on assessing the whole process.

The whole process means all the different elements of the programme like:

● the mapping process during the first two group sessions
● the Strategic Learning Contract – developing and working on it
● the operation of learning groups
● supporters (own manager, mentor, tutors, etc.).

In small groups learners analyse how they have progressed concerning different elements of the programme – where they have succeeded, what kinds of problems they have had, what kinds of questions they want to bring up, what there is to learn for the next programme.

It is most important that the learner perceives and assesses progress within work and everyday life. Learning groups can act as critics or sparring partners for the individual learner. Assessment has to concentrate on how we learn, not just on what we learn.

At the end of the programme the results of the learning process are presented to the senior management and other parts of the organization. Final work can be presented either by individuals, by the learning groups or by the whole group.

CASE 2: THE S GROUP

The S Group consists of the 44 Finnish co-operative societies and trading companies such as SOK. Group businesses include food and groceries, speciality goods, department stores, hotels and restaurants, hardware and agriculture, automobiles and service stations. The purpose of the S Group is to provide benefits for committed customer-owners. It is one of the largest organizations in Finland with nearly 20 000 employees and a 25 per cent market share in groceries.

IMPLEMENTED SML PROGRAMMES

The Jollas Institute operates as the S Group's training and development centre and has been the focus of the S Group's initiation into using SML.

Initially a pilot programme was started with one learning group of five persons. The participants were all women in the age range 35–40, working in the back office or headquarters positions in various departments. Since they were volunteers their motivation was high and it lasted till the end. These women were all at an age in their lives when questions like 'What else am I going to do with my life?' are central and to the fore, and that is one reason why they were very much interested in taking part.

Encouraged by this pilot programme two other groups were ready to start their own programmes. One was an in-house programme just for managers in one group of hotels and the other was open to managers from various hotels and restaurants.

SOKOS HOTELS TURKU (TURKU SML)

Two Sokos hotels in Turku (a city in western Finland) took part in a one-year programme for their hotel and restaurant managers. The management defined the main need as to increase co-operation over traditional boundaries between those two hotels and inside each hotel. One reason was to help managers to learn more about the hotel business as a whole, including each other's roles and work, so that they would be able at any time to 'jump into the pants' of the other manager if necessary. The group itself described the main areas to be developed in order to reach the goal and they identified the following targets:

- to realize and to internalize their newly-enlarged roles
- to act as a good team
- to develop leadership skills
- to manage changes better and to speed up their ability to learn
- to add openness, honesty, 'us'-spirit and willingness to win to the organizational culture.

The structure was similar to the one described above (Post SML) but with special focuses.

1. Mapping

Since the goals of the programme were concrete and accepted by everybody, the mapping phase was simpler. The hotel directors actively supported the entire programme and provided input on the needs of the hotel business.

2. Strategic Learning Contracts

Most of the group had been working together for a long time. They had shared the same changes in the hotel business from the time of recession with its strict cost savings to the better times with growth and good results. They had also had lots of training arranged by the hotel chain management. They were very much aware of how an excellent manager should behave, but they needed to make this happen more effectively.

A very strong focus was given to personal welfare and endurance: how to keep up a spirit of joyful working in the hardening competition and in the turbulent world; how to foster that strong motivation to work, which makes it so easy to work long days but must not be allowed to turn in on itself, resulting in burnout.

(Motivation among the managers is very high, the hotel directors being good role models. They are all typical entrepreneurs – business issues in mind night and day. Their goals included plans on how to gain more time for their private life: family, exercise and hobbies. The Finnish Nokia mobile phones have become very dangerous – you are easy to reach whenever and wherever!)

3. Learning group

Learning groups were built by the managers themselves. Four groups of five people were created. These were as heterogeneous as possible as to experience, age, sex and work role. They started to work by themselves having received just a few instructions and a draft of the rules. After having written their Strategic Learning Contracts each group was set a challenging project by their own managers to work out during the programme. Three of the groups asked me to be a learning group adviser for a while and then they continued to work alone again using the help of their networks. Above all they wanted to keep one day per month as an 'air hole' in the middle of an otherwise very hectic business life.

4. Inputs to the groups

Members of the groups had varying learning needs, as might be expected. However, there were some common needs in areas such as language learning and information technology. Courses were arranged on these subjects so that the learning groups could keep their focus on learning to learn from each other. Also managers agreed to read various books and they reported on what they had read to their groups.

SOKOS HOTEL MANAGERS (HOTRA SML)

The other SML groups in the Sokos Hotel chain were chosen in a different way. The participants were selected by their managers. The most important criteria were: 1) the participants are motivated to develop their skills as active learners; 2) they have not for a while and will not in the near future participate in any long lasting training programme; 3) they are seen to have developmental potential; and 4) they work in different hotels/restaurants and in different parts of Finland.

The general goals for the programme were:

- to add readiness to take responsibility for one's own learning and to manage change;
- to strengthen continuous learning by improving participants' learning skills;
- to support the development of self management and entrepreneurship in work teams.

Ten participants divided into two learning groups of five people started on the first one-year programme. Five men and five women gave the groups a nice balance.

The structure itself is very similar for both the hotel programmes described here. However, the focus for this second programme is somewhat different.

Strategic Learning Contract

The groups started by working on their own Strategic Learning Contracts. The biggest difference in comparison with the Turku programme was that the participants represented various hotels from different operational environments. Hence they did not have a common theme, as was the case in Turku.

Whole group sessions

The sessions for all ten participants (five sessions of two days in every two months) could be described as a forum of organized questions and discussions. Only a couple of hours were given to the one or two outsiders (visiting experts). The rest of the two-day session was used for interesting conversations on problem solving (and learning). While checking-in time usually takes a maximum of half an hour, this group used almost half a day. We are certainly living in a world of accelerating changes – in the two months between meetings there always seem to have been some big changes concerning this group of ten people.

The openness and trust among the group made it possible to handle very personal issues, too.

> Books talk to our mind, friends to our heart, heaven to our soul and everything to our ears.
>
> (Chinese proverb)

Learning groups

Learning groups seem to have played a very important role in the programme. People gave and gained lots of support when building and carrying out their learning contracts. They also had the opportunity to handle situations (changes and problems) offering learning experiences which were not planned in advance.

Mentors

During the programme each participant was linked to a mentor. As in the two other programmes it was the person's own responsibility to find a suitable mentor after having considered their developmental needs. In the Turku SML programme, which concentrated more on professional development, a mentor was not used so much. Here, where the learning included more whole personal development, everyone found one.

RESULTS

The best feedback from the Post programme is the growing interest about the programme and yearly increased number of applicants. Additionally, since many managers whose employees have passed through the programme have requested a similar type of programme for themselves, Finland Post has started a development programme, which is based on SML and aimed to the entire higher management (150 directors, senior managers and specialists).

The SML programme provided a way for the values of Finland Post to be put into practice. It has supported people in making the organizational values real, bringing them into operation in everyday work. The concept of Partnership Thinking (with customers and suppliers) has also become true through people networking more effectively than previously, both inside and outside the organization. In the past people didn't get involved with other departments, nor really know what they did. But through sharing information and knowledge while on the SML programme, people have come to feel responsible for the organization as a whole, not only their little bit of it. There is more understanding of the business as a whole.

WHAT ARE THE ADVANTAGES FOR LEARNERS?

Feedback from participants in the S Group and in the Post programmes reveal the same positive outcomes for learners themselves.

Commitment and enthusiasm

Generally speaking they have been very committed to the whole programme. In the beginning there was usually some confusion: what is this all about? Programme by programme the confusion has taken up less time as the programme tutors/leaders have learned more about the process.

Challenging goals

As we know from theory people usually set harder goals for themselves than their managers or programme leaders do. Especially young people seem to be very demanding; to themselves as to others. Most considered that the programmes stretched them considerably.

Learning to learn

> We have learned to use our own thinking in learning more than before; we have learned to observe things in different ways.
>
> (One of the participants)

'What can we learn about this?' has been my favourite question when working with the participants of the SML programmes. In the beginning the answers handled mostly content. This is what we were taught to analyse at school. Little by little people have learned to analyse processes too and that is what I have found to be the most important progress. Through this thinking process people learn to stop, reflect, analyse and make conclusions. These are important tools to deal with personal learning throughout life. People learned more about their personal way of thinking and found their strengths and weaknesses: what is easy for me in the learning process and when do I have to strain thinking or need support from others. Target-oriented learning has altogether increased target-oriented action. People have also learned to see learning more comprehensively than before (not only in the form of training).

> Changes always revolutionize competitive positions and the quickest learners take the biggest advantage of them.
>
> (Jere Lahti, president of S Group)

Authority is near by

Efficient learning is also received from colleagues in-house, not only from authorities and gurus from outside, whom people in the beginning so easily turned to in order to learn more on any subject. At the end of the programme participants have learned to trust each other's help when trying to find knowledge and wisdom among themselves. This has added to the feeling of self confidence. This is a very good direction in a country like Finland where proverbs like 'I am nothing – and shortly not even that' were born.

It seems that growth has happened:

- in self knowledge and self confidence; people's own values have become clearer;
- in independent initiative and courage; taking responsibility for the whole.

Entrepreneurship has been emphasized in the programmes, which means risk-taking, tolerance of mistakes and failures, and exceeding limits.

> The idea of development has become real and personal. Self-confidence and self-reliance have increased.
>
> (One of the participants)

Learning together

Participants have learned how to use teams and networks as a resource – people seem to feel very lonely in their managerial positions and have felt better when given opportunities to share problems and difficulties with each other. In the middle of tough times they have been able to look at tomorrow, seeing things in a longer term perspective. Working as learning groups has offered opportunity to develop various interpersonal and leadership skills by doing – leading self-managing teams as a coach, counsellor and mentor.

Participants have also learned to run meetings better after having had rather poor meetings: schedules did not hold, items other than those agreed were discussed, some participants monopolized the meeting, etc. By analysing their mistakes participants learned both how to run meetings better and how to learn from setbacks and mistakes.

> Much I learned from my teachers, more from books, but most from my own hardships.
>
> (Isaac Kaminer)

The 'total view' has increased

In all the programmes sooner or later better understanding of the whole (own department, the whole Post, our hotel, etc.) has arisen as an important development need. It has been considered as a necessity to understand better challenges connected to one's own work. The participants experience their total view having grown and they realize how dependent people are on each other.

> I feel considerably more engaged in my company than before the programme started.
>
> (One of the participants in Post)

Even top management learns from the active participants. After having been interviewed and challenged by them, one of the directors appeared to be sincere when saying after the meeting:

> There were really good questions and I feel I have achieved a lot from discussions with the participants. I am not sure whether they learned from me nearly as much as I learned from them.

Leadership skills

The whole process has developed leadership and interpersonal skills; those new skills needed when leading self-managed teams or managing knowledge people. Also human understanding has changed to become more positive, which adds trust in people and facilitates empowerment.

The mentoring system works

Especially in the Post, where training and supplementary material were arranged for people starting as mentors, the mentoring process has created an interest in working this way.

WHAT WAS DIFFICULT – NEW CHALLENGES

> In the beginning I did not understand what it was all about.
>
> (One of the participants)

Though most of the participants considered the process to be excellent, there were in each group one or two persons for whom it was a confusing experience. Self Managed Learning as a way of thinking, especially linked to a large organization accustomed to training, is not always easy or even self-explanatory. It may be easy to understand the principles and the philosophy and to have knowledge about SML; you may also be very motivated; you have the correct attitudes – but it is not easy to get rid of old habits which have been developed over many years. Positive changes in behaviour take time.

The major challenges are as follows:

- Changing attitudes towards learning away from traditional training and participation in courses to Self Managed Learning – about 5–10 per cent of people preferred the more traditional courses they were used to. The SML programme does not work if a person does not feel good about it. In such cases we have tried to find reasons by talking with the person. If that does not help we allow them to quit and try to make sure that there are no bad feelings, just understanding the differences among people and their life situations.
- Informing and involving all superiors equally, especially in programmes where people are working in different parts of the organization. Although it is the

participant's responsibility to inform their managers of the programme in the beginning and during the process, much more supportive material is needed to help managers to understand the idea of the process. In Finland Post a booklet on leadership challenges in learning organizations and self managing teams was written for the managers.

- Abandoning the traditional roles of supervisors and participants – and accepting responsibility for learning.
- Taking enough time for common discussions in the group meetings. A rewarding network does not develop unless time has been granted for it.

Paradox management

SML based programmes have not been heavily promoted or marketed. This has caused uncertainty and the programme may have been considered as a bit mysterious. The explanation for this is that since the pilot, and using experiences achieved in both organizations, the programme has been developed and the goal has been to find an optimal strategy, where the seemingly opposite issues can be combined:

- freedom – control
- looseness – tightness (in the programme)
- individuality – doing things together
- difference – equality
- breaking limits – discipline
- present tasks – new challenges.

SML demands that people balance these seeming opposites. This is both a strength and a weakness. The strength lies in the fact that excellent management requires just such balancing acts. The weakness is that some managers don't recognize this and hence feel confused by the SML approach.

CONCLUSIONS

SML programmes in both Finland Post and the S Group have been successful. The evaluations of the programmes show that they have benefited individuals and their organizations. This has been recognized by top management. SML is still relatively new in Finland but the evidence of these programmes shows that it could expand greatly. To some extent SML fits the Finnish culture where learning is valued. However, it is also a challenge to traditional education and training approaches.

NOTE

1. Much of the information in this section is based on a paper given by Asko Saviaho, CEO of Finland Post, at the Management Centre Europe Global Human Resource Conference in Vienna, April 1998.

Lifelong learning and Self Managed Learning in Ericsson

10

Robert Lines

INTRODUCTION

This case study looks at Ericsson Limited (ETL), the UK subsidiary of the Swedish-based Ericsson group. Self Managed Learning was introduced into ETL by a number of line managers in 1998 and was seen to compliment activities aimed at achieving a corporate objective of 'Lifelong learning for our proactive employees'. The objective is part of the group's overall approach to strategy that has been driven by scenario planning for the year 2005.

Ericsson's early SML programme participants included line managers, software designers and testers, project managers and administrators. The approach has subsequently been adopted by the Human Resources department and is now an integral part of the company's two-year graduate induction. It is also planned that SML will be included in the ETL management leadership programmes.

THE ORGANIZATION

Ericsson is one of the world's leading suppliers of telecommunications equipment. Operating in 140 countries, it employs over 100 000 people worldwide. In the UK 5500 employees are based at sites including Burgess Hill, Guildford, Basingstoke, Warrington and Swindon.

Ericsson has been in the UK for more than a hundred years, but significant growth did not occur until 1984 when an order was won from British Telecom to replace its analogue telephone exchanges with a digital network. The organization's profile remained low until the explosive growth of mobile telephony in the late 1990s. Ericsson is now the world leader in digital mobile networks and has captured over 40 per cent of the market. Ericsson sees its future in the 'New Telecoms World' where communications solutions will combine telecom and data technologies with freedom of mobility for the user. Its target customers will include the media industry, network operators, businesses and consumers.

Ericsson has a strong and long-established culture. The company quotes its guiding values as professionalism, respect and perseverance. Internally there is firm belief that the organization's sustained success is due to this strong culture. Ericsson has always invested heavily in technical development and in recent years its research and development budget has exceeded 20 per cent of sales. In 1998 the investment in this area was £3 billion.

BACKGROUND

During 1997 responsibility for a major telecoms software project fell to three ETL line managers – Alan Slater, Martin Springell and myself. The aim of the project was to allow BT to access the Ericsson Intelligent Network (IN) which in turn offers rapid and flexible service deployment. The project was significant because it followed a period in which our design team had run into serious problems during the development of a similar product. The implementation had been based on poorly specified internal requirements and this had affected all parts of the design process. Things had gone from bad to worse and the cost of re-work escalated as the time-scales doubled. The designers and testers worked exceptionally long hours in an attempt to recover, but without success.

Motivation to learn from the earlier mistakes and to introduce new ways of working could not have been higher in the Intelligent Network project. The design process was replaced by formal methods in which the output at each stage of the design could be rigorously checked against the original requirements. The learning that took place during this period was immense and it was clear that this type of working environment did wonders for morale and motivation. Because the methods and tools were brand new, there were no standard courses and the teams found alternative ways of learning. This included collaboration with the third party tool manufacturers, reading manuals, learning from experience, and much trial and error. Each afternoon a group of four or five of us would meet to discuss the challenges that had emerged during the day, and the potential strategies we might employ to overcome the difficulties.

Although the Intelligent Network implementation was extremely successful, the introduction of an entirely new design process is clearly not a practical measure for every project. However, we were interested to know if it was possible to find other ways to encourage the enthusiasm for learning that had had such a positive effect on the team.

It was clear that a great deal of learning had taken place during the IN project, but we had not pursued a deliberate learning strategy. Looking back to previous projects we were aware that things do not always run smoothly, and there can be a number of difficulties in managing learning and development. For example:

- We would ask people to document their training plans and records, but they would never get round to it. Where training plans did exist, they would soon become out of date.
- People would complain to their colleagues and managers that they had not received any training for years, when in fact we had sent them on a number of courses in the past few months. (As one test engineer put it, 'That course wasn't proper training, it was just for the project.')
- In the middle of projects, when time was short, we would send people on courses and far too often they would return and tell us that they had learnt very little.

We drew a number of conclusions. Firstly that people had lost confidence that there was any value in a training plan. One designer stated, 'Even when we send our training plans to HR, they never organize the courses we want.' In fact our HR department never has been responsible for organizing technical training. It was also apparent that in general people did not value courses that they had simply been 'sent on'. The question arose as to whether it would ever really be possible to organize other people's development effectively – particularly as for our team of 30 designers it would require a huge amount of time and considerable insight.

At around the same time, the company had provided the opportunity for its managers to study on a sponsored MBA programme run by the University of Brighton. The Action Learning mode employed for the MBA part-time course has been popular and participants have become familiar with the benefits of learning 'sets'/groups and learning objectives. We were keen to explore the possibility of introducing this type of learning in a way that would allow participants to pursue individual learning goals.

THE OBJECTIVES

The learning and development objectives that we wanted to achieve within the design team were:

- to provide an approach to learning that people would enjoy, perhaps along the lines of the Intelligent Network project where collaboration was highly visible and people took a creative approach to identifying sources of learning;
- to encourage people to take charge of their own development so that they would not be waiting passively for others to organize courses or learning activities;
- to get the most out of the time that people were investing in learning activities;
- to increase the employability of our team. In previous years concerns about a less than certain future had been a major distraction. We wanted to be in the

position where as an organization and as individuals we would be confident that we could adapt to whatever types of future roles might be required.

As well as aiming to achieve our local objectives, it was apparent that SML was also in line with the strategic direction proposed by our parent company in Stockholm. Scenario planning activities started in the early 1990s in an attempt to understand the future, and to identify what the organization needed to do in order to survive and prosper. Scenarios have been defined for the year 2005 and common objectives to support these include the following:

- 'We have an environment of continuous learning and development that fosters lifelong learning for our employees.'
- 'We have people who proactively take initiatives.'
- 'Ericsson shall have a Research and Development organization set for speed and flexibility.'

THE IMPLEMENTATION

Our first step towards SML was to organize a workshop in May 1997. Here members of our team worked in groups to develop individual learning contracts. The session was held away from the office and facilitated by Ian Cunningham.

Some of the themes covered during the day clearly struck a chord with many of the participants and these issues were discussed at length back at base:

- It is quite valid to pursue a career defined in terms of learning. In fact this view makes a great deal more sense than the traditional view of the hierarchical organizational levels.
- It can be extremely helpful to view change in terms of learning, and a way to manage change is to consider learning at an individual level.
- Learning objectives concerned with longer term strategic goals are important if individuals are to be adequately prepared for the future.

Much of the workshop was spent working in groups and it was apparent that support from colleagues can be valuable during the creation of a learning contract. In the months following the workshop, people met with their managers on a one-to-one basis to discuss progress.

In early 1998 we decided to run a larger programme which would include learning groups. Almost as soon as the group work had started at our previous workshop it had become obvious that the learning group had a great deal to offer. In the interim period a number of organizational changes had taken place and this resulted in Alan, Martin and myself taking jobs in separate parts of the ETL organization. This had the positive side-effect of allowing us to plan learning groups with people from more diverse backgrounds.

The programme was presented to potential participants as a pilot that was open to volunteers. We hoped that this would ensure:

- that people would approach SML with an open mind;
- that people would be prepared to give feedback on what they thought of the process;
- that aspects of SML implementation could be tested in order to establish what worked well within Ericsson, for example different start-up venues, different group compositions, etc.

A pilot trial of SML within Ericsson was agreed and 90 participants from the Mobile and Fixed Line divisions embarked on 10-month programmes which commenced in May and October 1998. It was planned that the programme should comprise the following elements:

- A two hour introduction with an opportunity for questions and answers
- A one day off-site workshop to include group formation
- Six 5 hour learning group meetings
- A half-day reflection at the end of the programme.

External learning group advisers were asked to support the scheme in order to increase the likelihood of the groups functioning effectively. We felt that norms accepted within Ericsson would be challenged, and that there would be new angles on solving problems. Academic credibility was important and we also felt that the independence of the set advisers would result in an environment that was seen to be safe for open discussion.

Three different venues were used to host start-up events. Normal practice would have dictated that the events would be run at the company's main training centre in Haslemere, Surrey. However, it was decided to emphasize the importance of stepping back from normal work by arranging venues that would not be associated with everyday business.

Ian Cunningham presented at each of the sessions, although the majority of the time was spent working in groups under the facilitation of the external learning group advisers.

PROGRAMME PARTICIPANTS

The programme was publicized at line management and team meetings. Although primarily driven by the needs of the business, a conscious effort was made to ensure that a diverse as possible population enrolled in the programme. As a result, the programme comprised:

- department and section managers
- software designers
- project and product managers
- administrators and secretaries
- group supervisors and team leaders
- human resource officers.

The largest number of volunteers were software designers and it was from this group that came the greatest level of enthusiasm.

INTRODUCTORY PRESENTATION

All members of the programme and their managers were invited to a presentation 10 days ahead of the start-up workshops. This provided an opportunity to explain SML and the main components of the programme. Approximately 40 people attended.

START-UP WORKSHOPS

Although identical in content, the experience of the three days may have been different because of the change in environment. On Monday, 11 May 1998 the workshop was held on the Brighton University Campus. The environment was academic and all those involved seemed relaxed after the weekend. Two days later the venue was a conference centre in Surrey where the environment was far more business-like. It was an extremely hot day and it appeared that there was less of the sense of energy that had accompanied the sessions on the Monday. The third start-up day was held on a Friday at a small conference centre in West Sussex.

Of the three workshops it was perhaps the first and last that most effectively achieved a change from the normal working environment. It seemed that this was important if people were to consider their medium and long-term goals.

FORMATION OF LEARNING GROUPS

Sixteen groups were formed over the three days of workshops. The main concern in allocating people to learning groups had been to ensure that people worked with others at a similar level in the organizational hierarchy. Almost half the programme participants were software designers and hence it was straightforward to put together groups where people could work with colleagues from other parts of the wider organization. However, in the case of the managers it was more difficult to find delegates at the same level from across the organization. Consequently four groups were formed that comprised part or all of a line management team.

Thought had been given to the possibility of allowing participants to choose their own groups, but this approach was not adopted due to time constraints and concerns over difficulties caused when people find themselves isolated due to logistical and other reasons.

LEARNING GROUP MEETINGS

Each group took responsibility for scheduling six group meetings over the 10-month period. In general meetings were held at Ericsson sites, though some groups chose to use hotels and group members' homes as alternative venues.

OUTCOMES

A number of activities were undertaken in order to evaluate the programme. Focus groups were held and asked to discuss their experiences and thoughts on the programme. From this, a survey was derived and this was used to test the focus groups' views across the whole participant population. The learning groups were asked to submit lists of learning areas that they were pursuing.

WORKING WITH OTHERS TO PURSUE LEARNING GOALS

As with most research and development organizations, teamwork plays a significant part of everyday life within Ericsson. Much of the work of software design involves consulting with others in order to resolve technical issues. Peer reviews and inspections are the primary method of quality assurance and control.

However, in the past training and development has not seen such an emphasis on teamwork or collaboration. For many of the participants on the Ericsson SML programme the idea of learning groups was novel. In a survey of the entire programme population it was this aspect of SML that participants rated most positively. Eighty-eight per cent of respondents agreed that group members had helped to generate ideas or to provide solutions to problems that they had encountered in pursuing learning goals. One designer discussed the support that he had received during the start-up phases.

> If I had had to work on my own I think I would have found the learning contract difficult to put together. However, other members of the group came up with all sorts of ideas, particularly on how I might measure the outcomes of my objectives.
>
> I was surprised it worked. In the early days I couldn't see how a bunch of people from different areas would be able to help other people learning different things. But I guess with SML you don't always need to be told the answer. Sometimes people suggest something that leads you to the solution indirectly. Often just the opportunity to discuss an issue makes you realize that you knew the answer all the time.

161

Other interviewees discussed feeling a greater sense of commitment to their learning goals once they had shared the ideas with the group.

> Having spent several weeks considering priorities, and explaining to my group why the areas of learning I planned to pursue were important, I felt obliged to carry them through to the end! I have to say that I did feel some pressure from the group and the adviser to succeed.

In the past ETL, like other organizations, has found that projects perceived to be 'HR initiatives' have not always received a positive reception from the technical specialists. One designer on the programme spoke of his surprise that his colleagues were enthusiastic about the SML approach.

> The people I was in a group with were very pro the scheme. I had expected them to be anti, and see this as just another HR initiative that would be 'here today gone tomorrow'.

Working in learning groups did not suit everyone, and some found the experience uncomfortable. It would be hard to generalize, as it is clear that individuals vary in what they feel happy to discuss, or hear discussed, in their groups. However, it was apparent that people were far happier to work in groups with people that they didn't previously know than with colleagues that they worked with on a regular basis. It is clear that programme organizers have a responsibility to ensure that groups provide as safe an environment as is practicable.

EMPOWERMENT

For a number of the participants, SML has presented an opportunity to take charge of their careers. During interviews, people talked about a sense of empowerment. Over recent years the importance of empowerment has been recognized and discussed at length. However, its implementation has been far less straightforward. One line of argument suggests that individuals only become empowered when they choose to be so. If this is true, it would seem that learning and development might be an aspect of working life where motivation for 'taking charge' can be high.

Across the telecom industry future directions are less than clear. Some interviewees discussed their concerns about the future, and their awareness of the danger of waiting to be told what was going to happen to them. For the vast majority of people within the company career progression in terms of promotion to new jobs is not entirely within their control. Much depends on opportunities and in some areas these may be shrinking or at the very least becoming difficult to predict.

People reported that they were happier to view their careers in terms of learning and development as this made it possible to take a proactive approach to their future direction. One senior designer in an area about to face change stated:

> I see in myself and in my colleagues that we are just waiting to be told what to do. I think SML will challenge that, and empower us to go and find learning resources for ourselves.

Similar thoughts from a project manager:

> [SML] will build a different type of culture where people are responsible for their own futures as opposed to thinking 'My manager knows what I need to learn – I'll just wait for him or her to let me know.' 'Empowerment', that's the word I was looking for.

EXTERNAL LEARNING GROUP ADVISERS

Many participants rated highly the opportunity to work with external group advisers. In particular it seems that people valued the chance to discuss aspects of work with people that were entirely independent of the organization. In budgeting for an SML programme it is clear that the cost of external set advisers can be significant, and this is an expense that needs to be taken into account. It was recognized that on a wider rollout of the scheme group advisers from within our own organization might produce a solution to the logistical problem of finding the large numbers of external advisers that would otherwise be required.

LIFELONG LEARNING

When the idea of running an SML programme was first floated, it was of interest to know how well this approach would line up with the company's vision for 2005. The relevant chapters of the strategy document describe the desire for 'lifelong learning for proactive employees'. The two approaches seemed to be well aligned, but we were keen to produce results that could be used to demonstrate to other areas of the organization that SML could indeed support an objective that otherwise could be hard to achieve.

Inherently lifelong learning is a difficult concept to work with since it could always be argued that data from several lifetimes is necessary to produce valid evidence. A decision was taken to use John Kotter's definition of lifelong learning where he discusses mental habits that he believes support lifelong learning:

- Honest assessment of success and failures, especially the latter
- Aggressive collection of information and ideas from others
- Propensity to listen to others
- Willingness to view life with an open mind
- Risk taking and a willingness to push oneself out of comfort zones.

(Kotter 1996: 183)

We believe that the SML programme addressed each of these characteristics. Although risk-taking was not specifically explored in the evaluation, this type of behaviour is likely to be encouraged by an increase in confidence that three-quarters of those involved in the programme believed would result. One respondent to the survey added the following comments:

> I feel that I have benefited from an increase in confidence that I can change things and learn. I guess it has made me more positive about trying new things.

OPPORTUNITY TO CONSIDER LONGER TERM OBJECTIVES

For most people in the organization, it seems that normality is a relatively hectic schedule. Many described their jobs as requiring 'fire-fighting' skills. SML can provide an opportunity to step back from day-to-day business. A significant majority of the survey respondents felt that a benefit of the programme was that it had allowed focus to be given to longer term goals and objectives.

LEADERSHIP DEVELOPMENT

The identification and development of potential leaders was seen as a value of SML by managers, for example:

> For me personally, the experience of SML has been valuable in many different ways. One unexpected benefit has been that the process has identified enthusiasts that are comfortable with the roles of mentor, coach, collaborator and, of course, self-managed learner. Perhaps for some, the behaviours encouraged by the SML process are natural and obvious. However, for many these roles and their associated skills developed over the course of the group meetings.
>
> Historically there has been a tendency to place emphasis on technical competence when considering appointments to positions such as group supervisor and technical coordinator. Unfortunately this has not always resulted in an entirely positive experience for the teams. Leaders also need human skills that will allow them to share knowledge and build their team.
>
> As a manager, I am now more confident that I can predict which people in the organization are likely to make effective team leaders and members of a management team. Of course, it would not be wise to rely on any single source of data when appointing leaders, but the experience of SML has added to the information store that can be accessed when critical decisions need to be made.

LESSONS LEARNT

DIFFICULTIES

Participants were asked about difficulties they had faced during the course of the programme. Time spent attending group meetings was mentioned on a number of occasions and we are aware that not all participants were able to attend every meeting. We also asked if participants had felt under pressure from their managers to give higher priority to normal work than to attending group meetings. However, this was not reported to be an issue by any of those involved.

It can be difficult to persuade managers who are not familiar with the SML process to spend their budget on a programme that does not promise an increase in specific competences. There also seems to be a problem in justifying the expense of external learning group advisers even though programme participants rated highly the opportunity to work with independent facilitators.

A small number of the participants were decidedly uncomfortable with the SML approach and cited an unwillingness to disclose information regarding life outside work (which they felt as being too personal). Although difficult to draw too many conclusions, this seemed to be an issue particularly for participants that use a noticeably hands-on approach to the management of a technical area.

WHAT WENT WELL?

Learning groups worked well where their members were drawn from across the organization and were at a similar level of the hierarchy. The approach also seems to be popular with those who have an interest in supporting other people's learning. Perhaps those who seem to get the least out of the approach are those who are focused purely on their own personal short-term goals. Here, the value of the learning contract is recognized, but the value of the group meeting is less obvious. Where there is an understanding of the wider organizational development and the high possibility of emergent learning, participants are more enthusiastic.

Of the 11 groups that started, all but one ran their planned course. One group decided to stop meeting after three sessions. A member of this group fed back that he 'resented sitting around for five hours in a meeting'. Here there seemed to be a feeling that the learning group meeting comprised 'active' and 'passive' periods. It was not clear if there was an understanding that the group members would remain engaged in the process during the periods when other people were presenting their progress and (perhaps) hoping for support. The group that ended early queried if they were getting less out of the process because they were used to organizing their own development activities, and already felt in charge of their careers.

For many, the learning group was seen as a safe environment. Groups reported they had provided support by giving feedback after specific work-related activities. One group had met on a number of occasions to listen to a presentation that one of their group had wanted to practise. The learning group was then able to provide feedback and coaching.

In another example a contract item had been to increase the person's influencing skills. Although the person had attended a course, she felt that there was no obvious improvement. Having discussed what had been taught on the course, the group then agreed to give feedback on how well the learning was applied in real meetings. The group created a checklist that included items such as:

- Do contributions start positively?
- Are phrases such as 'I've just got a couple of things I need to say?' and 'I don't want to bore you but . . .' avoided?
- Are contributions made early in discussions when there is still the possibility to influence the outcome?

So, here the group did not just support the initial learning, but also supported the application of the learning. The safe environment seemed to be especially useful to those who wished to build up their confidence in particular areas.

CONCLUSIONS

The SML programme was initiated and run by the line. This seemed to create far more of a sense of ownership from the target population than we have seen in the past for this type of initiative. Indeed the SML process has now progressed beyond the 'initiative' stage to become part of Ericsson's learning and development strategy in the UK. This links back to the idea of lifelong learning. If this latter concept is to be meaningful it needs to address the issues we tackled in launching SML. One important aspect of this is helping people to develop a long-term commitment to managing their own learning. Lifelong learning needs to be based on this.

A key aspect of the fact that it was the line that started the process has been the opportunity we have had to model a way of working taken from the business. If learning and development is pushed off to HR then it is not seen as being owned by the line. As managers we need to lead the process and show that we see the long-term benefits of investing in learning.

With regard to the SML programme itself, we are clear that it has been a success so far. Most people have enjoyed it and benefited from it. Whilst it has required a good deal of work, we can see that the organization will be more effective in the future as a result of using SML.

Self Managed Learning and Continuing Professional Development

11

Ben Bennett

INTRODUCTION

The growing pressure for greater results from fewer people is undeniable. Charles Handy has characterized the employment market of the future in the formula 'half by two by three' – half as many people paid twice as well, and delivering three times the added value (Handy 1995). These pressures are a manifestation of a host of changes affecting people in organizations. For example, those identified by the Institute of Personnel and Development (IPD) from a survey of their members included greater decentralization and devolvement of decision making, flatter and empowered structures, total quality, and more flexible, cross-functional and team methods of working (Institute of Personnel and Development 1995).

In these circumstances there is no option but to invest heavily in learning. One expression of this is evidenced by what Faulkner characterizes as the 'mushrooming' of formal Continuing Professional Development (CPD) schemes over the last ten years (Faulkner 1996). As well as being concerned with maintaining and developing skills and knowledge, which professional bodies have always encouraged their members to do, Faulkner sees the growth of interest in CPD as a contemporary response to the demands of change. He proposes that 'the underlying philosophy (of CPD) is relevant to us all whether we are members of a professional body or not' (Faulkner 1996: 48). In fact, as Woodward points out, citing evidence from the former UK Department of Employment (DE), the spread of occupations which might be grouped under the heading of professions has grown and diversified considerably (Woodward 1996). For Woodward, CPD is associated with 'learning activities that are undertaken throughout working life ... to enhance individual and organisational performance in professional and managerial spheres' (Woodward 1996: 1).

Woodward also draws our attention to other trends that indicate the need for greater flexibility in the provision of CPD. For example, increases in participation by women in the labour force, in part-time and self-employment, and in employment growth in the small firms sector all point to forms of participation in CPD other than the traditional, formal, 'off-line' model. That model is based on the assumption that continuing formal education and training is the primary learning mode to invest in. However, we know from our own research that much learning at work occurs in informal settings and that other people can be an important source of help (see Cunningham 1999). (The 'we' here includes B. Bennett, J. Cooper, C. Cunningham and G. Dawes.) This is confirmed by others' research. For instance, in a study of 120 managers, professionals and technicians in the engineering, business and healthcare sectors, Eraut and colleagues found that the individual's learning was strongly situated in the work itself and its social and organizational context (Eraut *et al.* 1997). Similarly, having investigated the contribution of this kind of learning to continuing professional development in seven professions, Gear *et al.* concluded that everybody should have an ultimate focus on continuing learning rather than continuing education (Gear *et al.* 1994). Such a focus makes distinct demands on learners. As Eraut and colleagues express it, individuals should be 'helped to become more capable learners, who can be both more reflective and more self-directed, more proactive and more able to recognise and use emergent learning opportunities' (Eraut *et al.* 1997: 16). In a similar vein, the IPD concluded from its survey that the desired outcomes of development should include a greater degree of self management in organizations, individuals who have been helped to take on greater responsibility for their own development and growth, and organizations stimulating and supporting ownership by every employee of their development (Institute of Personnel and Development 1995).

This chapter is about the links between Self Managed Learning and CPD, drawing on research into learning. In particular I will draw on the study undertaken by Gear *et al.* at the University of Hull (Gear *et al.* 1994). They interviewed 150 members of professional bodies about substantial episodes of informal learning that they could identify and isolate from the flow of everyday interaction and experience. The professions represented were architecture, mechanical engineering, law, medical general practice, nursing, social work, and obstetrics and gynaecology. The kind of informal learning that was a particular focus of their study was what they term 'developmental learning'. This is described as dynamic, progressive and cumulative and manifested in what Tough calls 'learning projects', that is time spent by the individual developing some aspect of professional knowledge, skills and competence to the point where some of it can be passed on to a colleague (Tough 1971).

In their study, they attempt to distinguish clearly between informal and formal learning. By the latter they mean institutionalized provision, planned curricula and formal methods such as lectures, classes and seminars. Formal learning relies heavily on written texts and is typically assessed through set tests and examinations. They use the term 'informal learning' to refer to learning by doing, typically on the job. Included in this definition is the acquisition of knowledge and skills under the supervision of a more experienced practitioner. This continues until professional independence is achieved by the person concerned. They propose that this kind of learning is largely self directed and relies heavily on oral communication. Where assessment of learning is concerned, judgements are made about observable levels of competence or performance. These conclusions are echoed in the considerable research literature produced by the Institute for Research on Learning. Their findings, reviewed by Cunningham, point to the idea of basic social units for learning. These are the 'communities of practice' in which people come to develop and share ways of doing things as a result of their joint involvement in activities (Cunningham 1999).

Formal and informal learning are seen as the two traditions inherited by the professions. This view is supported by Madden and Mitchell (1993) from their survey of 20 professional bodies representing a cross-section of contemporary professions in the UK. They were able to identify two models of CPD policy and practice, the 'mandatory' and 'voluntary'. These two models make a number of distinctions. For example, the mandatory approach is one in which the monitoring of CPD is undertaken exclusively by the professional body concerned to ensure compliance with its requirements. With the voluntary approach there is self monitoring of learning activities and outcomes. The former of these two models is more prevalent than the latter (Madden and Mitchell 1993). As pointed out by the Hull researchers, the education of professionals in the twentieth century has become more formal, both in the early stage and subsequently with regard to CPD. Thus their desire to undertake their research was motivated partly by a concern that the current and welcomed growth of interest in CPD could lead to an overemphasis on purely formal and apparently accountable activities, at the expense of less obvious and less public ones. In particular, that the formalization of CPD could have the opposite effects to those desired and intended by professional bodies. I also share their concern. Professionals are likely to be put off CPD and find that the only reason they are doing it in any of the forms deemed to be legitimate and accountable is because of the prospect of the sanctions imposed by their professional bodies if they do not. This feeling was echoed by human resources specialists in the Kent region. Chesterman reports that their reluctance to comply was not matched by a reluctance to learn. He concluded that there was a strong motivation to invest in learning with the support of others, as long as it was not prescriptive or bureaucratic (Chesterman 1999).

As a result of their study, Gear and colleagues are better able to express the need for informal learning to be incorporated fully into CPD. This follows from their expression of concern that we should all focus our attention on continuing learning rather than continuing education. They cite three reasons for this.

1. We should concentrate on the learning 'outputs' rather than the educational or other 'inputs' (e.g. courses, conferences, reading material, etc.). The latter are merely a means to an end – a contribution to learning where the end is more effective practice.
2. It happens anyway. As they suggest, the very concept of a profession implies individual autonomy and responsibility such that continuing learning should be initiated, organized, controlled and indeed evaluated by the individual.
3. Professional people employ a wide variety of means and resources to continue their learning.

In recommending that we adopt this focus they identify what they see as a number of potential problems. These include lack of time and resources and, further, what they see as a particularly significant inhibitor to continuing learning. This is an individual's lack of awareness of the nature of the learning process, despite their obvious involvement in activities that contribute to their learning.

I will bring an SML perspective to bear on these and their other findings, concerns and recommendations. The broad thrust of these comments will be that within an SML frame all their concerns can be addressed. From an SML perspective, the key requirement for professionals and others is to create a situation where learning is structured and planned and yet in such a way that the process of learning and development matches the desired outcomes. I will argue that, through SML, CPD can be structured, performance related, resourced and accountable, at the same time as being self-directed and driven by on-the-job needs (while also using institutionalized provision where appropriate). This argument is intended to encourage thought and discussion amongst those with an interest in CPD.

I will comment first on the distinction between continuing learning and continuing education. In particular I will show how SML enables the former without sacrificing the benefits of the structure and organization typically associated with the latter. I will then go on to discuss the kinds of learning identified in the study and demonstrate how SML can broaden, deepen and integrate these, and in such a way that awareness of the process of learning is enhanced. In the remainder of the chapter I will explore and comment on the implications of the continuous learning approach for CPD. I will do so using the perspectives adopted in the report of the Hull study, namely the implications for management in organizations followed by the implications for professional bodies.

CONTINUING LEARNING AND CONTINUING EDUCATION

Continuing learning is associated with self directed learning (i.e. learning that is initiated, organized, controlled and evaluated by the individual). This, in turn, is associated with lack of structure and organization. Structure and organization are seen as properties of formal education. This is the model associated with the initial phase of professional education, in which the learning is directed by educational institutions, not with the continuing, self directed, informal phase. However, self directed learning need not be unstructured and disorganized. The fact that it is so often seen this way is because those making a distinction between 'formal' and 'informal' learning commonly confuse structure with control.

Contrary sometimes to popular opinion, the SML process is not unstructured. However, it is not structured in the same way as that implied by the distinctions between formal and informal learning above. As explained in Chapter 2, SML has a very clear structure but it is not the same as that on a taught course. Taught courses are typically highly structured and, at the same time, control the content and trajectory of participants' learning. SML is structured (through timetabled events, learning contracts and learning groups, etc.) but not controlling, so that each participant has the opportunity to make their own decisions about their learning.

One inevitable consequence of high structure and high control at the initial stage of professional development is that, apart from the planned curriculum, there is also the creation of a 'hidden curriculum' of dependency. If the distinction between structure and control is clear, then relevant institutions can provide the former while also encouraging and enabling the development of real independence and interdependence amongst learners.

SOME MEANS OF CONTINUING LEARNING

Three kinds of continuing learning are identified in the Hull University study:

1. Specific learning: driven by, and often limited to, particular cases and problems that are part and parcel of everyday professional work.
2. General learning: keeping 'up to date' generally with developments in a profession and not related to any particular problem or activity.
3. Developmental learning: with which the Hull study is mainly concerned.

There are similarities between these kinds of learning and the outcomes of SML programmes identified through evaluation studies. However, what comes across in the latter is the greater degree of integration between them and also that, in practice, participants in SML programmes typically report having broadened and deepened their learning beyond the narrow limits of knowledge, skill and competence. For example, the evaluation study of a nine-month consortium SML programme discussed in Chapter 4 showed how the benefits of SML included specific issues or problems addressed in new or different ways, the application or development of new capabilities or techniques, and an increased capacity to learn from experience integrated with other aspects of personal development.

As illustrated by this evaluation evidence, and that reported in the other case studies in this book, undertaking CPD through SML can provide professionals with both a clear structure within which to undertake their professional development and opportunities that are likely to take them beyond the minimum requirements of their professional body. One of the reasons for this is the particular SML structuring device of the Strategic Learning Contract. As outlined in Chapter 2, and covered in detail in Chapter 12, participants in SML programmes have opportunities to direct their learning towards task, career and life goals. This takes their learning potentially further, deeper and over a longer time period than that suggested by the findings and recommendations of the Hull study. Doing this also fits with policies that are espoused at national and European levels about lifelong learning, and represented in the UK by initiatives like the University for Industry (UfI).

For individual professionals who are looking at least some way ahead, there are two reasons for travelling as far as this with CPD. Firstly, they are likely to be operating at levels professionally in which any continuing development has to be placed clearly in an organizational, business or managerial context in order for it to be undertaken successfully (and also probably associated with other learning related directly to these contexts, such as in business skills or a range of specific managerial capabilities). Secondly, professionals working in organizations are in large respect no different from others in terms of their need to manage their own development in the face of the organizational changes highlighted in the IPD survey and other research. For example, if we want key outcomes of CPD to include increased self management, the individual's ownership of their longer term development and learning which Gear *et al.* call 'developmental' (as well as learning which is 'specific' or 'tactical'), then we need a process in which professionals adopt a strategic and self managed stance towards their own learning.

LACK OF AWARENESS OF THE NATURE OF THE LEARNING PROCESS

The Hull researchers conclude that one of the main inhibitors to CPD is lack of awareness of the nature of the learning process. Typically, despite their active involvement in continuing learning, people do not recognize that involvement as learning until they are encouraged to provide an account of it. The implication of this is that, in the absence of the need or opportunity to render such an account, activities central to learning can go unnoticed and undervalued by the individual because they are not coded or labelled as learning.

These findings echo those of our own research on learning and personal development in organizations. We have also found that people often need assistance in construing their professional and other experiences in terms of learning. Recalling educational experiences (i.e. structured and controlled experience gained in educational institutions and in training programmes) is often not a problem for individuals although, interestingly, when they do have the 'label' for learning, educational experiences *per se* do not often figure as having made a significant contribution to it.

SML surrounds the learning process with a tangible structure and, in the Strategic Learning Contract, provides an umbrella under which the individual can choose to place a range of continuing learning (and education) projects. Also learning groups provide the ideal environment for individuals to reflect on both the substance and the process of their learning.

IMPLICATIONS FOR MANAGEMENT

The implications for employing organizations and their managers are categorized in four ways: time, resources, contact and ethos. I will comment on each of these from an SML perspective.

TIME

Those interviewed reported lack of time as one of the major obstacles to continuing learning. This is seen as a growing problem for continuing learning, given the increasing pressures in modern organizations towards greater productivity. Perhaps, in the end, it may be counter-productive to push productivity to the limit given that continuing learning 'inhabits the interstices and margins of organisational life and, if there are no margins left, then there will be little or no learning' (Gear *et al.* 1994: 75).

In SML, individuals have the means to address issues concerned with time and its availability. Through their Strategic Learning Contracts they have opportunities to clarify and tackle the 'problem' of shortages of time for learning and other purposes. Also, as evidenced in the evaluation study discussed in Chapter 4, participants on SML programmes typically report significant personal learning in this area in terms of getting a better balance between various facets of life and work.

Together with 'resources' and 'contact', the existence of problems in these areas will be affected by what is termed 'ethos'. Although a commentary on this is provided below, its immediate relevance can be noted here. By ethos we mean the presence or absence of a culture of learning in the organization. Where such a culture is present one would expect to encounter support for individuals' continuing learning. Minimally and tactically, this would mean a culture in which individuals find that their learning is not pushed completely to the 'interstices and margins'. Optimally and strategically, this would mean one in which the manage ment of any of the kinds of changes reported in the IPD survey would include planned opportunities and resources for continuing learning. The fact that the latter is unfortunately rarely the case is evidenced by the apparent lack of success of so many fashionable initiatives in organizations in areas such as total quality or knowledge management.

RESOURCES

Several of those interviewed warned that one of the dangers of emphasizing informal learning is that it gives organizations the pretext to reduce funds for formal learning. This is likely to be the case only if, within the organizational ethos, notions of the formal and informal are seen as an either/or choice. My comments above about the distinction between structure and control are relevant here. In principle there is no reason at all for organizations not to provide 'formal' support for 'informal' learning through SML. This formal support could include the structures of learning groups and Strategic Learning Contracts and the capacity to provide workshops or other learning materials in a flexible way to meet the needs of self managing learners. The desire on the part of organizations to reduce funds for learning will be lessened considerably with the recognition that SML is a highly cost-effective way of providing support for learning.

Where specific materials designed for learning are required these can be more closely targeted to meet individuals' real learning goals under the umbrellas of their Strategic Learning Contracts. This process can be further enabled through a system of 'learning budgets' in which amounts budgeted for within agreed Strategic Learning Contracts can be used by individual participants and/or by learning groups to access established or specially created workshops, seminars or open learning materials to address areas of individual or common interest. For instance, in some in-house SML programmes and SML qualification programmes, participants have defined and resourced many topics that they have felt were relevant to their learning contracts. The SML MBA programme discussed in Chapter 8 involved facilitating the resourcing of precisely tailored workshops which, combined with the other vehicles for learning chosen by participants, meant that the programme covered more than the complete range of subject areas typically included in an MBA, and without imposing a curriculum.

The constraints on the availability of potential learning resources can be determined as much by the limits of human imagination as by their cost. As pointed out in Chapter 12, there is much that can be resourced with minimal additional costs by using people from within the organization who are specialists in the areas of interest to learners. So, what might be gained by an individual from a short course, can be gained from one or a short series of meetings or coaching sessions with a specialist colleague, or, if it is clearly an interest common to a number of people undertaking CPD, by the use of the specialist as a contributor to a workshop. This can add to networking in the organization, to the continuing learning of the specialist and, along with the development of other relationships of this kind, to the creation or maintenance of a learning ethos.

The many different ways of drawing on colleagues and others in resourcing learning in SML is one illustration of why contact between people is so important. Other aspects of this are highlighted in the next section. Another example of its occurrence and consequences is provided by Eraut and colleagues (Eraut *et al.* 1998). They found that only a minority of respondents made frequent use of written or audio-visual materials such as manuals, videos or computer-based training. The majority tried to get round the need for materials by getting the information they needed from other people within their own work group, from other members of their own organization, from customers or suppliers or from wider professional networks. Clearly, SML structures can be used to legitimate, support and further develop these processes. In doing so, they also provide the means for learners to overcome what Cunningham (1999) identifies as a potential problem with the complementary social learning that occurs in learners' everyday communities of practice (their particular work teams, functions or organizational departments). The problem is the inherent conservatism of such communities – they can exclude people who do not fit and they can inhibit productive change. In SML, learning groups are typically formed from the members of different communities of practice in order for established ways of thinking and acting to be challenged constructively.

CONTACT

As indicated in the section above, the findings about contact between people support those from our own research and from that of Eraut and colleagues, that is, such contact is essential. It can be an integral part of everyday patterns of work or of regular meetings. Also evidenced was the importance of contact with others when not ostensibly working, for example whenever professionals are together and can 'talk shop'. Opportunities for contact are formally part of the process in SML through membership of the learning group where the primary focus is on individuals' learning.

Research also highlights the significance of contacts between senior or experienced staff and junior or novice staff in the context of 'apprenticeships' and role modelling in professional development. In SML, relationships of these kinds can be assured through one or a combination of:

● learning group membership;
● learning community membership where there is more than one learning group in a programme;

- individuals' decisions to initiate and develop such contacts as part of their Strategic Learning Contracts; and
- mentoring or coaching relationships.

Access to and the development of mentors is often an integral part of the design of SML programmes. In these ways, through SML, people have opportunities to develop both the professional independence and the interdependence increasingly required in modern organizations.

ETHOS

As noted above, the culture of the organization can have a significant impact on continuing learning. Organizations that facilitated or encouraged continuing learning were characterized by openness, interest and supportiveness and those that did not by rigidity, remoteness and short-sightedness. Organizationally, SML is most closely associated with an ethos encapsulated by Cunningham in his notion of the 'learning business' (Cunningham 1999). This is an organization where learning is:

- organization-wide rather than restricted to a few
- resourced
- large scale
- linked to the organization's purpose/values/mission/vision (or whatever other term is used for this area)
- visible and valued
- multi-functional, i.e. crossing functional boundaries
- long term.

These characteristics correlate with what is often described in the management literature as 'strategic'. The time, resources and contacts for CPD are most likely to be available in organizations that corporately adopt a strategic approach to learning. In practice, individuals undertaking CPD, along with those who were the subjects of the SML evaluation study cited earlier, are likely to experience their organizations as one or a combination of four kinds. These were identified in earlier research into the extent and ways in which a range of organizations in the south of England provided support for development (Cunningham 1991). In addition to the strategic category the other three are:

- Apathetic/antagonistic organizations
  These organizations tended to be unsympathetic to development. Either they did not care and could see no benefit in it (the apathetic) or they were actively opposed to it (the antagonistic).

- Reactive organizations

  Organizations in this category were prepared to finance someone going on a course if they asked for it (or, in some cases, if they actively pestered their managers). These organizations reacted to initiatives taken by others, especially their own staff, but they might respond to external pressure too.

- Bureaucratic organizations

  Here were examples of many large organizations that were doing lots of training and sending people on educational courses. However, there was no necessary relationship between this activity and the strategic direction of the organization. Often Training/HR people were detached from the places of power and were mechanistically following structures within which learning was highly controlled. Such activity was frequently out of line with individuals' motivations and personal strategies.

Unfortunately, but not unexpectedly, organizations in the strategic category were in the minority (in both the private and public sectors). SML provides the means for organizations more effectively to adopt a strategic approach to learning. It can also provide individuals with a level and quality of support that can compensate them for the lack of these in their normal organizational environments. I will return to this and other aspects of organizational ethos in the next section.

IMPLICATIONS FOR PROFESSIONAL BODIES

Many bodies are setting up systems to encourage, provide, monitor and evaluate CPD. These are placed roughly on a spectrum ranging from passive acceptance, through positive recognition, to the active requirement of CPD, however that is defined. Three ways in which professional bodies can contribute to CPD are proposed in the Hull study: feeding continuing learning, stimulating and monitoring continuing learning, and communicating and monitoring standards. In what follows the first and second of these are combined.

FEEDING, STIMULATING AND MONITORING CONTINUING LEARNING

Feeding continuing learning requires professional bodies to organize and provide resources and sources for it. Stimulating and monitoring continuing learning should involve the recognition of private activity (through the use of personal learning plans, logbooks and portfolios) as well as participation in public events. From an SML perspective, the means identified to recognize private activity can be incorporated in the preparation, pursuit and updating of Strategic Learning Contracts. In terms of the provision of resources, self managing members of a profession, pursuing their Strategic Learning Contracts, would be a source of stimulation to professional bodies to provide or organize resources closely targeted to meet their needs.

As shown in earlier chapters, we know from evaluation studies that one of the features of SML programmes most valued by participants is the learning group. This suggests that learning groups could be another important element of the resources organized by professional bodies for their members. Learning groups would be of particular value to those members whose organizational environments do not incorporate the three preconditions for continuing learning identified in the Hull study: a degree of openness to new ideas and initiatives at every level; a measure of security and trust which allows people to share not only innovations but problems; and some rewards for (or at least the absence of sanctions against) informal learning and development. Participants on SML programmes typically report that one of the reasons why they value learning group membership so highly is precisely because, in the learning group, they experience higher levels of 'openness', 'security', 'trust', and 'rewards' for learning than elsewhere. As well as compensating for the inadequacies of some participants' organizational environments in these ways, the learning group is also a context in which the individual who wishes to can gain support in finding ways of changing or developing their immediate organizational environment to become more open to new ideas, more trusting and so on. The desire to do so may emerge in response to problems encountered by them on route to achieving the goals in their Strategic Learning Contract. Alternatively, establishing or developing the necessary organizational conditions for their own and others' continuing learning may be an important and integral part of their longer term goals.

COMMUNICATING AND MONITORING STANDARDS

As far as communicating and monitoring standards are concerned, these are seen as inevitably problematic. These activities potentially involve a number of interested parties, all of whose responsibilities overlap – the individual, the professional body and the state. CPD depends on the individual having a perception of standards which are 'internalized' and control over these is exercised by members acting individually and as a collegiate body. This raises questions about who the final arbiter of standards should be. The importance of these questions is highlighted by the fact that the quality of learning that happens informally and that is self directed is dependent on the quality of the people engaged in it.

As covered in the section on structure, control and responsibility in Chapter 2, SML is clear about these issues. In enabling the learner to take responsibility for their learning and others to be responsible to them to assist them, SML provides a context in which the interests of various parties can be represented, in which internalized standards can be made explicit and developed and in which control is both individual and collegial. Professional bodies could see the provision of learning groups for professionals as examples of the 'resources' and 'sources' that need organizing or providing.

Another important feature of SML that is relevant here is the assessment process. The evidence from the Hull study is that most of the people who embarked on informal learning projects were satisfied with what they had learned. However, concern is expressed that these were only subjective judgements (with the implication that 'objective' ones would carry greater weight). At the same time there is acceptance that the individual professional's self evaluation should be taken seriously, given that making judgements is an integral part of professional activity and that such judgements are not made in isolation but in the context of interaction with peers. Issues such as these are addressed directly (and resolved) in SML programmes. Even where individuals' learning is not 'formally' accredited for CPD purposes or for a qualification, assessment is undertaken in SML programmes during and, particularly, at the end. The full-blown, rigorous, multi-level assessment of SML qualification programmes is described in Chapter 8 and that in non-qualification programmes in Chapter 12 (although, as pointed out there, assessment may not be the most appropriate name for it). The process begins with the individual learner's self assessment against the goals of their Strategic Learning Contract to which the other learning group members and learning group adviser respond, either confirming the person's claim or challenging it.

In these ways SML recognizes and values the fact that these judgements are 'subjective' but are not made in a vacuum. The issue is to make the process as explicit and rigorous as possible. This is particularly relevant to CPD where senior professionals are role models for their more junior colleagues. Ethics also have a part to play here. Given the comparatively greater material and other rewards that senior professionals receive for being in a position to make judgements about more junior colleagues who report to them, senior professionals have a moral responsibility to demonstrate to others their willingness and capability to make and act on judgements about their own effectiveness.

Aside from any moral obligations to engage in an assessment process, participants in SML frequently find that, although it is difficult, the process is also unexpectedly rewarding. They are often challenged to make more explicit the evidence for changes they have made. In the process, they become clearer, themselves, about their own continuing development. In responding to their self-assessment, other learning group members may bring up evidence of learning of which the person had not been consciously aware. The more our learning is made conscious, and the more we are aware of it, the more we seem to be able to integrate it. For these reasons, undergoing the SML assessment process contributes to the kind of awareness raising about the learning process discussed earlier. Providing an account of one's learning, and recognizing it and valuing it thereby, is of course an apt description of what members of an SML learning group do when meeting for assessment purposes and at other times – in fact, from the time they first meet to devise their Strategic Learning Contracts!

There is one aspect of standards that is sufficiently significant for questions about self direction and self and collegial control to be raised in the Hull study. This is that there will be areas of work which are so critical and common to the exercise of the profession that, in taking responsibility for them, the professional body has to require its members to gain particular skills and knowledge. If this is not done then the quality of the services provided will suffer. Apart from the harm done to clients in these circumstances, there are the possibilities of an increase in the number of clients seeking legal remedies or in calls for greater regulation of the profession concerned by the state. The SML process is a powerful way for pro-fessional bodies to take collective responsibility for ensuring that critical areas of work are performed to the required and expected standard. Hopefully this has been made clear in the commentary and discussion in this chapter. Of most impor-tance perhaps is the fact that SML offers the means for professionals to operate collectively in this way without at some point having to abandon autonomy, self direction or self control. The argument here is that self direction and self control are only open to question in this way if the questioner makes a distinction between 'formal' and 'informal' learning which, with all its logical entailments, confuses structure and control.

If SML was a feature of CPD then an ethos of continuing learning could be devel-oped in the professional body itself. This ethos would include both cultural elements and the necessary structural ones to support the SML process and cultural change. If, by these means, CPD was undertaken seriously by all in the profession concerned, one might reasonably expect to see both tangible and con-tinuous improvements in the services provided by members plus, collectively, an enhanced and better informed dialogue between them about fundamental issues to do with professional values, practices and standards.

CONCLUSIONS

Gear *et al.* (1994: 77) argue that 'the primary responsibility for CPD has to rest with the individual, although the organisation in which they work can have a powerful environmental influence.' Thus, they conclude, 'the role of the profes-sional bodies is ... likely to remain secondary and indirect rather than direct' (1994: 77). From an SML perspective, these conclusions about the role of others' are more limited than they need to be. The distinctions between structure and control and between the two kinds of responsibilities with regard to learning (responsibility for learning and responsibility to learners) indicate that both individual professionals and others (colleagues, professional bodies and employing organizations) have different, but complementary, primary responsibilities.

Through their Strategic Learning Contracts individuals negotiate their learning with their immediate professional peers in their learning groups plus, where relevant, colleagues from their organizations and their wider professional community. With SML, continuing peer review is an integral part of CPD and undertaken in the light of ever-increasing expectations and standards. Most importantly the quality of the dialogue in the learning group means that the members have frequent opportunities to pause, reflect on and explore what it really means to be a professional.

Part III
Making Self Managed Learning Work

INTRODUCTION TO PART III

This part goes into more detail on aspects of SML that have already been outlined in earlier chapters. In Part I we introduced the idea of SML and provided some background on its importance. Part II covered an array of cases of the use of SML without going into the fine detail of how aspects of SML processes and structures work. In this part we have provided three chapters that each take specific elements of SML designs to show more about how SML works in practice.

Chapter 12 elaborates on the use of Strategic Learning Contracts and Chapter 13 covers the way learning groups are used in SML. Chapter 14 discusses a range of other ways in which SML processes and programmes can be supported. This part of the book is not meant to be encyclopaedic but rather to move from the cases of the last part to show the way specific key SML methods are applied. Our hope is that the cases will have whetted your appetite sufficiently for you to want to know more about these issues.

12 Strategic Learning Contracts

Graham Dawes

INTRODUCTION

In previous chapters the central place of a Strategic Learning Contract (SLC) in the Self Managed Learning approach has been described, and participants in SML programmes have spoken of their experiences with SLCs and the contribution these make to learning and development. In this chapter the Strategic Learning Contract is examined in more detail and in more depth.

The importance of setting goals will be discussed as this is one justification for the role of SLCs in Self Managed Learning. This speaks to the 'whys' of Strategic Learning Contracts. There are also the 'hows': how SLCs are developed and how they are used within an SML programme, along with their role in any assessment process at the end of a programme.

We will also provide an overview of the kinds of goals SLCs contain, and the different formats in which the SLC can be presented. Lastly, there is the question of how Strategic Learning Contracts can be used beyond the context of an SML programme.

THE STRATEGIC LEARNING CONTRACT WITHIN SELF MANAGED LEARNING

The Self Managed Learning approach provides an integrated and coherent context for learning and personal development. None the less, if its major components had to be identified they would undoubtedly be the learning group and the Strategic Learning Contract. The Strategic Learning Contract can be viewed as the backbone of SML. It provides the focus for most of what is undertaken during the programme. Participants work on developing it in the early phase of the programme and then for the rest of the programme work to achieve the goals it embodies.

This is not to suggest, though, that an SLC can fully encompass all the learning that takes place through participation in an SML programme. One of the characteristics of SML programmes is the prevalence of beneficial side-effects. These typically come in two forms. There is what might be called the 'opportunistic learning' that takes place during and through the pursuit of the goals in the learning contract. By its nature it was neither expected nor intended and so could not have featured in the SLC. None the less, it may turn out, when reviewing what has been gained from the programme, as having been of more significance than even the learning that was intended.

The second form of positive side-effect concerns the process of 'learning to learn'. Those who engage wholeheartedly with the SML process learn a great deal about the process of learning itself. This goes beyond a recognition of how they are best able to learn, and involves their having stretched their ability into modes and manners of learning which may not initially have been their preference. In other words, they have expanded the ways in which they are able to learn, and they have had the concrete experience of having learnt without relying on being fed predigested information or instruction by others. The upshot is that they have become active learners – to whatever degree (and this will vary considerably). Ultimately, being an active learner may prove to be of more value than both intended learning and opportunistic learning, for both of these may be made irrelevant or obsolete by the changing circumstances of a changing world.

Despite the importance of these other areas of learning, they are only made possible through the focus on, and pursuit of, the learning goals that feature in the Strategic Learning Contract. The SLC, therefore, enables even the learning that is not its own focus. It is in this sense that it can be said to be the backbone of the SML approach.

WHY 'STRATEGIC'?

A Strategic Learning Contract is designed to be strategic in that participants on SML programmes are encouraged to take a strategic approach to their own learning. That is to say, their view is broadened upward and outward, beyond the immediate needs of the job to a consideration of their career, and even as far as taking a perspective on their life as a whole.

All too often, goals for learning (as with any other kinds of goals) are chosen to deal with a present situation. Therefore, they tend to be short term. Yet any goal of today or tomorrow sets a direction into the future. If the implications of that direction are not considered we can find ourselves in futures of our own making, but not of our intention, nor to our satisfaction.

Being strategic means setting learning goals that lead in the desired life direction. Once that general direction is established, the short-term steps along the way can be identified. There is nothing wrong with having short-term goals. Short-term goals are useful. It is only important to ensure that they will take you into the long-term future you want.

One issue that frequently arises when people attempt to formulate strategic learning goals is that they experience difficulty identifying the strategic direction of their organization. Obviously, the organizational strategy has a bearing on what their own strategy might be. In addition, participants are encouraged to take account of their organization's strategy as it sets the context for their own learning and development.

It is sometimes possible to discover an organizational strategy, either from published sources or from senior managers, though all too often it is not. This can be due to lack of communication within the organization or simply to the lack of any clear strategic direction. More often, though, there is a general strategy though it lacks sufficient specificity to guide the choice of learning goals. This presents a dilemma for the participant wanting to ensure that their own learning reflects the needs of their organization. However, it is every bit as difficult for an organization to establish a clear strategic direction as it is for an individual, often more so in that there may be a number of stakeholders with diverging ideas about where the organization should be heading.

Ultimately, the individual needs to be clear about their own strategic direction even when the organization is unable to be. The individual learner needs to step back from the day-to-day issues with which they are dealing and to cast their vision wider – to take account of what is happening in the surrounding context and out in the world at large. Their situation must be viewed dispassionately enough to provide useful guidance, yet the learning goals they formulate must be ones that excite the requisite passion to bring them into being.

WHY 'CONTRACT'?

Many organizations have embraced the concept of learning and development. Unfortunately, they often go about it in a misguided way, jumping from the concept straight to the provision of courses. A strategic approach to learning and development is rarely taken. In many instances, this means the closest people come to experiencing it is in the context of appraisals. Yet these tend not to be very strategic either. Interestingly enough, they are widely accepted and rarely evaluated on a cost–benefit basis.

Appraisals often lead to the formulation of a Personal Development Plan (PDP). These are sometimes seen as having the same value as a Strategic Learning Contract. This is rarely the case. More often than not, when compared to an SLC, a

Personal Development Plan can be rather ill-focused and sloppy. It is not that they look sloppy; on the contrary they often appear very precise. But being activity-led there is a lack of clarity about goals and many of them end up as little more than a list of courses which it is assumed will fulfil those development needs the appraisal has identified. Some of the differences between the Strategic Learning Contract and the Personal Development Plan will be covered below, others will be easier to understand, and to recognize, when we examine the five questions that provide the framework for contracts.

DIFFERENCES BETWEEN PERSONAL DEVELOPMENT PLANS AND STRATEGIC LEARNING CONTRACTS

When organizations that use Personal Development Plans in their appraisal system begin Self Managed Learning programmes the question is often raised as to how the Strategic Learning Contract differs from the Personal Development Plans that they have already written. There are many differences between the two forms, some of which are listed below:

PDP	SLC
Tactical	Strategic and tactical
1 year	3+ years
Now	Now + Future
Work	Work + Life
Competency	Capability
Performance	Learning

A PDP is usually designed to last for a maximum of one year. It rarely takes into account anything beyond that timescale. An SLC, though its active life may be for less than a year, encourages thought about how the goals of that period relate to future aspirations. That is to say, it encourages participants to look at both the short term and the long term, and to align the short-term goals with the long-term direction toward which the person is aiming.

A PDP has a far more restricted focus. When developing an SLC, people are encouraged to take a more holistic view of their development. Their whole life – past, present and future – is relevant to their learning goals. People vary considerably in how much they are ready to contemplate and work on the larger scale of their whole life, but there is no artificial narrowing of their vision.

There is a tendency for PDPs to get caught up in a deficiency perspective. Appraisals put much of their focus on performance issues and development needs are seen as being what is required to bring the person's performance up to the required level. In such cases, the focus of the PDP may be less on learning than on performance. Performance goals are set between the person and their manager, but such goals do not necessarily imply any learning. To reach an increased performance goal the person can simply work longer hours (with the poor effects this is likely to have on both quality of work and quality of life). If they are to work differently, to accomplish more in the same amount of time, then they will have to learn to do something different. Whether that learning is from someone else or the result of their own creativity, it is still learning.

This difference between performance and learning is important. Results may also feature in an SLC, though here they will be used to demonstrate the achievement of a learning goal. But when our attention is solely on the result it is all too easy to forget the learning that is required to get us there.

For similar reasons, PDPs often get tied to competences. The limits of such a perspective have been suggested by many (among them Cunningham 1999). Competences all too often fall into a 'ticking the boxes' approach, which will usually limit the integration of what is being learnt. Many organizations have become attached to their competency lists. As a checklist of things to take account of in relation to particular roles they can be useful. Where they slip from usefulness to tyranny is when attempts have been made to nail them down to nitty-gritty specifics and it becomes mandatory that all learning be in terms of this specification.

As was implied earlier, when learning does feature explicitly within a PDP it often means an agreement that a manager will put the person on a course. Within an SML programme a far wider variety of options is possible (as will be seen later), and these are reflected in a person's Strategic Learning Contract. This difference is not so much a feature of PDPs themselves as of a more general (and limiting) orientation to learning. It is also reflected in the frequent lack of consideration given to supportive structures, for both performance achievements and learning. When a PDP is agreed, the person is pretty much left to themselves to just get on and accomplish its goals. Even in the best cases, where a manager makes time for a quarterly check with the person on their progress, this is not frequent enough and it also needs to be remembered that there may be good reasons for not being completely candid with one's manager. Within an SML programme, a Strategic Learning Contract is supported both by the structure of the programme and, more directly, by the participant being part of a learning group.

This raises the question of 'ownership'. It is widely recognized that there is a far higher tendency for people to achieve goals that they feel they have chosen, and have made a commitment to achieving. While the rhetoric of appraisals and PDPs is that these are negotiated between the person and their manager, the nature of the reporting relationship makes for an unequal negotiation. All too often people end up feeling that the goals were imposed on them. The assumption that they were mutually identified only makes this feeling more painful.

An SLC begins with the individual making their own choice of goals. This may be within constraints, such as the theme of the programme, or even an imposed competency framework. None the less, the process begins with a personal choice. Those goals are then put before their learning group where they will need to be justified against the questioning and challenge of the group. Usually they are also put before the manager for a response, but the context makes it less likely that unwanted goals will be imposed. (Partly this is because the goals in such a pro-gramme focus on learning and not on performance, as we have seen.)

The individual also has the choice of what to put before their manager. It may not be the whole of their Strategic Learning Contract. It need be only those parts that are felt to be relevant to the manager, for example job-specific goals. There could be other goals that may be left aside, yet still worked on with the learning group. These may be things that concern the person's private life or career goals beyond their current job. It is important that participants on SML programmes should not be restricted to those goals they feel comfortable showing to their man-ager. That would be to unnecessarily limit the learning and reduce the holistic quality of the contract.

In this regard, it is worth emphasizing that the person works for the organiza-tion and is not owned by their manager. This is often assumed in the way man-agers talk about and act in relation to 'their people'. One CEO made clear his view of loyalty to the organization when he said managers should be perfectly willing to let their best person work in another area when it would be for the good of the organization.

THE IMPORTANCE OF GOALS

In this section I will explore some of the factors that make goals especially useful in the context of learning and development. Many apply to other contexts, as these are general factors concerning goal setting, and so may be familiar.

Although goals are recognized as being important to organizations generally, there is some research that emphasizes their importance to the individual espe-cially. Most people are familiar with the general creativity exercise that challenges the individual to come up with as many uses as possible for a particular everyday object: a brick, a paper clip, a paper cup, or whatever. The psychologist Liam Hudson (Hudson 1966; 1968) used this exercise in research which demonstrated the significance, and efficacy, of setting a goal. What he found, on averaging out his results, was that when the exercise was set in the usual way, as described above, only 7 per cent of people were able to find 25 different uses for the object. However, when people were told that the goal of the exercise was to find 25 differ-ent uses for the object, 65 per cent of people were able to find 25 uses. This result shows unambiguously the enormous difference in what was achieved when the only difference in variables was that a goal was set.

In making a goal explicit, especially where this is reinforced by putting it down in writing, and even more so by making it public, we create a focus for our attention. Such focused attention seems almost magnetic. It encourages serendipity. We notice anything relevant to our goal and tend to find information, assistance and opportunities drawn to us. Some people experience this as the universe responding to their desires. Those of a less mystical bent understand it as the result of focusing attention.

WORKING WITH GOALS

There is convincing evidence that setting goals does work. But how does it work? The influence of focused attention can be elaborated through the model of Robert Fritz, a colleague of Peter Senge. Fritz (1984) describes what happens in terms of 'structural tension', which he metaphorically equates with an elastic band. Rather than leave the build-up of structural tension to chance, he suggests we frequently and explicitly bring our awareness to where we are now, in the present, and then review and re-associate to our goal. The structure is that there is a difference between the present and the not-yet-achieved goal. It is this difference that creates the tension and, as it were, stretches the elastic band. His point is that, as with all such tension, there is an inherent and natural tendency toward its resolution. That resolution brings with it the fulfilment of the goal.

The process of working with SLCs in the context of a Self Managed Learning programme, when examined in the light of Fritz's model, can be seen to embody structural tension through the frequent revisiting of learning goals. What he adds is the idea that it is important explicitly to put attention on both where you are now and where you want to get to and, most particularly, to notice the difference between the two.

GOALS, META-GOALS AND DIRECTIONS

When the importance of setting goals is recognized, the ability to do so can be refined. We have seen that once we focus our attention on a goal we are drawn toward it. However, we have also seen that SLCs encourage a view that pushes out beyond the immediate goal. Consequently, participants are encouraged to identify a meta-goal or a direction.

A meta-goal establishes what the present goal (the one in the SLC) is in service of. For instance, the learning goal may be to become familiar with a software package and the meta-goal is to enhance the impact of reports and presentations. Or the goal may be to work in another department, while the meta-goal it contributes to is becoming an all-rounder, familiar with many different aspects of the organization and its work.

Often a specific meta-goal cannot be identified. Either the future is unknown or it is inherently uncertain and all that can be established is a direction. Here attention is not narrowly focused as with a goal or meta-goal. There can be benefits to such broad-band attention. It allows the individual to take advantage of whatever comes up, without being wedded to a specific 'one-point' goal. For instance, through working to develop an SLC an individual may become clear that they want learning and development to play a big part in their work. However, they may be quite unclear what that will mean in practice. It might mean a role in HRD or it might not. At this point, it is only the direction they want to go in that can be identified. The particular goal this leads to in the long term will depend on the possibilities they can realize in their situation as it unfolds. None the less, they may have a short-term goal to do with familiarizing themselves with learning and development theories and methods.

When it comes to our career, or our life, we may feel we are only able to identify a desired direction, and not a specific and precise goal. Today, it is impossible to tell whether most fixed long-term goals will still be there by the time we reach them. In a changing world it may be more appropriate to identify a direction for the longer term and, in the shorter term, to identify specific goals along the way. This gives the advantages of specific goals while avoiding the dangers of a fixed goal in the distance which may disappear or be irrelevant or even problematic by the time it is reached.

Both meta-goals and directions can be addressed by asking oneself, in relation to a specific learning goal, such questions as:

● What is important about achieving that goal?
● What will achieving that goal do for me?
● What will reaching that goal make possible for me?
● What is there that is more important to me than that goal, but which achieving it will take me toward?

There is an obvious advantage to considering meta-goals and directions in that they ensure our immediate goals are taking us into the future we want. They act as a check on those goals on which we are focused during the SML programme. There also seems to be another advantage, akin to an increase in structural tension. Because our sights now stretch further toward the horizon, the goals that are closer to us appear much more easily attainable. Since motivation is always, ultimately, psychological this is no trivial matter.

To sum up, the benefits of goal-setting are enhanced by writing them down, frequently revisiting them, and being specific about them as well as noticing where you are now in relation to them. In addition, goals are best held in relation to meta-goals or directions. Lastly, in an SLC it is important that goals be about learning.

THE FIVE QUESTIONS

A Strategic Learning Contract can be constructed in whatever way an individual finds useful. Almost everyone, though, finds it useful to have guidelines. The five questions covered here provide a framework for points to consider when creating a Strategic Learning Contract. Most SLCs are explicitly constructed around these questions, using them as headings and dealing with each in turn (though they need not be done in that way). Here, we will take each question in turn, expanding on its meaning and how it might be answered.

WHERE HAVE YOU BEEN?

This question invites a global review of the result of the past learnings with which the individual arrives on the SML programme. The influences of such past learning contexts as family, schools, work, or life in general can be identified here.

On beginning an SML programme our attention may be totally on what we want to do (or on the difficulty of knowing what that is), and looking to the past, particularly the long distant past, can seem an unnecessary chore. We want to rush into the future, not to be dragged back into the past. However, within this review of the past lie recurring patterns of thinking and action, some of which are beneficial, and to be drawn upon, and some of which may be limiting your future, and will need to be resolved. Thus the past may provide resources to use as well as things to address while on the programme. We could adjust the familiar saying to read that those who refuse to learn the lessons of (personal) history are condemned to repeat the mistakes of the past.

My first attempt to address the five questions was in the context of an Independent Study programme at what is now the University of East London. (Ian Cunningham was one of the developers of this precursor to his development of Self Managed Learning.) In setting about this first question I found myself at a loss. I was in my thirties and if I detailed all my significant experiences I would be writing for months, if not years.

Yet I could identify no basis on which to decide what to include and what to leave out, and there was no learning group on that programme with whom to think it through. I began what was, essentially, an autobiography, writing whatever seemed significant in my childhood and adolescence. A dozen or so pages into this process I noticed patterns in those events I identified as significant, and it was this that enabled me to condense what I had written and encompass it within a few pages.

One of the valuable lessons from this laborious process was that my past, indeed anyone's past, offers a multitude of potential stories. The question is what story a person tells. The selection of events to recount relates to the individual's present precisely because it is that present self that is choosing them.

For this reason, people should be given the widest possible landscape across which to stretch their past. Yet people come on SML programmes with a restricted view of what is appropriate to a programme conducted under the auspices of the organizational or academic worlds. They assume such a programme countenances only a slither of the total world of experience, and will thus cut their past accordingly.

This tendency can be offset because the first question is usually addressed at the start-up event for the SML programme and presented live to the members of one's learning group. This is done through a 'lifelines' exercise. It takes its name from one way of illustrating the answer to this question. A line can be drawn on the board or flip chart to indicate a life chronology and around this line can be woven a rising and falling line which shows enjoyable times and difficult times in the person's life. Other modes can be employed. For instance, the individual can identify the 10 most important things that have happened to them, be these good or bad, as a way of giving insight into their life thus far. Many other methods can be used to fulfil the same purpose.

The lifelines exercise is begun by the learning group adviser presenting their own lifeline. The other participants are given time to work on theirs before they present in turn. When in the learning group adviser role, I have seized this opportunity to show that the bounds of the programme are wide by choosing things not normally mentioned in such contexts. These include, along with some of the more colourful incidents from my past, mistakes and failures of mine and aspects that have nothing to do with the work context. This encourages learning group members to take a wider view across the landscape of their lives. There would be little purpose to their reading out their CV (though this, too, would be significant in its own way, suggesting the participant was uncomfortable about revealing anything to learning group members).

In addition to the various frameworks that can be used for lifelines, whatever approach is taken, each event can be considered in terms of what one has learnt from it. This may be difficult to do initially, depending on the time available, and might be the subject of later reflection. The following questions assist this process:

- Constants – is there something that is there all of the time, for example a personal quality?
- Is there something about you that appears from time to time?
- What skills and abilities did you use in order to move out of the 'lows' and to progress?
- What patterns are emerging?
- How do you feel about these patterns? Are they weaker/lessening or stronger/increasing?
- How would you like them to be?

- What is still unfinished, or your next task?
- Looking back over your life experiences, what skills/qualities/abilities have you gained?

These questions give an idea of the wealth of information that is available for both the participant and their fellow learning group members. When sufficient time is given, the above questions can be explored within the learning group while an individual is presenting their lifeline. The process can alert them and other group members to patterns that can be drawn on in the future, or the presence of which might be cause for concern.

This last point was illustrated when a participant on a Masters degree programme, in talking us through his lifeline, said, in a number of ways and about a number of events, 'I felt I let myself down; I didn't make the best of the opportunity.' Once this pattern had been recognized it became a yardstick for evaluating that person's use of the programme. That this remark could not be repeated about their participation in the programme became an element in the assessment on which the award of the Masters degree was based.

In the opposite situation, when a learning group has identified patterns that have held the person in good stead at other points in their life, they can be reminded of these when struggling with a situation in their present. It is often the case that we fail to use those strategies that have worked for us in the past, perhaps because we consider the present situation so different, or simply because we have not identified what was useful about our response to past situations. This is one of the benefits of being part of a learning group – other people can point out to us those things we have not noticed ourselves, be they useful patterns or limiting patterns.

There is a side-effect to doing lifelines which should be mentioned. Precisely because it grants us a privileged insight into what is behind the faces that sit before us it helps the group to gel as a group. This is so even when the people are known to one another. It is rare, within a work context, for people to know all that much about the backgrounds of their colleagues and co-workers. Yet this can make quite a difference to how we feel about people. This is another reason for learning group advisers to be willing to open up the personal realm when presenting their own lifelines. With this goes the fact that the more people feel free to bring to the group what is important to them, the more learning there will be. The simple principle is: the learning group *can* only work with what people bring to the group. Any restrictions on what they feel comfortable to work on lessens the learning they will have.

WHERE ARE YOU NOW?

Just as a high jumper needs the ground to leap from, we depend on our starting point to reach our goals. All too often, though, we give it scant attention. Robert

Fritz emphasized the importance of maintaining in our awareness both where we are and where we want to get to. With only our goal in mind we are creating structural slack.

A colleague told a story, from his time in Africa, about a man invited to visit friends living on a far distant farm. Nobody could go to meet him so it was arranged that he have a plane fly him to the nearest piece of flat land, where a jeep would be left for him with a map of how to drive to the farm. As the plane flew in to land he saw the jeep waiting there for him but, from the air, there was no sign of habitation anywhere on the horizon. He found the map in the glove compartment of the jeep, marked with an 'X' to indicate the farmstead. He was about to wave the pilot off when he realized that although he knew where he had to get to, he had no idea where on the map he currently was. This was a graphic instance of the uselessness of knowing where you want to get to if you don't know where you are starting from.

This question invites the individual to make an audit of their current situation, including their knowledge, abilities, qualities, and the possibilities open to them. This audit provides the basis for the person's goals so it makes sense to do a thorough and broad audit and ensure that all the relevant factors of the present situation are taken into account. This process begins with the individual but it is useful to gain the perspectives of others, both as a check on one's own perceptions and for the benefit of having things brought to one's attention that might not have been noticed otherwise.

Some of these sources are to be expected, such as upward feedback and information that comes from appraisals. Many people find it useful to conduct their own 360-degree feedback process, to ensure they do not forfeit relevant perspectives. Less often considered is what can be learnt from jobs applied for, whether or not they were gained, and whether or not they were within your present organization. The fact that you applied for a particular job indicates what you assume to be your level of knowledge and ability. Where you did not succeed in getting the job you may also have found out why you did not.

Diagnostic instruments and psychometric tests feature in some training contexts and can give useful mirrors in which to see oneself. They should not be relied on singly, nor without other supporting indications, and are often most useful if different instruments focus on similar abilities and qualities. Even if they seem to be giving different findings this is a useful stimulus to one's own reflections. Friends and family are an often overlooked source of information. Although these people may not know us in a work context, they may also be the people who know us best, and what they have to say can be worth taking account of.

As is always the case, it should be emphasized that what anybody, and any diagnostic instrument, tells you should not be taken as an absolute truth. While it is important to take other people's opinions into account they are only opinions and need to be seen in relation to the other information you are gathering. It is also important not to swing to the polar opposite and dismiss other people's opinions out of hand just because they do not fit with our own prejudices. Here is where the learning group can assist with the working through and thinking through of the information being gathered, as they respond to the draft versions of your answer to this question.

The time that can be given to answering this question depends on the length of the programme. In a two-year qualification programme, where learning contracts are not agreed until six months into the programme, a greater depth and thoroughness is expected than on shorter programmes where, at the other extreme, you may only have a few hours to take stock of where you are now.

WHERE DO YOU WANT TO GET TO?

Here is where the goals are set. They should be informed by the previous two questions just as their pursuit will be informed by the two questions to come. As has been mentioned, these goals are learning goals. We are much more used to thinking of goals in terms of performance goals. This is where a learning group can be helpful in ensuring that the focus of goals is on learning.

Goal setting in an SML programme has a wider scope than most such exercises and it can be helpful to think of the following different types of goals:

- Job goals
  These relate to learning you may wish to undertake to improve your performance in your current job. You may also want to change aspects of your present role and would include these under this heading.

- Career goals
  You may wish to set goals in relation to your future career. This may cover job changes you would like to make and any development you feel you would need to go along with this. Career goals may not always include assumptions of upward progression: some people find it helpful to consider sideways moves, for instance.

- Life goals
  Increasingly, people want to ensure a balance in their lives – between, especially, work and home – and to specify what precisely they want to create in the future. In the SML approach there is the opportunity to open up these issues and explicitly work on them.

All the above are inter-linked but it can be helpful to use these headings as a starter for analysis.

While it is useful for meta-goals and directions to be included in the contract, it is important that for each there are goals in relation to the length of the programme. It is these goals, not the longer term ones, that the individual is committing to accomplish by the end of the programme.

Because concrete goals are valued in organizations there is a tendency, even in learning programmes, to put aside many important, but hard to specify, goals. This is not necessary. An SLC can accommodate an interim goal which is to identify precisely what goal would be useful and appropriate in a particular area. In fact, I had a similar goal myself on one SML programme. My goal was to formulate a Ph.D. proposal. It was not to have the proposal accepted, nor to be registered on a Ph.D. programme. It was a goal to specify a goal (what the Ph.D. would be about). This was accepted by my learning group and was one of the things I worked on during the programme.

In terms of crafting a goal, the discipline of Neuro-Linguistic Programming has much to offer. Here are a set of considerations that are useful in evaluating a first attempt to formulate a goal and which assist in the process of refining it.

Stated in the positive

Frequently, our attention is on what we don't want. We may wish to avoid getting caught up in our colleagues' political machinations. But, while this tells us what to avoid it doesn't tell us where we do want to go. It is like backing into the future, without even a rear-view mirror. All the attention is on what to avoid. For instance, people tend to think of dieting or losing weight more than of the weight, shape or feeling they want their body to have. Where you put your attention the mind follows, as illustrated by the phrase, 'Don't think of a blue elephant dancing in a pink tutu.' You can't not think of it without thinking of what you are not to think of. This means that when a goal is stated in the negative that is where the attention stays, and this makes it much more difficult to change. Much better to keep the mind focused on what you do want and to have that be the magnet that draws you on.

Feasible

It may seem obvious that it is not worth formulating a goal that is not feasible. None the less, it is always valuable to evaluate whether any particular goal is within your grasp; not someone else's but yours. Also whether it is feasible within the time-scale of the programme.

Within your control

Any goal is a lot more feasible if it is under your own control, if it is something your own efforts can bring about. The more that it requires the agreement or, even more so, the active involvement of others the more your goal becomes a hostage to fortune. It is no longer in your own hands. Obviously, we are far more able to commit to goals that we, ourselves, can bring about.

Specific as to behaviour

This moves us on to question 5 in that it requires us to be able to state, in a very concrete behavioural way, what we will be doing differently when the goal is attained. It is only through doing this that we can be sure to know when we have reached the goal. Although goal setting is considered important within organizations, many goals, even many of the most important ones like organizational change goals, are formulated without identifying the specifics of the intended result. When asking organizational members whether a culture change programme achieved its objectives, and just what those objectives were, there is often an embarrassed silence.

Gets you what you want

In deciding on a goal we are making the assumption that it will be beneficial to us in whatever way. This is an assumption well worth examining. For if it is incorrect we can expend all our energy to achieve the goal, yet achieving it will not bring us what we want. Such an evaluation is not as simple as it might appear. By definition we are not at our goal, in all likelihood we have never been there, so we have to understand that things will look very different from there than they do from here. We look to that goal in the distance and imagine its benefits, whereas we might best put some thought into imagining what it would be like to be there, in order to identify whether or not it is likely to bring about the benefits we hope for.

Ecological

This term is usually applied to the relations between the natural world and human society, particularly in terms of the effects of pollution. Here it refers to applying the same systemic view to our own lives, and to thinking through what will change for us as we achieve a goal. For instance, gaining control of a high-profile project might affect our relationships with those who did not get the role but wanted it. Also, the extra hours it is likely to entail will affect our relationships with our partner, our children, our friends, etc. The point is to examine the ripples that will fan out from our attaining our goal, so as to allow us to prepare for them or to rethink our goal if we do not like what it brings with it.

In organizational contexts the process of goal setting is often taken for granted. Yet we have seen many different aspects to it, each worthy of attention. SML advocates that the process is done in a rigorous, thorough and thought-through manner.

HOW WILL YOU GET THERE?

The goals have been identified. Now it is a matter of how they are to be accomplished. The only limits here are usually:

- your imagination and creativity
- the resources available
- any social, cultural, legal or policy constraints.

People tend to overestimate the policy and resource constraints, and underestimate their imagination and creativity. Following identification of a learning need, people's experience of organizational life may lead them to a knee-jerk response – they must go on a course. Unfortunately, this can often be the least useful mode, as well as being the most costly in terms of time and money.

In choosing vehicles for learning the most important thing is to be clear about just what it is you need or want to learn. Even conventional lecture or training modes may find a place once you are clear what you want out of them. Going into them with that in mind means you are much more likely to get the learning you want.

One of the most underused resources are the people in your own organization. Frequently, individuals identify a goal such as learning more about the financial side of their business. Then the mind jumps to the thought of a course on 'Finance for the Non-Financial Manager'. What is being ignored is that their own organization has financial people, and that those financial people know precisely the role of finances in that particular business. Approaching one of them, after having thought through precisely what you want to know, the chances are that through spending a lunchtime or few (or having an after-hours drink) with them you can learn what you want to know. The same, of course, applies to other disciplines represented in your organization.

The list in Figure 12.1 may give a sense of the wealth of ways through which we can learn, and indicates which approaches are more strategic and which are more tactical.

Once our goals have been established, it is within the means and methods through which we pursue them that most of our time during an SML programme is spent. If we choose inefficient ways we will need to spend longer at them; if we choose unimaginative ways we may have more difficulty sustaining our interest. A great deal of thought may need to be given to how we pursue a given goal. Sometimes, following identification of the goal, this will need to be a focus of attention in learning group meetings.

HOW WILL YOU KNOW YOU'VE ARRIVED?

For most people this is the most difficult question to answer. In most goal setting it

STRATEGIC

Learning contracts   Mentors
Learning groups   Networking
Learning organization   Organization development

TACTICAL

Courses   Workshops
Seminars   Conferences
Projects   Coaching
360-degree feedback   Away days
Secondments/job swaps   Research
Counselling   Voluntary work
Team development   Development centres
Distance learning   Deputizing
Learning Resource Centre

METHODS

Visits   Shadowing
Reading   Tapes (audio or video)
CD-ROMs   Interactive video
Packages   Internet
Computer conferencing   Dialogue
Presentations   Writing
Meditation   Thinking
Case studies   Reward for learning
Feedback   Observation
Role plays   Psychometrics
Simulations

Figure 12.1   Development approaches

is simply assumed. But what it is asking us to do is to establish the criteria, the standards, against which the achievement of our goals will be evaluated.

In draft contracts it is common for rather vague answers to be proffered. Even when contracts are finalized the answer may not be fully specified. It must be refined over time; a process that becomes ever more important as the end of the programme approaches (especially so for qualification programmes). To bring vague responses into a more concrete form it can be useful to ask how the person themselves will know they have achieved a particular goal, and then how the other members of their learning group will know.

Actually, two aspects are required here. Firstly, there is the issue of what will be the evidence for, or a demonstration of, the goal being achieved, and, secondly, there is the different issue of the level or standard to which it is achieved.

Essentially, this is a matter of identifying the parameters of the goal. The issue of level is important. For example, returning to the person who wanted to learn more about the role of finances in their organization, there is little likelihood they would ever learn as much about finance as their finance director, and they have no need to do so. What level of knowledge do they require? This can only be set by the person themselves. But to set it they need to think through their reasons for learning about finance, and make a judgement about just how much knowledge of the area will satisfy those reasons. To do this may require some investigation. For instance, they may need to talk to their manager about what the business might require of them.

In considering this last question, the consequences of a standard education make themselves felt. We were taught (unintentionally) that our aim must be to satisfy the authorities that we have learnt, whether or not the means of doing so were of any relevance to us. Typically, this was through examinations. When an SML programme leads to a qualification this can result in people suggesting essays as the way they will demonstrate what they have learnt, just because this is what they think they have to do. Although this pattern is less prevalent with in-company programmes there is still a tendency to think that something onerous need be done, just to make the whole process seem real. The challenge is to make everything of relevance. Since people are expected to choose learning goals that are relevant there is no reason they should prove their attainment with irrelevance. Finding an appropriate way to demonstrate the achievement of a learning goal can require some creativity but is, by definition, much more rewarding.

AN EXAMPLE OF THE LINKS ACROSS THE FIVE QUESTIONS IN AN SLC

By way of illustration, an individual goal will be shown as it might be addressed in terms of each of the five questions. The goal is time management, a topic that frequently comes up in development programmes.

1. Past

A person might indicate that this has become a growing problem as they have gone through their career but that, at times, they have managed their time better, for example because their work pattern was simpler. This might prompt ideas of how to simplify current work practices.

2. Present

Here the person might specify the problems they currently face. Some people have kept a time diary to record how they spend their time. They have discovered that they waste time, for example, by not structuring their day effectively or through not having their paperwork in order.

3. Goals

Some people have set goals around how much time they want to spend at work. Others have set goals for improved productivity, that is getting more work done in the time available.

4. Means (to achieve the goals)

Often the first thought is to go on a time management course. However, this is usually not the most cost-effective solution. Sometimes direct one-to-one coaching is most effective, though people have gained benefit from watching videos or reading books. For others it has been more important to work better with their secretary/PA in order to create a new pattern to the working day.

5. Measures

One person who set the goal of reducing time at work set a measure that he would get the 6.39 train home at least four days a week. (His answer to question 2 on this was that he typically caught this train a maximum of once a week and normally he was still at work after 8 or 9 p.m.)

We have now examined the five questions. They constitute the most often used framework for drawing up a Strategic Learning Contract. We have considered the relevance of each of the questions to the setting of goals and the process of learning. As has been made clear, to answer the questions is not a simple process. The nature of the questions, and the perusal of the answers by a learning group, resist a slipshod response. As with so many things, the more individuals put into the process of answering the questions the more benefit they get out of them.

DEVELOPING THE CONTRACT

The process of developing a Strategic Learning Contract is designed to be an iterative one. No one is expected to be able to dash off an adequate response to the five questions all in one go. In the design of SML programmes up to a quarter of the length of the programme may be given over to the development of the contract. This is a mark of what it involves and also of the importance it is accorded.

For those who have not engaged in developing a contract, such a length of time may appear too long. But it is not that learning only begins once the contract is agreed. There is much learning along the way. There are occasions where the work done in defining a goal adequately has meant that the goal was completed before the contract was agreed. That this should be possible is not so odd when we consider that in order to know what you need to know, and to be able to define that knowledge sufficiently for a contract, you may have to find out a good deal – and sometimes you will have found out enough.

There are other cases where the refining of a goal will lead in an unexpected direction. When formulating my goals, through the five questions, for my own undergraduate programme at the School for Independent Study, I began with a rather grandiose project, the intention being to delineate what I saw as a new Image of Man (which at that time meant humankind as a whole). I viewed this emerging image as an aspect of the evolution of consciousness. Moreover, I felt that by delineating what was then only beginning to take shape I would be contributing to that evolution. A long shot, perhaps, but I considered it a worthwhile task. However, whether it was a feasible task would have been a fair question. As I began to explore what would be involved in getting a sufficient grip on the *Zeitgeist*, the enormity of the task dawned on me. As one of the many areas from which I expected to draw the lineaments of this new Image of Man, I examined the emerging discipline of Neuro-Linguistic Programming (NLP). It had relevance to my theme in a number of ways but in order to discover its precise relevance I would have to explore it in depth, and that would be impossible within the terms of my current goal. For some days, I wrestled with this dilemma. In the end, I completely re-jigged my contract so as to concentrate on an exploration of NLP. The fact that it had practical relevance was of huge appeal and, by contrast, I could see that to operationalize the new Image of Man would require of me the talents of a politician or, at least, a motivational writer. Even then the chances were slim.

It is unusual that the requirement of answering the five questions will lead to such a sweeping reformulation of aims, but it is equally as unlikely that the process will have no effect at all on the person's starting point.

STARTING WITH THE START-UP

The 'start-up' process for an SML programme may vary between two days and a week-long residential, but in that period the process of formulating learning goals is begun. Typically, people go away from the start-up event with the rudiments of a contract and work on it prior to the first subsequent meeting of their learning group. Just prior to this they will circulate their draft contract, at whatever stage it has been brought to in the interim, so learning group members have a chance to peruse it and arrive at the meeting with their questions and responses prepared. Those questions and responses can be exceedingly helpful in the formulation of the contract.

Learning group members respond to the individual's draft contract in terms not only of what is written within it but also of what they have heard from the person during the start-up. This may lead them to wonder whether a particular goal makes sense in terms of what the person has said about their overall direction, or their past, or their present place in their organization. The questioning assists the person in really thinking through what they are aiming for. Not only is their own perspective on their aims sharpened by the process but, through responding to other learning group members, they are, in effect, taking account of five or six other perspectives also.

A person's manager will usually be involved at some stage in the development of the contract. The manager may be asked for initial advice on which learning goals the participant might consider, or they may be shown a fairly advanced draft for their responses. Any resource implications of a learning goal will also need to be checked out with them. If a manager wants someone to take on a particular learning goal it requires them to be sufficiently convincing that the person comes to agree with them.

It is always important for participants to know that the version of their Strategic Learning Contract that they show to their manager need not be exactly the same as the one with which they work in the learning group. For instance, they may prefer to remove references to their personal relationships and social life which they, none the less, feel will be important for them to explore through the agency of the learning programme.

When members of a learning group, along with a person's manager, all give their individual responses to the SLC it would be strange if it were not affected by these different perspectives. My own experience on the Post-Graduate Diploma in Management (by SML) is an example of this. Having already had the experience of answering the five questions, for the School for Independent Study, I felt I was ahead of the game. In addition, I had a personal computer when they were still relatively uncommon, which gave my draft contract the appearance of a finished document. However, this did nothing to daunt my learning group who proceeded to question me at some length. Their questions forced me to think my ideas through more thoroughly and one person's response, especially, gave me a surprisingly fresh perspective. The woman in question had an art school background and was working in video production, a completely different realm from mine. Yet she was able to see something I had not. She pointed out that all the learning goals I was proposing to work on were examples of the same underlying theme. This recognition was such a revelation to me, and so valuable, that I have often said that at that point the programme had already justified its cost.

While all responses cannot be as useful as that one, it is rare for anyone to go through the process of developing a contract without gaining immensely from the questions and challenges of their learning group. The finished contract is often significantly changed from an individual's first thoughts. There are two processes involved in this. There is the process of getting clear on the goals, what they are as well as why you have them and how they will serve you. Then there is the process of specifying them, of making them concrete, precise and in a form that can be evaluated. Obviously, the extent and rigour to which this process can be taken will depend on the length of the programme. A lot more will be expected when the process is given six months (as in a two-year qualification programme) than when it is given a couple of months or so (as in a nine-month in-company programme).

AGREEING THE CONTRACT

As would be expected, the process of agreeing the contract will be more thorough and more rigorous in the case of qualification programmes than for short-term in-company programmes. Qualification programmes are dealt with in Chapter 8. Even when the process of agreeing the contracts is not overly formal it is in the nature of a 'contract' that an agreement is made. That agreement involves all parties to the contract. In this case, those parties are the individual, the learning group members and their learning group adviser. In terms of its practical implementation, it may also mean their manager, although the manager would not be present during the learning group discussions in which the agreement is negotiated.

To provide a framework for agreeing a contract, it may be useful to have a checklist of criteria. Chapter 5, on the Sainsbury programme, shows one example of this (p. 79). This sheet simply lists some of the points that have already been made in relation to SLCs, and makes of them a checklist. Its value is that it ensures that these points are given explicit attention. Of course, in the process of agreeing a specific contract there may be much debate about whether or not it satisfies these criteria. But when it does, then in all likelihood it will prove a useful document to work from during the programme.

CHANGING THE CONTRACT

Participants often seem to see it as a paradox that so much attention is given to formulating the Strategic Learning Contract and yet it is not 'set in stone'. Making a thorough job of developing the contract is useful for all the reasons we have seen. At the same time, it must not be inappropriately reified. It is a working document. And it has to work effectively. It must accord with the principle that everything is to remain relevant to the individual's needs. Those needs can change and, if they do, then so must the Strategic Learning Contract.

ASSESSING THE CONTRACT

The full-blown, rigorous, multi-level assessment of a qualification programme has been described in Chapter 8. For in-company and other non-qualification programmes, assessment does not have the same requirements. None the less, there is value in some form of 'taking stock', though assessment may not always be the most appropriate name for it.

When the assessment format is applied to non-qualification programmes it is an assessment against the goals in the Strategic Learning Contract. It is simply a less formal and less painstaking version of that undertaken in qualification programmes. The individual presents their learning as a whole, that is to say, bringing together all they have gained from the programme. This will often include 'opportunistic learning', learning that was not set as a goal in the contract but which has resulted from pursuing goals that were, or learning that in some other way has resulted from the person's pursuing an SML programme. In their presentation the person is making a claim that, taken as a whole, what they have learnt constitutes an effective fulfilment of their contract. The other learning group members respond to this presentation in terms of the learning they have witnessed and for which they have evidence, either confirming the person's claim or challenging it.

A separate aspect of taking stock is to ask people to address the question of whether, and to what extent, they feel they have made good use of the learning opportunity they have had (through being on the programme). It was mentioned earlier that, over and above the achievement of the individual's learning goals, an added benefit of an SML programme can be in the 'learning to learn' area. This is the path to becoming a self managing learner. Consequently, this question allows participants to reflect on how they approached the programme and how effective they were in dealing with the various issues with which it confronted them and in engaging in the various learning tasks it required. Such a review enables them better to prepare themselves for future learning opportunities.

WHAT DOES A STRATEGIC LEARNING CONTRACT LOOK LIKE?

This question is often raised at the beginning of SML programmes. Understandably so. People set off on a journey which they rapidly discover is into more of an unknown (as far as the process is concerned) than they may have anticipated. They want something to hang on to. However, this presents a dilemma for those running such programmes. Knowing the tendency to take an example as a prescription there is concern that a participant's own options will be curtailed by sight of an existing contract.

Nevertheless, in the present context there is benefit to having a concrete representation of what is being described. Of course, contracts will differ, so there is no possibility of showing a 'representative' one. The point has been made that they will differ in relation to the length of the programme and, inevitably, they will also differ in terms of their quality. It follows that there is no 'good' or 'bad' contract outside of the particular context for which it is formulated.

There are obvious issues of confidentiality prohibiting the use of a real contract. However, dummy contracts have been drawn up for a number of organizations. These are used in development workshops for those who are to take on the role of learning group advisers. Typically, they are given the dummy contract and charged with responding to it in terms of how it might be improved. For this reason, the example given here in Figure 12.2 should not be taken as exemplary.

Figure 12.2 shows some elements of the job-related goals for a mock/dummy contract. This particular dummy contract was created for a well-known financial services company. It was used as a briefing for the directors of the company prior to the launch of a 360-degree feedback exercise. The headings for the three learning goals were from categories in the 360-degree feedback questionnaire. Also in this company the SLCs were labelled 'Development Contracts' – it seemed that, for the CEO and the directors, 'development' was a more acceptable word than 'learning'!

When this dummy contract was shown to directors of the company, to assist them in thinking through how they would create their own contracts, they were very critical. They had plenty to say about what was wrong with it. It has to be said that SLCs are easier to criticize than to create. This is not unexpected – criticism tends to be a dissociated process, whilst creating one's own Strategic Learning Contract involves deep consideration and a lot of self questioning. This is a much tougher undertaking.

This dummy contract has its learning goals grouped under three headings, with a separate form for each. In this example, there is no column for the first question on past experiences. This tabular form of summarizing aspects of the SLC has been used extensively and people seem to find it especially useful for communicating to their manager. What the tabular form may miss is some of the more descriptive aspects which a learning group might welcome.

WHAT IS IN A CONTRACT?

The point of an SLC is that it be individual. In this sense, an SML programme has a separate curriculum for each person on the programme. None the less, the learning goals that people choose have commonalities. We have seen how people are encouraged to make, or to consider making, choices within the three realms of

Learning goals: Leading

Current situation	Development goals	How to achieve these	Measures of achievement
I got a low rating on 'giving support and coaching'.			
1. My team think that I don't spend enough time with them and don't support them enough.	In six months time I will be spending appropriate amounts of time with each team member.	Agree time with each person – allow two hours per person each month. (*2 hours × 5 people = 1.5 days a month*)	I will have kept to all meetings, except for dire emergencies.
		Create space in my diary to see what current activities I can get rid of. *Book two hours.*	
		Agree clear ground rules with each team member on how to use the time.	
2. I am seen as too directive and don't question them about what they want to do or what ideas they have.	In six months time I will have the ability to question people to help them to learn, so that I can achieve a balance between questioning and telling.	Arrange *half a day* coaching with Development Adviser. (*£600*)	All team members will have produced, within the next six months, a development contract as a result of my coaching.
		Arrange for Development Adviser to observe two discussions with each team member. (*4 hours × 5 = 20 hours = £3500*)	
		Arrange *two hours* with Fred to find out what strategies he uses (he has a reputation as an excellent coach).	
Conclusion Because I am not coaching or supporting them, my team members do not have development contracts and are not developing their full potential. I need to do something about this.		(Also see goals on planning for success, because I need to improve my time management in order to do this.)	**Overall** Get a feedback rating on this question from my team in six months time – this should show the desired change in levels.

Figure 12.2 A dummy Strategic Learning Contract (*continued*)

Learning goals: Teamworking

Current situation	Development goals	How to achieve these	Measures of achievement
1. I am seen as 'taking all the glory' and not giving any credit to my people.	I will have talked to each of my teams every three months, to identify their successes and how to publicize them	Agree time with each team member – allow two hours per person per month. (*2 hours × 5 people = 1.5 days per month*)	The overall staff satisfaction scores will have improved by 2 per cent by the next survey.
	I will continue to talk about my success, but acknowledge (to my team) what part my team have played in creating that success.	Agree some clear ground rules with team members on how to publicize our successes.	The turnover figures will have decreased by five per cent within the next 12 months.
	I will say thank-you to my team when they have completed good pieces of work.	Arranged *two hours* coaching with Team Leader. Practice!!! – identify at least one opportunity each month to say 'thanks'.	At the next appraisal all my team will get at least 'met' ratings.

Conclusion
Because of this my Staff Attitude Survey results are low, the turnover in my team is higher than average and my team are not performing well.

Overall
Get a feedback rating on this question from my team in six months time – this should show the desired change in levels.

Learning goals: Creative thinking

Current situation	Development goals	How to achieve these	Measures of achievement
1. My team don't think I look for the positives in their ideas.	In nine months time I will have the ability to give praise and sound genuine. I won't feel embarrassed when I do it. I will identify what's good about ideas, before I start to pull them apart.	Arrange *half a day* coaching. *(£600)* When I am reviewing work, identify what is good about it.	Get feedback from my team after I have reviewed each piece of work.
2. The team think that I always question and challenge them, and make them feel threatened.	In nine months time I will have the ability to challenge and question people to help them identify gaps in their thinking, without threatening them.	Arrange *two hours* with Bert to find out what strategies he uses. Work with the person who has produced the work to help them identify areas for improvement, rather than telling them what to do. Agree clear ground rules with each team member about how to review their work. Arrange for my Development Adviser to observe two discussions with each team member. *(5 people × 2 hours = 10 hours = £1750)*	All team members will have implemented one new idea within the next 12 months

Conclusion
Because of this my team are not able to fulfil their potential, because they don't see the point in coming up with new ideas. I need to do something about this.

Overall
Get a feedback rating on this question from my team in six months time – this should show the desired change in levels.

Figure 12.2   A dummy Strategic Learning Contract (*concluded*)

their current job, their career and their life in general. Obviously, there is a limit to what goals they are likely to identify within each of these categories, even though each person will bring their own individual perspective to bear on each specific goal. The following gives a sense of what people address in a Strategic Learning Contract in relation to various areas.

Present job

Depending on how long people have been in their present role there may be technical learning of one sort or another, or it may be a matter of improving their existing abilities or of making the most of their situation. Goals may be established in relation to doing things that the person wants to do but has been putting off, wrestling with time management issues, various facets of planning, and in developing their ability to influence others.

Career

Goals relate to finding a future role, preparing oneself for it, and doing whatever is needed to get that new role. These general goals may involve many more specific goals having to do with the ability to influence, to present oneself well, to find out relevant information about opportunities, networking, establishing one's own strategic alliances, learning new abilities that will be required by the new role and so on.

Self development

Something like self confidence, for instance, is either tackled directly or can come about as a beneficial side-effect of other accomplishments. There may be very practical goals, such as getting one's finances in order. Or there may be issues like changing one's self concept as, for instance, when being newly promoted to a management role after having long identified oneself as simply one of the team. This can be a lot less trivial than it might first appear if, for instance, the individual comes from a background in which no one was ever a manager.

Family and social life

There is often a general issue about achieving a balance between working and non-working life. More specifically this can mean spending more time with one's spouse, being able to assist children with homework (rather than returning from work when they are already in bed), maintaining friendships by seeing your friends (rather than only exchanging Christmas cards), ensuring cultural and non-work stimulation through going to the theatre, movies and concerts and taking time for healthy activities such as country walks or more vigorous sports.

Organization

In large and complex organizations people often feel the need to make sense of their organization. This is relevant to their knowing of opportunities that might lie in areas with which they are unfamiliar. This is also a good reason for initiating a mentor relationship with someone who, by virtue of their seniority, is able to answer questions about how the various parts of the organization fit together and what happens in each. A similar desire can exist to understand the internal politics of the organization, essential if one has particular projects one wants to implement. Finding out about this is often a more delicate matter as there is usually an implicit taboo on admitting that internal politics exists. Finally, there is the issue of where the organization is going. This has huge relevance, of course, in terms of one's own future employment, quite beyond its relevance to future possibilities. Despite the extent to which this is a preoccupation of organizational gossip there are few organizations in which people feel they know as much as they wish.

Industry/market

Here there is the same question of wanting to make sense of the industry or market in which your organization operates. To answer these questions may require establishing a network within that field, or information may be obtained from newspapers and journals or, increasingly, from specific Internet sites. In taking this industry/market perspective, it can be a definite advantage to have a mentor in the same field but outside one's own organization (though this is not to preclude also having a mentor within the organization).

Life in general

Goals in this area relate not just to the big picture, but to the biggest picture. Identifying them requires stepping back sufficiently far to be able to view one's life as a whole and evaluate whether it is proceeding as one would wish. Most of the time our attention is drawn by the more immediate requirements of work and living, but for that very reason we can find ourselves veering away from where we want our lives to be heading. The kinds of considerations that come into play here often relate to spiritual concerns and spiritual development. They may also include a desire to undertake voluntary work. More often the perspective taken at this level finds its expression in goals at the levels of self development and family and social life.

RELATION TO ORGANIZATIONAL NEEDS

While the emphasis of our exploration of Strategic Learning Contracts has been on the individual's choices it has hopefully been apparent that those choices are not made in a vacuum. This book takes the organizational application of SML as its focus and within that context the organization will be a significant influence on all aspects of the programme, especially so when it is an in-company programme. Of the three levels to be considered in relation to learning goals – job, career and life – the first is completely reliant on the specific organization in which the participant is working, and, in all likelihood, in the second, the organization, if not the only player, is the major one.

STRATEGIC LEARNING CONTRACTS BEYOND THE PROGRAMME

The most direct way in which SLCs go beyond the programme for which they were devised is when people choose at the end of a programme to develop a continuation contract, to take them from that point on into their future. Essentially, they create a second edition of their SLC, adding new goals, taking long-term goals another step forward and continuing with any goal not yet completed to their satisfaction.

Another concrete way in which contracts have a life beyond the programme is when they contain interim goals in relation to longer term meta-goals or directions. There will almost always be some of these to continue on with afterward. I have mentioned my own interim goal of developing a Ph.D. proposal. This I accomplished within the time of the programme, and I subsequently registered for a Ph.D. and used this as my next learning context.

Through developing a Strategic Learning Contract a person becomes familiar with using that particular structure. Over and above its immediate use in an SML programme, it embodies a way of thinking that can be applied to any situation where goal setting might play a part. The experience of having been on an SML programme may make it all the more likely the structure will be used in other contexts. The more experience people have of the Self Managed Learning process, the more likely are they to become self managing learners and to take an active approach to learning in the future. And thus to make the best future use of Strategic Learning Contracts.

SUMMARY

This has been a long chapter. That needs no justification in that, within the chapter, the case has been made for the central place of Strategic Learning Contracts in the Self Managed Learning approach. At the same time, we have seen that they can be useful in their own right, outside of an SML context, though their use, alone, does not make the approach into SML. The use of learning groups, within which to work with SLCs, makes all the difference, as is shown in Chapter 13.

The importance of establishing goals, and the importance of those goals being strategic, has been argued in the context of learning and development every bit as much as it might in the context of an organization's business. How the five questions are used to elaborate a Strategic Learning Contract has been covered at length, and the way in which SLCs are used throughout the life of an SML programme has been explained. Lastly, the SLC has been seen as a method whereby an individual can engage in the process of lifelong learning. The creation of SLCs can be a continuous process, whether they be seen as separate contracts or as one ongoing and continually revised version that reflects the individual's changing circumstances and the achieved goals that mark the path they are creating.

13 Learning groups

Ian Cunningham

INTRODUCTION

In this chapter I will explore a number of issues about the use of learning groups. Already in other chapters we have emphasized the value and importance of this element of SML. Here I will cover the following factors:

- why the label 'learning group'?
- why have learning groups?
- the nature of learning in a group setting
- some qualities of dialogue
- things to do in a learning group
- using projects in groups
- problems in learning groups
- groups over time
- the difference between a learning group and everyday interactions
- other group structures that can be used in SML
- online groups.

In SML we define a learning group as a group of about five or six people, with an adviser, which meets over a period of time (anything from six months to two years typically) at intervals of perhaps one day per month. In SML programmes a specific requirement of such a group is that each person has their own Strategic Learning Contract. The purpose of the group is to assist the learning of the members in it and its efficacy should be judged as to how well it achieves that aim (and not whether it's a comfortable group or whether people always enjoy being in it – though one hopes that it is usually a good experience).

WHY THE LABEL 'LEARNING GROUP'?

In earlier writings about SML we used the term 'set'. This term is used in action learning and we wanted to honour the fact that we had learned the value of such small groups from action learning. The learning set, of about five or six people, has been a cornerstone of action learning practice for many years. However, the use of the term 'set' in action learning has been associated with a group setting where individuals usually carry out project work and where Strategic Learning Contracts are not used. It can, therefore, be confusing if we use the term 'set' to describe a group where everyone does have a Strategic Learning Contract and where project work just happens to be one of many options that a person can use as a mode of learning.

Hence we have started to use the term 'learning group' instead of 'set'. One advantage of this labelling is that it is low on jargon: the label does say it all and in common parlance. However, there is still the need to explain what it means in our context – and that will be one aim of this chapter.

WHY HAVE LEARNING GROUPS?

One argument put to us is that using learning groups does not suit everyone. In one organization with an optional SML programme for senior managers around 10 per cent said that they preferred not to be in a group, and hence did not take part in the SML programme. There seemed to be a number of reasons for this. A legitimate concern was that in a highly political environment it might not be wise to open up about learning needs to colleagues. In the best arranged SML programmes it is normal for people not to be grouped with close working colleagues, for example people from the same team. However, when one gets to the top levels of organizations this becomes a problem, as there are not sufficient people to get this mixing. That is one reason we have favoured consortia arrangements for very senior people (see Chapter 4). Certainly it is almost impossible to see it work for a person in a CEO role to be part of an internal learning group.

A less legitimate reason used against learning groups is that of the highly independent managers who want to work on their own. In the organization mentioned above it was apparent that a number of managers who were against learning groups were maverick individuals who did not operate in a collaborative way in the organization. These managers were also ones who had a poor reputation for managing their staff and were viewed as bullies or uncaring people. The issue here, then, comes down to whether it was appropriate for them to be working as managers at all. It is arguable that such people may be better suited to acting as individual contributors or as outside consultants. Note that I am not saying here that poor 'people managers' should be excluded from managerial roles – only those who are a) poor; b) know it; and c) have no desire to learn to be better.

The company concerned certainly saw some of these managers as creative people who had a potential value to the business. The problem was that they created so much mayhem around them that it was dubious as to whether they really added value. Obviously this issue is part of a wider problem which includes the choices the company was making at selection (were these 'selection errors'?) and in putting these individuals into 'people management' roles.

Another dimension of the problem is people's earlier educational experiences. Most educational activity emphasizes a highly individualistic mode of learning. If you work together on something it's called 'cheating' – and is punished. Yet in organizations sharing learning and supporting each other is crucial to organizational performance. In an era where knowledge sharing is seen as vital it's difficult to see how organizations can avoid addressing the problem of excess individualism. And it's definitely apparent that any attempts to create learning organizations are doomed to failure if individuals refuse to work collaboratively with colleagues on learning issues.

My stance, then, is to be suspicious of managers who refuse to join a learning group. In Sainsbury's people were not given the option and by and large it worked. That's not to say that everyone was happy with the SML mode. But what the process did was to create a culture where mutual support was engendered and where there was increased collaboration.

After a learning group has existed for, say, a year individuals may opt to continue in this mode or to cease to use the learning group. That seems fine as by then we usually find that internal networks have been set up which provide the basis for continued sharing and collaboration (see, for example, the PPP case in Chapter 7). Also evaluation research shows that managers take this way of thinking and working back to their own teams and encourage increased collective learning activity.

THE NATURE OF LEARNING IN A GROUP SETTING

When thinking about a name for learning groups one option was to create a TLA (Three Letter Acronym). After all they are much loved in the management literature (BPR, TQM, etc.). One thought was 'Intentional Learning Groups' – this would denote the fact that such groups are not just any old grouping and that there is a serious intent behind forming them. Another label could have been 'Dialogic Learning Groups'. The main reason for not using that title was that it moves into a more jargon-oriented mode (and we definitely wanted to avoid that).

However, the invocation of 'dialogue' as a term could be apt. Figure 3.1 indicates a spectrum of possible interactions in groups and I will explain that spectrum a bit more here. The four factors in the spectrum are, to some extent, crudely distinguished one from another. But my intention here is not to present a neatly packaged truth but to indicate some simple ways of making choices about how a learning group can best work.

Figure 13.1   Spectrum of possible interactions

'Direction' indicates a mode of communication which is one-way and has a 'telling' dimension to it. It could be seen as characterizing a particular mode of leadership or a way of teaching. In the latter case the teacher directs people – 'This is how things are', 'This is what you are to do', etc. It is associated with didactic authoritarianism. The 'command and control' model of leadership clearly fits this category.

'Debate' is often seen as superior to 'direction' because it has a two-way dimension to it. Debating requires response to what is said. However, debating has a quality of polarizing about it, as exemplified by political debates. One side says something and the other side automatically disagrees. So debating has a win–lose quality and can create a closed mind interaction (as witnessed in parliaments the world over). In a learning context debating can be as inefficient as direction. If a group gets into debating it can create conflicts and unnecessarily entrenched positions.

'Discussion' potentially moves us out of the polarized, position-taking, debating mode. It allows for a more open airing of views and more give and take. It is characterized by seminars and group tutorials (as opposed to lectures) in a traditional higher education setting. Discussion is also multi-way as opposed to one-way (direction) or two-way (debate). People can air a variety of views and, in the best discussions, do not have to take a position. Or if a person does take a position they may change that in the light of new information arising from the discussion.

The downside of discussion, in a learning context, is that it can encourage a superficial 'out-there' mode of interaction. A group can discuss, say, leadership as an abstract topic and may degenerate into debating the best leadership style. But none of the people in the group may own up to their own leadership style or even consider it as something to contribute to the discussion. Hence the learning may be about theories of leadership but no one in the group changes anything about the way they lead.

This problem characterizes the case study syndicate on a typical MBA. Such a group may come up with idealized solutions to a case through rigorous discussion and/or debate. However, none of the group will have to implement the solutions proposed and none of them may have considered at all their own possible real-life actions if faced with the case. Hence the learning stays at the level of knowing about something but not knowing how to do it.

'Dialogue' is different. It requires people to own their own feelings and their personal involvement in issues. It encourages deep learning through the active engagement with issues of real importance. In earlier chapters, where there have been quotes from participants on SML programmes, you will see examples of people saying that they had to re-examine previous assumptions; they had to face challenges to their own beliefs and values – and, in the process, they may have changed quite radically.

Dialogue, then, creates real personal involvement. I always say to a new learning group that people can raise what they like so long as someone owns the issue and has a personal stake in it. This is one way of differentiating dialogue from discussion. However, it can seem paradoxical that dialogue may often need to begin with something that looks like monologue. That is, it needs the problem owner to elaborate on the problem, sometimes at length, before the group can engage in dialogue with the person.

A typical example of an issue is someone struggling with a career choice. Should they go for a new job or stick where they are, for instance? This kind of problem may require the person to talk about their values, the constraints on any decision they need to take (family etc.), the impact on others and so on. Dialogue can begin when the group has enough information to engage with the person.

In the process other members may be challenged to think about their own values and assumptions. For instance, someone may ask the 'problem owner' about money and job security. The fact that they ask about these is likely to indicate that the questioner values these. The problem owner may respond by saying that those factors aren't important to them. This can then move the dialogue on: both parties may need to consider what they value – and if they changed their values what that might mean. This kind of open exploration pushes people to understand each other in greater and greater depth – and develop the deep learning that evaluation studies show is of such importance.

One of the important learnings for such a group can be about how to take this process into other contexts. A team leader may realize that a dialogic approach can be used in their team meetings, where appropriate. This is an example of why I see such learning groups as having an important role to play in wider issues such as knowledge management. In Chapter 7 one respondent in the PPP evaluation study commented on how the group had fostered real knowledge sharing through moving tacit (internalized) knowledge into explicit (externalized) knowledge.

SOME QUALITIES OF DIALOGUE

It may be worth summarizing here some of the qualities that one might look for in effective dialogue:

- *Openness* by all concerned, but to a level that is appropriate (and that is not always easy to judge, though groups seem to develop their own norms on this).
- *Authenticity* group members need to 'tell it like it is' and not cover up or pretend.
- *Choice* the person starting the process has choice about what to raise and how to raise it.
- *Meaning* meanings are clarified, and this has long-term value in a group meeting over, say, a period of a year.
- *Non-defensiveness* it is important that the problem owner does not act in a defensive manner when their cherished ideas are challenged.
- *Giving up control* one person explained this as follows:

When I joined the learning group I lost control because, when I brought up a subject to discuss there were so many people feeding back and contributing that I could not push the conversation in the direction I wanted. Now, however, I have realized that by controlling I was not actually going into real depth on an issue because the depth was limited by my own perspective and control at that time. In the group I lost control and by so doing, gained more information and knowledge from my fellow group members who all have diverse backgrounds, knowledge and intents.

THINGS TO DO IN A LEARNING GROUP

Given that dialogue needs to start somewhere, I have reproduced in Figure 13.2 a handout that I use to help people see what they can bring to a learning group. As mentioned, this list is not meant to be comprehensive. It does, though, reflect real examples. What would not be apparent from such a list is how it can provide the basis for dialogue and in-depth exploration. However, in the context of a learning group, even a simple request for information might lead to a more searching examination of why the person wants the information, is it the right information to ask for and so on. And it also might not go in this direction – sometimes a request for information just leads to giving it.

USING PROJECTS IN GROUP SETTINGS

As I mentioned earlier, one reason for moving away from the term 'set' was to avoid the trap of seeing such groups as being purely for the purpose of supporting

These are just a few ideas, based on past experience, of how people have used a learning group for their own benefit. The list is not meant to be comprehensive but rather to assist your thinking about getting the most from the group. It also does not mean that a group is likely to use all these. Each group needs to establish its own culture about how it uses its time.

1. Update the group on actions you have taken to fulfil your Strategic Learning Contract.
2. Ask for information, for example who in the group knows about some resources that you could call on.
3. Ask for feedback on some specific issues.
4. Explore a work problem that you would like assistance on.
5. Try out a presentation you are about to make.
6. Test work plans, for example a new strategy, a possible re-organization, etc.
7. Rehearse some options for handling a tricky situation such as a disciplinary interview by, for instance, doing a role play in the group.
8. Explore career choices.
9. Ask for assistance in finding ways to meet goals identified in your Strategic Learning Contract, for example recommendations for books to read or courses to attend.
10. Report on projects undertaken.
11. Use the group as a safe environment within which to explore personal issues.
12. Conduct a brainstorming session in order to get new ideas, for example on how to tackle a problem.
13. Ask for coaching from a group member on some specific issue (such coaching could take place inside or outside the group meeting).
14. Ask the group just to let you vent your feelings about some problem.
15. Ask the group to let you ramble on about something (as you won't know what you think about the issue until you've talked it through).
16. Ask for assistance in generating an action plan following a discussion in the group.

Figure 13.2   Notes on how to use the learning group

project work. Whilst we tend to advise organizations away from compulsory project work, we sometimes find that they are keen to use such modes, believing that projects ensure practicality in learning. That they usually don't is often confusing to CEOs, HR Directors and others making decisions about development programmes. Figure 13.3 reproduces a note I wrote for one organization to help its directors to see that if they wanted people in learning groups to do projects they would need to design in such activity with some care.

Figure 13.3 deliberately counterposes the two project modes in a rather crude way, but my intention in writing it was only to sharpen up thinking not to provide a magic formula. I would still see the ideal as projects (even action projects) being only an option rather than a compulsory part of a programme.

PROBLEMS IN LEARNING GROUPS

Most groups work well most of the time. However, we have experienced 'problem groups' over the years. We, of course, define 'problems' in our terms (i.e.

Good projects are ACTION PROJECTS – they require people to take action on real business issues. Less useful projects come under the heading of INVESTIGATIVE PROJECTS. Such projects require people to investigate an issue but take no action on it. The two kinds of projects are discussed below, with the ACTION variety identified first.

1 RISK

Action projects require people to take real risks in making something happen. People learn from having to work with the emotional and political dimensions of taking action in real life situations.

Investigative projects are low risk, as they demand no action: people can merely suggest ideas to others.

2 SIZE (NB Size matters)

Action projects need to be of a manageable size – and definitely not too large, as projects tend to expand over time (and not to contract). Projects need to be specified as to actions needed in a defined time frame and should not be open-ended.

Investigative projects tend to be large scale and open-ended (hence ensuring no action).

3 RESEARCH NEEDED

Action projects don't suck people into massive research activity. Often it's best if the research evidence is already there, but people haven't acted on it.

Investigative projects tend to be heavily research-oriented (though often the research can end up as second-rate sociological surveys).

4 PRODUCT

The product of an action project should be action – it may not require an output in the form of a report or a presentation.

Investigative projects often end in a report (which no one ever reads) or a forgettable presentation.

5 GROUP WORKING

Often the best way to ensure action is to give people individual projects. Then they are personally accountable for their actions. One problem with group projects is that some people can coast and let others do the work (but they may want to take as much credit as others do). If action projects are to work they need people to have clear accountabilities in the project. One way to do this is to allocate individuals in the group to act as leader at certain times.

Another approach is for the sponsor to take an active role in the delivery of the project, but the danger here is that the sponsor may become too involved, for example with too much hand-holding. This means that often there is no substitute for effective 'group advising', and the role of the adviser can be crucial. This is especially so if there are group dynamic issues to sort out.

6 LEARNING

Action projects demand that people learn to make things happen and they take learners out of their comfort zones.

Investigative projects are often comfortable and make only restricted demands on learners, for example presentation and report writing skills, analytical skills, etc.

7 ROLE OF SPONSOR

In action projects the sponsor is looking for a real problem to be solved. It must be a problem not a puzzle (puzzles have known solutions; problems don't). Sponsors often need help in defining a suitable project, as they may be unused to this mode of learning.

In investigative projects sponsors may only be interested in getting recommendations for action – or they have no real interest in seeing anything happen (they just dreamed up the project to provide a learning opportunity for the group).

Figure 13.3   Criteria for good projects

problems as regards learning): the group members in some groups might not see them as problems at all.

1. THE LOW RISK GROUP

This group may want to stay at a very safe level and not confront issues. It can be overly polite with people refusing to open up in order to avoid tricky issues. This problem is most likely to occur in highly politicized environments or where people feel themselves under great threat. It can call for the learning group adviser to be quite challenging in order for the group to move forward – but that can mean the adviser taking big risks.

2. THE DISCUSSION GROUP

A group can get into a discussion mode, as described earlier. People can start to talk in generalizations about problems 'out there' that no one owns. Again the group adviser may need to challenge why this is happening – and it can be a subset of the Low Risk Group.

3. THE SOCIALIZING GROUP

While the two problems above can occur early on in the life of a learning group, this problem may crop up when a group has been going for some time. It seems especially to happen when a group decides it no longer needs an adviser but will continue to meet on its own at irregular intervals after a formal programme has finished. If the group re-defines itself as social, for example just meeting for dinners in order to keep in touch, there may be nothing wrong in it. The problem arises only if the group deludes itself that it is continuing as a learning group when there is little learning going on.

4. THE PSEUDO THERAPY GROUP

This is rarer these days than it used to be but some group members can take on the role of counsellor or therapist, wanting to delve inappropriately into people's private lives. The point here is about 'inappropriate'. If someone wants to talk about life outside work that can be very sensible. But if they are pushed into areas they don't want to talk about that seems less acceptable. As with all these examples the learning group adviser has a key role in maintaining the focus of the group.

5. THE OVER-DEPENDENT GROUP

This is another problem that can occur early on in the life of a group. Members want the adviser to hand-hold and tell them what to do. The adviser needs to keep spelling out their role, as tactfully but firmly as possible.

6. THE SUB-GROUP SYNDROME

This is rare but has happened. For instance, two or three people who get on well may decide to meet up and work together on issues. They may well then exclude others in the group. In one case a person had taken a dislike to one of the group members so they lobbied others outside the group and met secretly to find ways to exclude the person. It is a very unusual occurrence but one that the group adviser has to address.

GROUPS OVER TIME

As indicated above, groups can display different qualities at different times. The start of a group can often be quite tentative, with people testing the water a great deal and considering if they can trust their colleagues in the group. Some writers have postulated a natural progression in groups; the most famous is probably Tuckman's notion that groups go through four phases of forming, storming, norming and performing. Banet (1976) gives a good summary of Tuckman's and other theories of how groups progress over time. He suggests three kinds of theories: linear models such as Tuckman's which see change as a 'progressive straight-line function'; helical (spiral) models which see change as 'a regressive, whirlpool movement from surface to core issues'; and cyclical models which view change as the interplay of forces which loop continuously round in a group (1976: 169).

On balance I tend to support a view that each group is different and that generalizations can be dangerous. However, there does seem usually to be something different about the start of a learning group from when it is fully functioning. After that period it's difficult to predict how a group will progress, though the ending is clearly important. We tend to favour a ritual ending that marks a clear finish of a formal programme even if groups might continue to meet afterwards. One good way to finish is for the CEO or someone at that level to meet with groups and hear how they have performed and what they have learned. In PPP this was followed by a dinner with the CEO so that people could socialize after the formal part of the closing event.

THE DIFFERENCE BETWEEN A LEARNING GROUP AND EVERYDAY INTERACTIONS

It may be obvious by now how a learning group is different from everyday meetings but those who've never been in one sometimes question why such a structure should be necessary. I have heard one CEO, impressed with what he heard of the use of learning groups, say that this is how all groups should behave. While that sentiment was meant as a positive exhortation to his managers to create more of a living learning organization it was unrealistic. Everyday meetings are closer to what I've described as a discussion mode. They are about tasks or issues 'out there' in the business. While it's possible to add a learning review at the end of such meetings it is usually trivialized and any learning is likely to be surface level only such as a new piece of information. A learning group provides a unique environment for each person so that they can get a focus just on themselves. And the dialogue that ensues is quite different from anything that a business meeting can (or should) create.

OTHER GROUP STRUCTURES THAT CAN BE USED IN SML

The next chapter covers other modes of working that can support or wrap around learning groups. All I want to mention here is the importance of the links to other structures. Learning groups do not stand alone and other collective modes can be important parts of SML programmes. Also evaluation studies show that continued collaboration through networking is important.

A further point to bear in mind is that learning groups themselves can open up to other techniques. An example is the use of a learning group to invite in visitors. One way to use a visitor is exemplified by a group in the NHS with which I worked which invited in the CEO of a public sector organization outside the NHS to quiz him about his role. The group consisted of people who had been identified as of CEO potential so they were able to use their visitor to help them explore the nature of the CEO role. Also at final assessment (especially for a qualification) out-side 'assessers' can be of great value. Often people invite their manager or some colleagues in to the group to give judgements about their performance on specific aspects of their Strategic Learning Contracts.

A growing factor in learning group operation is the use of modern technology and the next section will briefly cover these issues. The next chapter also has more information on this matter.

ONLINE GROUPS

Learning groups can function effectively through support that is not face to face.

The first example to consider is the use of groups that work online via the Internet or an in-company Intranet. The Internet has become increasingly used to support learning and clearly my interest here is to move away from mechanized modes to ones that encourage a shared way of working. The software is now well developed to allow effective learning group interactions via the Internet and this mode is becoming more important to support groups that are geographically spread. With increased globalization it seems likely that this mode will be needed more and more.

A good model is for a learning group to meet up for about three days to draft their Strategic Learning Contracts and to get to know each other (and how to use any relevant software). The group can then agree to log on to the Internet, say, once a week to do what might normally be done face to face, for example sharing issues, monitoring Strategic Learning Contracts and so on. The learning group adviser has a key role to provide support to the group. The group could then meet every three months face to face for a two-day meeting to go into more depth on issues. My experience of groups that meet less frequently is that they usually feel frustrated at having to use only the online environment for so long.

Of course, this can be supplemented with teleconferences and, where the technology is available, videoconferences. Note that I am here emphasizing continuing a group mode of interaction. I prefer to keep one-to-one contact, for instance by phone, to a minimum (e.g. for emergencies) as other group members cannot be party to such one-to-one contact (and hence feel excluded). Also where I had a group with members in Tokyo, Alaska, Sydney, California, Washington DC and the UK the asynchronous mode was of great value. Given time differences a tele- or videoconference would have been almost impossible to arrange.

International companies that are using SML are finding that their Intranet can be a powerful support for learning groups. A company with group members in Hong Kong, the USA and Europe found that it was essential to use its Intranet for group communication. One advantage of using this was to encourage senior managers to use this mode as a matter of course in order to foster learning across different parts of the company in different parts of the world. So networking here becomes not just phone and face to face but also shared through the Intranet. And we are back to the issue of improving knowledge sharing in a really effective way.

Some myths to debunk about online working include the following:

● People won't open up so much online.
This is just not true. If the group is well bonded after an opening event, people will be just as open online as they are face to face. In fact for some people the asynchronous mode gives them more time to think and so they give more information online than they would face to face. This can especially apply to those whose first language is not English. They can be disadvantaged in face-

to-face interactions and find great value in online working because it gives them time to compose their answers to questions.

- It reduces the adviser's workload.
  Also not true. In fact a really active group can increase one's workload as they come to expect regular responses to their work.

- It's a cold medium.
  It doesn't have to be. People can share feelings just as well online as face to face. The only problem is that the normal visual clues are absent so sometimes it's not easy to interpret the extent of someone's emotions.

SUMMARY

Learning groups are a vital element of SML programmes. This chapter has made that case along with showing some factors that influence effective learning group operation. I have made a case also for using the term 'learning group' instead of 'set' in order to distinguish SML groups from action learning sets. I have elaborated on the way learning groups are used and shown how such groups are different from other kinds of group settings. I have also shown how new technology is important and will become increasingly so in the future.

14 Supporting Self Managed Learning

Ian Cunningham

INTRODUCTION

We have argued, in earlier chapters, that SML requires support structures and methods. SML is not about leaving learners in the lurch and telling them to do their own thing. We have especially argued for such structures as learning groups and Strategic Learning Contracts. This chapter adds to the earlier discussions in this book and makes a case for the creative use of various support approaches.

The following issues are covered here:

- meeting the needs of Strategic Learning Contracts
- the use of other collective learning structures, including methods such as the café society, learning communities and large group processes
- possible methods to assist mapping
- the idea of the learning assistant
- the role of the learning group adviser
- mentoring and coaching
- the role of experts
- the emerging role of the strategic development adviser
- the use of learning resources such as learning resource centres, online support and company universities
- sponsorship support and the role of top management
- what happens after a formal programme.

Given that this book is about SML the treatment of these issues will focus on SML. I will not attempt to be encyclopaedic or totally comprehensive in my analysis. There are many texts that cover basic general problems in the area of learner support, for example material on coaching (Cunningham and Dawes 1998).

MEETING THE NEEDS OF STRATEGIC LEARNING CONTRACTS

In the chapter on Strategic Learning Contracts we showed how question 4 (How do I get there?) provides the bridge to achieving one's learning goals. In traditional programmes it would be a curriculum or syllabus but in SML it is where learners specify how they will achieve what they want to achieve.

We showed, in that chapter, how there are a range of ways to meet learning needs and we emphasized that there is a danger that people will fall back on those approaches that they know or that seem legitimate (for example training courses). In this chapter some of what I will discuss is about alternatives to those 'known' approaches. In some programmes we have given a budget to either the learning group or the individual and this can help to focus people on the cost-effectiveness of various approaches. For instance, on the MBA by SML discussed earlier some people thought it would be a good idea to invite in a particularly popular 'guru' only to find that his minimum fee was £25 000. They quickly decided that blowing most of the year's budget of the whole group on one session would not be wise – so they bought his book instead.

This personal and collective responsibility for budgets also encouraged members of the programme to be quite creative in meeting their needs. For example, one person invited in their own CEO to do a session (at no cost to the programme). Inside companies people can also become quite creative in drawing on the expertise of colleagues in the business. In the learning group with which I have been working in Ericsson we found that a number of people had the need to learn about particular technical items. It was mainly knowledge acquisition so when one person went on a course about that topic they came back and shared their notes and handouts with their colleagues. This avoided the need for large numbers of people to take time out away from work and also saved the company a considerable amount of money.

This kind of saving is one reason why we have been able to make the case for the cost-effectiveness of SML. Although there is a cost to arranging learning group meetings and to setting up the programme, this is often easily balanced by the kinds of savings I have mentioned. When one couples this with the pay-off from programmes (as discussed in Part II of this book) there is an impressive case for using SML.

THE USE OF OTHER COLLECTIVE LEARNING STRUCTURES

The 'other' in the title of this section means 'other than learning groups'. So, although we have stated the case for the centrality of learning groups, there are other collective methods that can support SML. The approaches briefly outlined here are optional extras; they may have a limited role in many programmes. The methods described here are also not meant to show all the options available. They are shown as exemplars of particular approaches and are designed to give a glimpse of the rich possibilities for methods that move away from didactic teaching or standard trainer methods such as syndicate discussions, exercises, case studies, role plays and so on. This is not to deny that the latter methods might sometimes have a place in assisting people to learn. However, they often limit people's thinking about alternatives, and especially those alternatives that are more in keeping with the spirit of SML.

CAFÉ SOCIETY

In organizing a conference in 1988 I chaired a team where we came up with the notion of the café society as a method for encouraging people to be more self managing with their learning. The idea was to provide an informal and yet structured context in which people could interact around a focal point. We invited guest 'experts' who could act as such foci and who could initiate a dialogue around a topic. Our idea was to mirror in some way a (probably idealized) model of a Parisian café in the late nineteenth and early twentieth century. I had in mind how artists such as the Impressionists would gather at favourite cafés to share ideas and provide mutual support – but without someone controlling such exchanges and without setting limits or boundaries for the interchanges that could go on.

In the conference we wanted to encourage a similar sharing but, of necessity, to structure it more than would be apparent in an actual café. We therefore asked various well-known figures in the field (in this case 'management learning') to sit at tables with a number of chairs round each. People were told who was sitting where and what the focal person would like to dialogue about. Participants in the conference were free to wander from table to table and pick up the conversation as it went on. Only the invited 'expert' (focal person) had to stay put. We let the session run for about a couple of hours so that people had the chance to wander around a few tables.

We learned from the first experience of doing this that one has to limit seating at each table otherwise some groups could become too large. Also we found that providing some props that replicated a café helped. For instance, having waiters coming round with drinks can add to the atmosphere – though you can take this too far if you are not careful (the smoking of pungent French cigarettes would not be welcomed in this day and age).

The model of learning exemplified by the Parisian café seems important in SML. It shows that people can use expert figures but in more creative ways that avoid presentations. When I first started as a trainer, in 1970, we ran what we thought were quite good one-week residential training courses for managers. We often heard people say that, whilst they enjoyed the formal sessions (which we made quite 'participative' with exercises, role plays and so on), they frequently gained more value from the conversations over meals or in the bar in the evening.

In developing SML one motive was to respond to these comments. If dialogue between people helps them to learn, why not make that the core of the learning process and spin the formal bits off around it. Hence the use of learning groups. Figure 14.1 shows diagrammatically the switch from a training course, with inputs as central and dialogues between participants as peripheral, to the SML model which inverts these processes. Note that we do not reject 'formal inputs'. It's just their location in the scheme of things that changes.

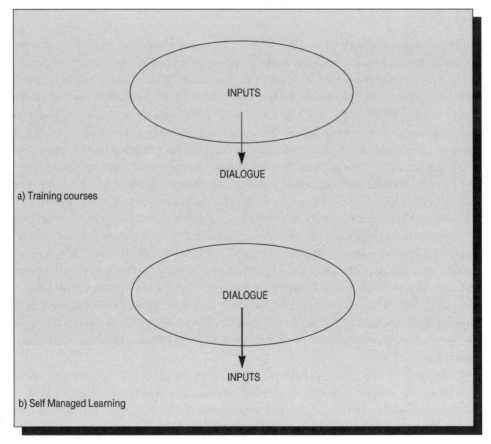

Figure 14.1   Training versus SML

The café society model is particularly useful when there are a number of learning groups on a programme as it enables them to come together to explore issues. There are variants of the basic structure but I hope that readers can see that the concept can be shaped to suit circumstances. What it also does is to help a loose network become more of a learning community. Networking is a popular concept but the downside of a network is that it is so loose that people cannot use it for learning purposes. People don't know each other well enough and it can degenerate into mechanistic arrangements for fixing deals. There may be nothing wrong with this unless the idea of the network is to support learning. In organizations where many people have gone through an SML programme it can be a waste if people are not linked more to each other so that they can generate continued mutual learning.

LEARNING COMMUNITIES

The above comments lead into the use of learning communities. The idea of such a structure is to move to something that goes beyond networking. All the learning groups on an SML programme can together constitute a learning community, but only if they are encouraged to act as one. A danger with learning groups that operate in isolation is that they can lose the value of a wider range of contacts. (See Cunningham 1999 for other comments on learning communities.)

Later I will mention the use of online working. This is starting to be a very effective way of promoting collaboration across groups. Intranets provide the opportunity for people to share across geographical distances that limit (or even preclude) face-to-face contact. In the MA (Organization Design and Effectiveness) at the Fielding Institute in California (see Cunningham 1999) we have found that a formally created 'Community Hall' on the web site allows learning groups to share ideas and contacts, set up special interest groups and so on. The asynchronous nature of online working also accommodates the increasing constraints on people's time; by allowing people to respond to each other in their own time the limitations imposed by tight schedules can be more easily circumvented.

If, however, groups can get together then structures such as the café society can be used to good effect. Learning communities can also use large group processes, as outlined below.

LARGE GROUP PROCESSES

The Sainsbury's case study shows one use of large group processes (see Chapter 5). There we found that such structures were very effective in initiating a Self Managed Learning programme. In that structure we were able to identify issues that needed addressing and we started to create a culture where people were prepared to collaborate across internal boundaries. This all helped to encourage people to take more responsibility for their own learning and development. Figure 14.2 shows how we developed the large group process at Sainsbury's.

We held an event for about 80 of Sainsbury's personnel people which lasted a day. The day was opened by a Board member introducing the context of the event including an overview of how the function needed to change and in what direction. We then structured the day to allow people to respond to what was happening in the business, with the aim that by the end of the day people would have had a chance to get their views over to others, explored options and committed themselves to action on the issues and problems. Part of the aim was to encourage more collective team working among personnel staff and to model a more empowering culture. Hence a method was needed that did not disempower people by dictating to them what they could work on. We also wanted to initiate a process whereby people could start to focus on learning issues (and then take part in an SML programme).

The agenda for the day is set out below, along with the aim of each session and the technique used.

Time	Aim	Technique
0900	Give backcloth to issues plus a steer on what needs addressing.	Board member presentation.
09.30	Explain the day.	Oral briefing.
09.50	Get the issues out.	Large group collage covering one wall of the room – people gave their views about the company (past, present and future).
10.20	Analyse the issues.	Small groups put the issues into words and identified the top priorities for action on one flip char per group.
11.20	Share issues and make choices about ones to work on.	Posting flips; people 'mill' in order to read each other's flips, then large group session to agree topics to work on.
11.30	Working on the issues chosen by the group.	Small groups with self selected membership to start work on what needed doing; freedom for people to move around groups, redefine tasks, merge groups, etc.
12.45	Check progress/action.	Preliminary report back to whole group.
13.00	Social interaction.	Buffet lunch.
14.00	Moving on.	Whole group – deciding topics to close off, what new issues had emerged, what issues which had been left in the morning could now be picked up, etc.
14.20	Working on issues.	Small groups – some the same as in the morning, mostly different groups working on new or redefined tasks.
15.30	Moving towards action.	Report back plus teasing out things that could be fixed there and then. Moving to action groups.
16.00	Getting action back at work.	Action groups – agree to meet afterwards to progress key problems, plan work to be done.
16.45	Wrap up, review, check action points.	Final large group session.

NB These timings were only roughly adhered to during the day. We modified things as we went along – always with the key objectives in mind. A second day with similar membership reported significant progress on all action points with most problems either solved or at least moved on.

Figure 14.2   Large group process in Sainsbury's

We have also used large group events to make links between organizational change and learning issues. Chapter 6 shows how Arun District Council used the 'large group' of 50 managers as a basis for setting up one of its SML programmes (for all 50 managers). Whilst, as Marcia Fellows points out, the programme itself produced some problems, the process of using a large group to take charge of the SML process did work well.

The major advantages of using large groups are that it involves a wide selection of people, it energizes action and it provides a secure base for future learning activity. Such structures do not, though, stand alone. Many organizations use such methods and then find that the energy is dissipated, as there is no sustained learning. The SML learning groups address this problem.

POSSIBLE METHODS TO ASSIST MAPPING

This section links to the last one. To some extent there is an overlap in the use of these methods. However, it seems useful to separate out the methods discussed here as they can be of most use at the start of a programme to help people to map out the territory and make appropriate choices for the content of their Strategic Learning Contracts.

WITNESSES

Rather than having straight presentations, for instance about business issues, it is possible to make the exploration of the issues more self managed. One process that works well is to use witnesses. The following extract outlines an aspect of a programme on Client Relationship Management for senior partners in KPMG.

> One session in the first phase of the programme uses three outside visitors ('external witnesses') who the learning groups get a chance to question. All were deliberately chosen because their organisations were service businesses, but dissimilar to KPMG. On the first of these programmes the external visitors were Barry Hearn, whose field of client relationship management is mainly in sport; Fiona Driscoll, who was running a major PR company and Mike Davis, the Group Managing Director of RCO Support Services, whose company does cleaning, portering, security work and related activities.
>
> The sessions with outsiders have given people an opportunity to explore similarities and differences in approach. Audit, tax and consulting partners could see that they had something to learn from how Barry Hearn managed Steve Davis or Herbie Hide.
>
> A shock sometimes for participants has been the very different language that the external visitors have used, compared with KPMG's often literal and analytical language. Barry Hearn often answered questions by telling stories. Fiona Driscoll used rich metaphors to respond to questions. For instance, asked about how she judged the level of motivation of her staff, she replied that she wanted her (largely female) staff to prefer to be at work rather than having sex with Tom Cruise! These

parables and metaphors could answer a question in a far more powerful way than analytical English.

A major challenge for many participants has been how they move from being able to relate to the issues faced by functional directors (for example finance or IT) to being able to talk with chief executives about wider business issues. All the visitors to the programme operated with this wider perspective at the most senior level in their client organisations. As with other sessions the challenge has been for participants to tease out 'the difference that makes a difference'. It requires questioning which digs behind the differences of style, context, and content and unearths fundamental aspects of client relationship management.

(Cramb and Cunningham 1998: 51–2)

As can be seen from this quote, the idea is to enrich people's mental maps by providing a stimulus to their thinking. It avoids boring up-front presentations and it encourages self managing by making participants take responsibility for getting out of the witnesses what they want.

LIVE CASES

There are many problems with standardized case studies. One of them is that they are based on 'dead' materials and learners cannot interrogate real people. Also there is often no way of checking if the action people suggest is valid or useful. On the PPP programme (see Chapter 7) we used live cases instead as a way of mapping the field of strategy and strategic implementation. The method is as follows.

A CEO is asked to produce papers on their company, say, five years ago, for example balance sheets, profit and loss accounts, product and market information, etc. These are copied ahead of an opening workshop (in PPP's case this was a three-day event to cover both mapping and learning group formation). At the start of the day participants are given a quick overview of strategy theory and then the CEO appears to give a five-minute introduction. The groups then go off with the material on the company and spend some time coming up with questions to ask the CEO. The groups come back together and the questions are put to the CEO about the state of the business five years ago. After the question and answer session participants go off into their groups to come up with a strategy that they think the CEO should have adopted.

The final session is where each group presents to the CEO what they think the CEO should have done. The CEO then responds with what he did do and gives financial and other data about how the company has fared over the last five years. This is followed by a general discussion about the issues that have come up. The method helps people to think about strategy and implementation and it can also help learning group bonding by giving the group a collective task to carry out.

OTHER METHODS FOR MAPPING

While above I've mentioned two approaches that show ways of working that are particularly aligned with SML values, it is quite possible to use any of the approaches outlined in Chapter 12 for answering our question 4 (How do I get there?). People read books and articles, talk to colleagues in the organization, watch videos, listen to audiotapes, go on the Internet and so on.

I will return to the issue of mapping under the later section on the role of 'experts'.

THE IDEA OF THE LEARNING ASSISTANT

We have suggested that the role of people like ourselves in SML programmes is best described as a 'learning assistant'. The implication of this title is that we are there to assist others with their learning, and the notion of 'assistant' provides the necessary humility required of the role. The learner is managing their learning but they can be assisted with it. Elsewhere (Cunningham 1999) I have suggested that there are four roles that can usefully be played in making a programme work and these are briefly described below.

1. THEORY

There is a role for creating and articulating theory. I use the term 'theory' to cover generalizations, concepts and models about SML and learning in general. It can be important to be clear about the theoretical basis of one's work. And those who claim to have no theory may only be indicating that their theories are somewhat unconscious or poorly articulated.

In SML it is valuable to be able to state theories of learning to participants and therefore, in the process, at the very least maintain intellectual honesty. However, we tend to hope that people will also recognize the theoretical basis of SML processes and see the links into the design of programmes.

2. DESIGN

We assist learners by designing programmes that we envisage will help them with their learning. Earlier chapters have covered a range of aspects of SML designs, from macro factors such as the design of a whole programme to micro factors (for instance aspects of this chapter). The designs obviously do not just happen. It takes effort to create appropriate designs.

3. MANAGING

SML processes and programmes need managing. This can vary from leadership of programmes (for example marketing and selling the approach) to back-up support such as administrative duties (booking venues, getting material copied and so on). Ideally a lot of what goes on under this heading, as with design work, will be relatively invisible to participants.

4. INTERACTION

This is the most visible part of the work we do. In the past it has been largely focused on the face-to-face interactions in learning groups. Increasingly, though, the influence of modern technology such as the Internet, Intranets and video conferences, has varied the role more. What all modes do have in common, though, is a basis for the direct assistance of learners as individuals and as groups.

Below I will take up some aspects of the interactive dimension of assisting learning. First I will say a little about being a learning group adviser and then I will comment on one-to-one roles, especially coaching and mentoring.

THE ROLE OF THE LEARNING GROUP ADVISER

The first thing to say here is that there is a role for someone to act as adviser to a learning group. The term 'adviser' isn't the right one but we have found it difficult to come up with an alternative. We particularly wanted to avoid using the label 'facilitator'. At one level 'facilitator' is fine because it has the sense of not being a teacher or trainer. Also the dictionary definition of facilitate includes the term 'ease'. So a facilitator eases the group along – they oil the wheels, so to speak. However, the term 'facilitator' has also come to be associated with a group facilitation role and has been linked to team development. And we are clear that a learning group is not a team.

In addition to this, facilitation has become associated with a role that has become professionalized (in the worst sense of the word). We, on the contrary, want to promote the idea that a learning group adviser is someone who behaves as a good team leader/manager would behave. It requires someone to be a good human being: to listen, to ask questions, to care about group members, to support them as people while sometimes challenging their behaviour and so on.

That being said there is a lot more that can be discussed in relation to being an effective learning group adviser. Cunningham (1999) has more on this along with further discussion about the role of learning groups. Also Burgoyne and Cunningham (1980) has a useful model of learning group adviser behaviour.

MENTORING AND COACHING

These two terms are often used interchangeably. We prefer to use them as separate terms to delineate separate processes. We see mentoring as a strategic process that has a more whole person focus. A mentor is someone who is available to assist a learner in the totality of their learning. A mentor will also typically have a long-term relationship with a learner.

On the other hand, a coach is someone who will be more concerned with assisting a learner to develop a skill or range of skills. The coach role is more tactical and can last a short time. In the latter case someone may assist a person on a one-off basis to learn a specific narrowly defined skill. An example would be someone coaching another person on how to use a software package on the computer. The coach in this case may have little or no interest in the person *per se* – only in getting the person to learn the specified piece of software. This would be different for a mentor who would more likely be interested in the development of the person in a total sense.

COACHING

There are various contexts in which coaching takes place, just as there are various ways in which it can be done. The spectrum ranges from the unplanned coffee-machine conversation in which ideas or information are picked up, and which would probably not be thought of by either party as 'coaching', to regular planned meetings, where progress is monitored on the way to clearly defined learning targets.

The concept of the coach is best known from the field of sports. In that context, the coach was frequently a former athlete who had become a 'teacher' of athletes. In the old model of coaching, the coach *tells* the athlete how to improve, most often by instructing them in what to do, and what not to do. Typically, sports coaches are more emotionally involved in how well their athletes do than are most school teachers. It is important to be aware of this image of the sports coach as elements of our thoughts about and experiences of them can be imported, along with the notion of coaching itself, into the organizational context.

In the organizational context, the concept of coaching has come to cover many different activities. Its early use often carried a remedial connotation. Someone needed to be coached because they were not performing. When this was the case, coaching could include a punitive element; the message to the learner was that this was the last chance, they were being coached to improve and it was either 'shape up or ship out'. While this idea of coaching has been largely superseded it is well to be aware that there may be people who still look upon it in this way.

Today, coaching is more usually seen as a means of developing people within organizations. As development has become increasingly the role of the manager, the manager has increasingly become a coach. However, this is a new role for many and there is clearly a lot to learn. Just as expertise in a technical area is not a preparation for a managerial role, neither is experience in a managerial role, necessarily, sufficient preparation for being an effective coach.

(For more on ways to develop coaches for SML programmes see Cunningham and Dawes 1998.)

PEER COACHING

There is a tendency for much of the literature on coaching to assume a senior to junior model: the coach is presumed to be more senior. However, one spin-off from learning groups is that people get to see the value of peer coaching. Group members often provide coaching for each other. This then can encourage the interdependence that is so important in developing a more effective learning culture in the organization.

THE ROLE OF EXPERTS

An expert in a particular subject can act as a coach. However, experts are often not good at coaching. What they find easy the learner may find difficult, and the expert may be unsympathetic to the struggles of the new learner. One spin-off from the vogue for knowledge management has been the desire to capture the knowledge of the expert so that it can be shared. Where this is done well it can be of great value for learning purposes. The elegant thinking of a real expert that gets posted on an Intranet for others to use is clearly valuable. However, this often does not happen. For instance, IT professionals may capture only the trivial or the mundane and fail to get inside the head of the expert. Or the politics of the organization inhibits experts from sharing their knowledge – if knowledge is power then you give up your power at your peril in a highly political environment.

Allowing for these difficulties we find that learners in SML programmes come to see that asking questions of experts can be a quick solution to learning needs. The finance expert or the lawyer can quickly help someone to learn all they need in that area if the learner asks the right questions. And here the learning group can be of great assistance in helping learners to formulate their needs prior to 'asking the expert'.

MAPPING REVISITED

As one of the elements of an SML structure, mapping was characterized (in Chapter 2) as a way of letting participants get an idea of what is in a particular domain, without foreclosing on their own choices. To do a mapping for an SML group is quite different from teaching. We found that experts in a particular field coming in to a programme varied enormously in their ability to keep to mapping and away from teaching. This is not always an easy matter. Mapping should bring a reflective distance between participants and the material, while the standard teaching approach can encourage them to accept it lock, stock and barrel as the 'truth'. When things are absorbed as truths they leave little room for individual thought. Of course, it is quite possible to respond to something presented as truth by treating it as one person's map. It is possible, but the more that truth is insisted upon the more difficult it becomes. However, an SML programme can assist in developing such a perspective.

Mapping is an important concept in releasing people from the tyranny of truth. While anything presented as truth can be viewed as a mapping, the truth mode of presentation does not tend to invite discussion. Presenting something as a mapping encourages an engagement with the ideas and concepts being put forth, not in terms of their truth but in terms of their benefits and consequences. This is far more fruitful because it begins to relate the ideas to action: what would result from using this model or theory?

One reason for having mapping in an SML programme is that people are being asked to create their own learning programme, yet cannot know to include elements that they don't know exist. Their choices are constrained by the fact that they don't know what they don't know. Of course, the same factor applies to the one who does the mapping. The limitations of a mapping are that the person doing it may not know some elements of the field in focus. Also, to focus on a particular field is to create a boundary which excludes many other factors, and cross-disciplinary practices show that this may be to exclude things of value. These are inevitable concomitants of mapping. There can be no map of everything. From this we see the importance of presenting a mapping as one way to view the domain, leaving it open for participants to forage further.

THE EMERGING ROLE OF THE STRATEGIC DEVELOPMENT ADVISER

Learning group advisers, mentors and coaches focus mainly on the learner or small groups of learners. However, a new role has been emerging in organizations. The best label is 'strategic development adviser' (SDA). This person is able to take a strategic focus on a business area and help people get the learning they need. The SDA may do coaching and mentoring themselves but they are more likely to be looking at the needs of all the people to whom they have a responsibility and to help them access learning resources of all kinds.

The SDA may facilitate people joining an SML programme and they may then ensure that support is available for people during a programme and after it. So they may set up programmes to develop mentors and coaches, they may link to learning resource centres in the organization and they may help people to use the company Intranet for learning purposes. The SDA may not be located in a central HR department but, especially in large organizations, may be located in a strategic business unit (SBU) and report to the director responsible for the SBU (not to HR).

THE USE OF LEARNING RESOURCES SUCH AS LEARNING RESOURCE CENTRES, ONLINE SUPPORT AND COMPANY UNIVERSITIES

Learning resource centres became popular in the 1980s and early 1990s. They focused on providing a fixed location for the storage and retrieval of learning resources such as books, video and audio tapes, learning packages, etc. With the evolution of more sophisticated computer-based approaches, such as CD-ROMs, computer facilities were added to such centres.

With the growth of the Internet and in-house Intranets, these have become more important sources of learning resources. In some companies electronic systems have totally taken over the provision of learning resources (and no physical learning resource centre exists). The good old World Wide Web is a grossly underused resource for learning especially if people can learn to use search engines effectively. SML programmes have often educated participants in the value of the 'Web' and this has provided a continued resource for people.

A major use of Intranets can be to support learning groups between meetings. Groups can continue to dialogue even if their face-to-face meetings have to be limited due to geographical distance. Figure 14.3 shows a note on the use of a company Intranet for a global SML programme. The software mentioned in it is the Sitescape Forum software which is particularly user-friendly for learning group dialogue.

Alongside these developments have come corporate universities in organizations such as Motorola, Unipart and Sun Microsystems. In most cases the corporate university is merely a re-badging of the training centre. In such cases they often do not provide the flexibility needed for SML. However, where organizations have created 'virtual universities', that is online, it at least gives more flexibility of access, as people do not have to attend a specific location to get materials.

People on SML programmes will frequently access their learning resource centre as a way of meeting some of their learning contract requirements. Indeed some organizations have seen a marked improvement in learning resource centre use as a result of setting up an SML programme. In the better examples, such as

WHY USE IT?

- With participants around the world this medium provides the best basis for continued contact for group members.
- People will have to learn how to use this mode – Intranets and the Internet are not matters for the future – they are here now and senior people will have to know how to use them.
- The best way to learn how to use this technology is – to use it.
- Asynchronous modes of working can have advantages over synchronous modes, for example they cope with time differences, allow people to ponder over responses, allow for cultural and language differences (people whose first language is not English benefit from this mode of communication).
- It is cost-effective.
- It has advantages over e-mail as it allows for group discussion and wider networking. The multi-dimensional threaded discussions enrich communication.
- Discussions are recorded so ideas are not lost. This supports better knowledge management in the business.
- Globalization of businesses demands a global mode of working – and this mode supports such globalization.
- Online working enhances networking across boundaries and can free up creativity and innovation.
- This medium encourages a wider use of teamworking.

ISSUES FOR PARTICIPANTS

- Some will be less computer literate than others so will need more help.
- People will have to learn how to use this specific software – it isn't complex but it will take some time for those unused to online working.
- People will have to learn to balance their communications, for example not too much writing and not too little; how to avoid coming over as too blunt and confronting.
- The medium is not as 'cold' as some make out – it is possible to work in some depth with people. However, the normal face-to-face cues are missing and people will need to get used to that.

ISSUES FOR LEARNING GROUP ADVISERS (LGAs)

- Working in this mode can be quite demanding and LGAs will need to be committed to it.
- LGAs will need to be in a position to assist participants with basic problems – and then know how to refer people on if they can't help them.
- LGAs will need ready access to the Intranet – including from home (so that they can keep in touch with their groups even if away from the office).
- LGAs will need to facilitate group discussions. Whilst some of the skills used face to face will apply, such as the ability to ask good questions, there will be added skill requirements, for example the ability to 'read' what's going on in a group without the advantage of the visual cues available in face-to-face meetings.

Figure 14.3   Online working – a background note for learning group adviser development

PPP, the learning resource centre has been designed from the start around the needs of SML programmes. Clearly this is our preference. In such centres material can be bought that responds to people's learning contracts and therefore waste is minimized. (In many learning resource centres there has been much costly waste where materials have been bought that no one uses.)

SPONSORSHIP SUPPORT AND THE ROLE OF TOP MANAGEMENT

Whilst programmes such as the one in Ericsson can be initiated by middle managers, there is no doubt that top level support makes things easier. Such support is made simpler if top managers have had personal experience of using SML. This, however, is not always easy to arrange. One use of consortium SML programmes has been to provide a facility for CEOs and company directors to take part in SML processes outside their organization. While it would be nice to think that top level leaders could form their own learning groups inside the business it often doesn't work out that simply.

In the cases quoted in this book we can see that, for example, the Arun programme, which involved the CEO and the directors as learning group members, was not a complete success. This was in part because there were serious level and status differences in the learning groups. However, Judith Evans and Nigel Broome (the two directors in Sainsbury's) were able to operate as a mini learning group (see Chapter 5). This was made easier because they had to collaborate anyway, given that the two of them managed the HR function between them (and if they hadn't got on together the structure would not have worked).

One reason for top managers finding SML in their own organizations to be a problem is the politics so often endemic at Board level. Directors and CEOs say that one value of using a learning group outside the business is the opportunity to talk about things that would never be possible in their own organization. CEOs especially emphasize the uniqueness of their role and, even if they could open up in their organization, they value being able to meet with other CEOs in a learning group.

Often when starting a programme it is not possible to give top managers direct experience of using SML. In such cases we have sometimes organized a mentoring/coaching workshop for the Board (e.g. in Allied Domecq) so that they at least have an idea of learning issues and how they can support their managers on the programme. Also just straightforward briefing sessions can be of value. Even if the top level managers do not fully understand all the ramifications of the programme at the very least they can support the Strategic Learning Contracts of their managers.

This latter point is important. Evaluation evidence such as that from PPP shows that support for reviewing learning contracts is important. A person on an SML programme will usually look for support from their line manager, even if it is just at the level of letting them attend learning group meetings. Ideally one wants more. This can include:

- regular review meetings around the learning contract;
- coaching support, where the manager can offer it;

- assistance with access to learning resources;
- assistance with networking and using contacts inside and outside the business;
- response to new abilities that the person gains through SML, for example giving the learner more responsibilities;
- support with secondments, career breaks, etc.;
- career advice and support.

All of the above are, of course, made easier if the manager has a real understanding of SML and an orientation to learning and development. Many managers, unfortunately, do not fit this profile. In these cases SML acts as a way of counteracting the influence of poor managers. A learning group can do what the manager should be doing and hence SML can rescue people from relying on their manager.

WHAT HAPPENS AFTER A FORMAL PROGRAMME

SML should not stop at the end of a formal programme. After a programme some people:

- carry on with their learning group – often meeting less frequently;
- form a new learning group – this can be valuable as it shows people that the success of their group was not just down to the chemistry of their group (and hence they can see the real value of the SML process);
- find a mentor – and re-write the learning contract to go with this new arrangement;
- work with their manager using a learning contract;
- join a learning group outside the organization, for example as part of a consortium;
- work with their current colleagues using their team as a replacement learning group;
- join an SML qualification programme.

Many of these approaches require organizational support, that is someone has to organize them. It can be important to build in some of this infrastructure before a programme ends. For example, mentors may need some development prior to them taking on the role.

CONCLUSION

This chapter has made a case for providing a range of support structures and processes for learners. SML programmes are not just about Strategic Learning Contracts and learning groups. However, the kind of infrastructure I have championed is in keeping with best practice in developing learning organizations. In order to keep this chapter in bounds I have, of necessity, limited the discussion of a number of key issues. The references point to other texts that elaborate some of these ideas further.

Part IV
Conclusions

INTRODUCTION TO PART IV

This part has only one chapter. The intention here is to make some rounding off remarks. This is, however, only a conclusion to this book, as we have to stop somewhere. It is not a conclusion to SML. Our work continues and each new programme throws up new learning for us. The principles of SML continue to be validated in practice, as this book shows. However, SML is a living process and new aspects of practical application continue to emerge. Anyone wanting to keep up to date on developments can access the Centre for Self Managed Learning web site at http://www.selfmanagedlearning.org

15 Looking to the future

Ian Cunningham

In this last chapter I will return to some themes already mentioned as well as raising some new issues. The sections of this chapter will cover the following topics:

- learning issues raised by earlier chapters
- why is SML not universally used?
- directions for SML.

While the chapter provides some 'concluding remarks' to the book it is not a conclusion to the development of SML. We see many possibilities ahead and we hope that this book will be part of the continuing dialogue about how to foster and enhance the use of SML. The cases presented in Part II are only some examples of what can be achieved.

LEARNING ISSUES RAISED BY EARLIER CHAPTERS

STRATEGIC SELF MANAGED LEARNING

Figure 15.1 shows two different ways of seeing SML. Figure 15.1a indicates how we see SML. It is a strategic approach to learning that makes the links from individual and organizational strategies to tactical and operational issues. A number of aspects of SML designs emphasize this stance. The Strategic Learning Contract is overtly about a person taking a strategic, big-picture approach to their learning. Also the fact that learning groups exist over time encourages a strategic perspective as opposed to a quick fix mind-set.

Figure 15.1b shows an aberrant view of SML. Many organizations claim to do Self Managed Learning yet all they do is leave learners to undertake miscellaneous random activities. This lack of integration can cause confusion for learners and whilst there can be some value in it, the approach tends to be low on cost-

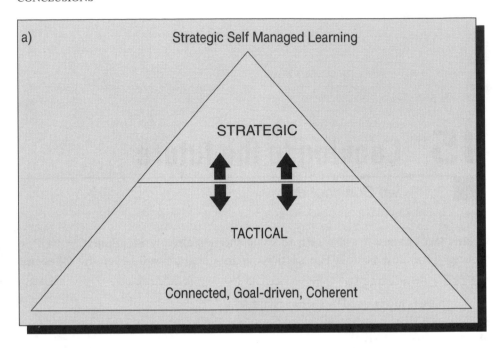

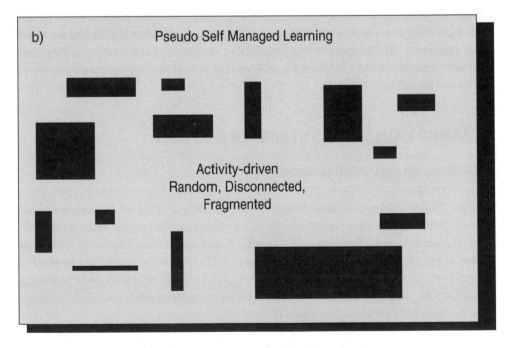

Figure 15.1 Two views of Self Managed Learning

effectiveness. We hope that the examples in Part II show the need for clear, well-thought through strategies.

LINKING KNOWLEDGE DEVELOPMENT

Knowledge management became a fashionable notion in the late 1990s. The idea of capturing and using knowledge more effectively is certainly attractive. However, it is apparent that many knowledge management schemes have foundered and are not cost-effective. One reason for this has been the confusion about what exactly 'knowledge' is and another factor has been the lack of attention to learning issues. Whilst a fuller discussion of these issues belongs elsewhere it may be instructive to take one aspect of this problem for further analysis.

My starting position is to postulate three levels of knowing, namely:

- first person knowledge – self knowledge that is internalized and often tacit (not made explicit);
- second person knowledge – knowledge 'in relationship', knowledge of others as people like oneself (not as 'it' or 'them'); it is personalized and connected to others and usually has an emotional content;
- third person knowledge – the kind of knowledge that is captured in mechanistic IT systems, text books and so on; the kind of knowledge that the educational world tends to see as the only legitimate knowledge; it has a quality of 'it/them' about it; it is disconnected from oneself and from other people as persons.

These three kinds of knowledge need to be integrated in healthy people and in healthy organizations. A severe imbalance can lead to pathological dysfunctions. For instance, if people are only aware of their own needs (first person) and of others as 'it/them' (third person) then it can, at its extreme, lead to a person becoming a serial killer, rapist or child abuser. Such a person has little empathy for others and only looks to get their own needs met. Paul Britton, the forensic psychologist, described the mass murderer Frederick West as follows:

> When Mr West was growing up and discovering his sexuality, his attention became focussed only on his own needs and wishes. He didn't really learn to see other people as separate, unique individuals who had the same rights, needs and wishes as he did. He could use the right words but he had no internal grip on the concept. Feelings for Frederick, as far as they existed, were 'my feelings'. He could never really grasp the notion that other people had feelings and theirs were just as important as his.
>
> (Britton 1997: 324)

While this is a dramatic example – and I am in no way implying that we come across such extreme examples in everyday organizational life – we do face lesser versions of the same syndrome. In SML we feel that it is essential to emphasize the integration of these three knowledge domains in order to promote healthy learning. The type of imbalance quoted above is only one of many. For instance, there is the person who denies their own (first person) knowledge in an over-veneration of theoretical (third person) knowledge.

In an organizational context dealing with another department or function as an 'it/them', as a depersonalized entity, is different from relating to them as a 'you', as real people with their own concerns, values and behaviours which are honoured as different but of worth. In SML we find that by mixing people in learning groups they use the first person knowledge base to move to the second person position. Learning groups can appear paradoxical in seemingly being highly first and third person, for example they are not meant to be teams. However, the understanding that people get of each other creates a new kind of learning. In the process people do become less defensive and more prepared to share knowledge – hence making real knowledge management work (as opposed to merely mechanistic systems that cause surface information to be shared but where functions and departments hold on to the really important knowledge).

In all this I am not implying that third person knowledge is less important. On the contrary, we see SML programmes helping participants to become more sophisticated in their theoretical knowledge, in part through using all three knowledge domains and hence avoiding irrelevant theory that does not connect to them and the people around them. So the effective manager develops a good sense of themselves, their values, their strengths and weaknesses, and of other people and of relevant theories of management. And they develop coherence across these domains. An example would be about motivation. The self managing learner understands their own personal motivations (first person), understands the people around them (second person) and has available good theory to make generalized statements about motivation (third person). And they test for integration of these so that they can act out of an integration of these three perspectives.

It seems that the best kinds of knowledge management schemes are moving in this direction. One example would be BP Amoco. Nick Milton (1999) relates how BP's Knowledge Management team helped BP Columbia to complete a successful business restructuring. As well as capturing the third person knowledge from previous restructuring processes they also gave the Columbian management team stories and anecdotes from managers who had led previous restructuring efforts in other parts of the world. This was all provided via a web site which also provided contact information and other means to make the information 'live'. As one of the Columbian management team said

> I wish all the stuff we read was so well put. I lived this process together with the folks that were quoted in the text. Not only did you capture the content, but also the souls of these people talking.

The integration of second and third person knowledge helped the Columbian managers to make links such that they could minimize the 're-inventing the wheel' syndrome.

THREE 'SIGHTS': FORESIGHT, HINDSIGHT AND 'PRESENTSIGHT'

It is well accepted that foresight is about looking forward into the future and hindsight is about looking back at the past. There seems to be a danger that we polarize our thinking and assume that these are the only ways to deal with time differences. I want to postulate a third mode which I will label 'presentsight'. I associate this process with the capability to see the present. An example may show why I'm raising this issue.

The *Guardian* newspaper of 30 December 1998 asked why people had not realized that Russia would endure such economic problems. As the *Guardian*'s leader said 'With hindsight it is clear that what Russia lacked most of all was the institutional infrastructure to deliver a market economy.' This is an interesting statement, and says more about the leader writer than anything else, perhaps. Having been in Russia five years earlier it seemed to me at the time obvious that the country did not possess 'the institutional infrastructure to deliver a market economy'. So why invoke 'hindsight' as an excuse? Wasn't 'presentsight' needed, that is just seeing what was there?

Others, of course, look for foresight – and the ability to see into the future. This approach can be anti-learning as it attempts to avoid learning by trying to control the future through prediction. And hindsight can mean that, despite rhetoric to the contrary, one does not learn from mistakes (but merely analyses them or uses the *Guardian* leader writer's get out for getting things wrong).

Burgoyne and Reynolds (1997) argue that we need to move from *effective practice* through *reflective practice* to *critical reflective practice*. I'll modify their typology as follows. The *pragmatic practitioner* just gets on with things, often muddling through with mainly first person knowledge. The *reflective practitioner* observes action in practice and modifies behaviour in the light of thinking through their actions. They are likely to add second person knowledge and some third person knowledge. The *self managing practitioner* takes this further in often reformulating theory and ideas as a result of their awareness of their experience and of relevant theory. They use 'presentsight' to a great extent, for example they have high levels of sensory acuity. But that is not enough. To take the example of Russia in 1993, the *Guardian* leader writer needed not just to observe and interact with Russian people and the concrete day-to-day experience of how the country worked but also to have theories of economic progress that he or she could test as they went along.

These qualities correlate with research evidence on what makes a person effective in working across cultures (a good test of the ability to self manage). It seems that a key quality of cross-cultural effectiveness is the ability to test hypotheses from past experience with the lived experience of being in a new environment. (See Cunningham 1999 for more information on this issue.) Hence a person going from one country to another will bring with them the accumulated knowledge from their past experiences. They are likely to have to modify these assumptions as they interact with the new environment – they will modify the first and third person knowledge they bring with them in the light of both new first person learning and of the learning with others in the new environment (second person knowledge).

It appears that people who are poor at learning to operate in a new culture either stick to their previous assumptions and theories (and hence do not learn to deal with the new context) or they come with poor third person knowledge so that they do not have hypotheses to test. In SML we help people to address these issues through a number of structures. The learning group encourages people to reflect on past experience (hindsight), to face current problems (presentsight) and to consider future actions. The Strategic Learning Contract pushes people to consider how they will integrate first, second and third person knowledge.

The case I'm making here, then, is that self managing persons can, through SML, develop an integrated mode of learning which transcends narrow formulations of what it is worth learning. I'm not implying that all participants on SML programmes go through some immediate magical transformation. It takes time to move in this direction – and not everyone responds fully to the opportunities SML provides. But I've seen enough people make these changes to be confident about making these claims here.

WHY IS SML NOT UNIVERSALLY USED?

We think that the varying reasons we present for using SML (like the one above) are pretty convincing. We have solid research, impressive case material and a coherent rationale for using SML. So why aren't all organizations convinced of the value of using SML? Below I have postulated some reasons.

IT'S A PARADIGM SHIFT

The notion of a paradigm has become overused but it may of necessity have to be invoked here. The prevailing educational paradigm is teaching and control-oriented. If we take the idea that paradigms affect the way people see the world then it's clear that some people just do see the world from a teaching perspective. They have little or no notion of how learning actually occurs and therefore cannot even begin to have a dialogue about such issues.

LACK OF AWARENESS THAT IT EXISTS

It's clear that many people have not heard of SML and that's one reason for writing this book. Those of us working in this field do have a continuing duty to make the SML processes better known, and on that score it's maybe our fault that SML is not better known. However, in mitigation of our position there are over a hundred articles, papers and books on the kind of SML we have covered in this text.

CONFUSING SML WITH sml

This is back to our distinction between strong version SML as described in this book and weak version self managed learning. The latter is often about sloppy self development or mechanistic pre-packaged learning materials or re-badged 'participative' training courses. In other cases 'sml' is an excuse for organizational abdication. We find this situation frustrating even though it could be seen as flattering that people want to use a term we invented.

LACK OF CONFIDENCE IN SELF

Even when organizations have made the move to SML we have been aware of the nervousness of, for instance, those taking on the role of learning group adviser. It can take some degree of personal courage to sit in a group and not know what is coming up. This especially applies to managers and trainers who are used to being in the driving seat in their other work contexts. We are aware that one of our roles in helping organizations to get started is to develop that confidence.

LACK OF CAPABILITY

While we do want to be optimistic about the ability of organizations to deliver SML programmes, it's apparent that some people find it too difficult to take on the roles we have suggested are necessary to make SML a success. If this stops people even trying then that is preferable to situations where trainers start an SML programme without a good design and without developing capable learning group advisers. The programme may go horribly wrong – and the idea of SML gets a bad name. Hence the organization is permanently put off SML as an approach.

LACK OF CONFIDENCE OR TRUST IN OTHERS

Some senior managers do not trust their staff. They believe that if you give people a chance to ask for learning that is relevant to them they will misuse the opportunity. My answer to that is that managers have to trust their staff every day. They have to assume that receptionists will not abuse callers, that salespeople will not alienate customers and so on. If you can't trust someone why are they employed in the organization?

All the evidence we have is that people do write serious Strategic Learning Contracts and they don't plan to learn how to rob the company or shoot the CEO. Most people want to do well in their work; it is a key part of their lives. And learning helps them to be more effective and get more satisfaction out of life. Apart from a perverse minority of sociopaths, why would anyone want to behave differently? (And real sociopaths don't want to do SML anyway.)

LACK OF RATIONALITY AND LOGIC – POLITICS AND FEELINGS

Decisions in organizations are made on all sorts of grounds, and often emotional or political decisions are dressed up as rational and logical. One political reason for opposing the use of SML is on the grounds of control. Senior managers may feel that they can control people through imposed training programmes. That they don't work as control mechanisms often only causes people to redouble their efforts in this direction.

Schools and educational officials from ministers down often get caught in this trap. 'Young people are not learning what we want them to learn so let's impose on them even more.' The fact that this is a failing strategy escapes them. People just learn to work the system – or if they don't, they learn to create their own system (for example become truants or criminals – or both).

REFUSAL TO LOOK AT RESEARCH EVIDENCE

This is quite common. We are asked to show that SML works by quoting research evidence – we do this, and still the organization refuses to acknowledge it. Mostly this syndrome is a sub-set of the one above.

FEAR, FOR EXAMPLE OF LOOKING FOOLISH

Doing something new can mean that it could go wrong. Many trainers prefer to stick to approaches they know, even if they have minimal efficacy. The standard training models appear safe and politically acceptable.

ANYTHING A CONSULTANT SAYS MUST BE A LIE

This is never said directly and probably not felt as strongly as this usually. However, there is a real (and understandable) suspicion about consultants peddling the latest gimmicks. Much as we may prefer not to be seen as consultants (with our humble 'learning assistant' hats on) we have to recognize that we are most easily pigeon-holed in this way. We often find that it is the word of organizations that have used SML that is the most powerful. In Arun District Council we arranged for a Sales Director from Allied Domecq to come and address the top 50 managers about his experiences of SML. That clinched their support more than anything we could have said.

CONSERVATISM, LAZINESS AND COMPLACENCY

The stance might be 'We know what we currently do is ineffective but it would be too much bother to change it.' Something similar was said to me by a training director from a large company. He said that he was convinced of the value of SML but he employed a lot of traditional instructors and they would not find it possible to work in this way (and he wasn't prepared to rock the boat on this). Sadly (but unsurprisingly) I learned some years later that his training department suffered huge compulsory redundancies because they were failing to deliver business results.

ANTI-LEARNING

Some top managers just do not want people to learn. That they can't prevent people from learning seems to escape them, but it does provide a basis for rejecting SML. Some managers who are fearful of their staff learning too much are prepared to support some training, so long as people do not come back from such training having learned things that will disturb the status quo.

ANECDOTAL EVIDENCE

Some people do not take to SML. Their voice may be disproportionately loud in the organization and even if 95 per cent of people have benefited (which is the norm) the few lone critics can get heard in high places. Sometimes we get trainers and managers who develop the 'premature evaluation disease'. They want to judge a programme after the first month. At this stage there can be significant numbers of people struggling to make it work. Some people find that writing a Strategic Learning Contract is not easy and they may be prone to being less than positive about SML at this juncture. Usually their views change during the programme and they become much more positive, recognizing the value of their struggles to create a Strategic Learning Contract.

We recognize that we have to tackle many of the issues we have identified above. Thankfully, over time, they are becoming less and less of a problem.

DIRECTIONS FOR SML

SML has evolved over the years and we assume it will continue to do so. One could describe the changes in the language of computer software. SML 1.0 was characterized by early experiments with linking sets (from the action learning world) with learning contracts. SML 1.1 was the Post-Graduate Diploma at North East London Polytechnic; the principles and design were the same as the early experiments but with the addition of a qualification. These ideas evolved into in-organization SML programmes and warrant the label SML 2.0. We refined those activities over the years and one could attach the label SML 2.5 to the large-scale programmes that emerged, especially where we started to develop in-house set advisers.

SML 3.0 is maybe where we are right now. One obvious change is in the language. We now talk of learning groups instead of sets and Strategic Learning Contracts instead of just learning contracts. Of course, language change may signify nothing much – and there are still organizations that are staying with the old language because that is what they are used to. More significantly we are linking SML to major organizational change and are involved with areas such as the learning organization and knowledge management. The specific stance we take on these issues is outlined in the earlier part of this chapter and in the opening chapter.

Another factor in the evolution of SML is its use in an increasing array of countries. We have shown examples from Finland in this book and in subsequent texts we hope to have other examples from different countries. Also we are currently involved in setting up some international/global programmes which promise to be both exciting and developmental.

An area we see as potentially important for the future is the link with the educational world. The chapter on qualification programmes (Chapter 8) has shown how problematic this is in higher education. But potentially the biggest impact could be in schools. We are not necessarily optimistic on this score. We can see that the structures we use in SML will work for people below school leaving age. Young people can write learning contracts and work in learning groups. They have to be set up on a different basis but the principles are the same.

The major issue here is that we do not see teachers or governmental agencies being prepared to address the issue of the waste of talent in schools by virtue of the current teaching approach. This is a global issue and is not restricted to wealthier countries. Tackling it could bring enormous benefits to humankind, and so, despite our bouts of pessimism, we want to find ways to work in this arena. We so often see people who have been damaged by the educational system coming onto SML programmes as adults and regretting the waste of their earlier years in school. Many of them have been stigmatized as failures because they did not pass exams or play the system. Solving this problem is going to take a long time and a massive effort. But we have to start somewhere. That corny old saying comes to mind: 'Better to light one candle than to curse the darkness' – and just because it's corny doesn't make it wrong.

References

Banet, A. G. (1976) 'Yin/yang: a perspective on theories of group development', *The 1976 Annual Handbook for Group Facilitators*, La Jolla, CA: University Associates.

Bohm, D. (1985) *Unfolding Meaning* (ed. Donald Factor), Mickleton, Gloucs.: Foundation House Publications.

Bohm, D. (1994) *Thought as a System*, London: Routledge.

Bridges, W. (1995) *Jobshift*, London: NB Books.

Britton, P. (1997) *The Jigsaw Man*, London: Bantam.

Brown, J. S. and Duguid, P. (1991) 'Organizational learning and communities-of-practice: towards a unified view of working, learning and innovation', *Organization Science*, 2 (1) (February), 40–57.

Burgoyne, J. G. and Cunningham, I. (1980) 'Facilitating behaviour in work centred management development programmes' in J. Beck and C. Cox (eds) *Advances in Management Education*, Chichester: John Wiley.

Burgoyne, J. and Reynolds, M. (eds) (1997) *Management Learning*, London: Sage.

Chesterman, D. (1999) 'A story about learning communally', paper to Kent Conference on Communal Learning, March.

Cramb, J. and Cunningham, I. (1998) 'Face value – the case of KPMG', in *People Management*, 4 (16) (13 August), 48–52.

Cunningham, C. (1991) *Report on Management Development and Training in Central Sussex*, Sussex Training and Enterprise Council.

Cunningham, I. (1978) 'Self Managed Learning', paper presented to Association of Teachers of Management Workshops (reprinted in I. Cunningham and G. Dawes (eds) (1996) *Self Managed Learning: Selected Writings 1978–1996*, St Albans: Centre for Self Managed Learning).

Cunningham, I. (1981) 'Self Managed Learning in independent study' in T. Boydell and M. Pedler (eds) *Management Self Development: Concepts and Practice*, Aldershot: Gower.

Cunningham, I. (1986) *Developing Chief Executives: An Evaluation*, Berkhamsted: Ashridge Management College.

Cunningham, I. (1993) 'A strategic approach to learning', *Strategic Direction*, July/August, 3.

Cunningham, I. (1994) 'Self Managed Learning' in J. Prior J. (ed.) *Handbook of Training and Development*, Aldershot: Gower.

Cunningham, I. (1995) 'Managing change' in S. Crainer (ed.) *The Financial Times Handbook of Management*, London: Pitman.

Cunningham, I. (1996) 'Action learning for chief executives: an evaluation' in M. Pedler (ed.) *Action Learning in Practice*, third edn, Aldershot: Gower.

Cunningham, I. (1999) *The Wisdom of Strategic Learning: The Self Managed Learning Solution*, second edn, Aldershot: Gower.

Cunningham, I. and Dawes, G. (eds) (1996) *Self Managed Learning: Selected Writings 1978–1996*, St Albans: Centre for Self Managed Learning.

Cunningham, I. and Dawes, G. D. (1998) *Exercises for Developing Coaching Capability*, London: Institute of Personnel and Development.

de Bono, E. (1996) *A Textbook of Wisdom*, London: Viking.

Department of Employment (1994) *Labour Market Skills and Trends*, Sheffield: Department of Employment.

Eraut, M., Alderton, J., Cole, G. and Senker, P. (1997) 'Learning from other people at work', in F. Coffield, (ed.) *Skill Formation at Work*, London: Polity Press.

Eraut, M., Alderton, J., Cole, G. and Senker, P. (1998) *Development of Knowledge and Skills in Employment*, Research Report No. 5, Brighton: University of Sussex Institute of Education.

Faulkner, M. (1996) 'Continuous learning', *Management Training*, March/April, 48–9.

Fleishman, E. A. (1953) 'Leadership climate and human relations training', *Personnel Psychology*, 6, 205–22.

Fritz, R. (1984) *The Path of Least Resistance*, Salem, Mass.: DMA Inc.

Fukuyama, F. (1995) *Trust: The Social Virtues and the Creation of Prosperity*, London: Hamish Hamilton.

Gear, J., McIntosh, A. and Squires, G. (1994) *Informal Learning in the Professions*, Hull: University of Hull.

Goleman, D. (1995) *Emotional Intelligence*, New York: Bantam.

Guinness, D. (1996) 'How we started self managing', *Open Mind*, 80 (April/May), 20–21.

Hamlin, R. and Davies, G. (1996) 'The trainer as change agent: issues for practice' in J. Stewart and J. McGoldrick (eds) *Human Resource Development: Perspectives, Strategies and Practice*, London: Pitman.

Handy, C. (1994) *The Empty Raincoat*, London: Hutchinson.

Handy, C. (1995) 'Life inside and outside the organisation', *Common Purpose Magazine*, Spring, 10–13.

Hofstede, G. (1982) *Culture's Consequences*, London: Sage.

Hudson, L. (1966) *Contrary Imaginations*, London: Methuen.

Hudson, L. (1968) *Frames of Mind*, Harmondsworth: Penguin.

Industrial Society (1998) *Self Managed Learning*, Managing Best Practice No. 40, London: Industrial Society.

Institute of Personnel and Development (1995) *People Make the Difference*, London: Institute of Personnel and Development.

Kotter, J. P. (1996) *Leading Change*, Boston, Mass.: Harvard Business School Press.

Madden, C. A. and Mitchell, V. A. (1993) *Professions, Standards and Competence: A Survey of Continuing Education for the Professions*, Bristol: Department of Continuing Education, University of Bristol.

Milton, N. (1999) 'Building and applying a global knowledge asset', paper to 'Making Knowledge Management work for you' Conference, London, July.

Peters, T. and Waterman, R. (1982) *In Search of Excellence*, New York: Harper

Revans, R. (1982) *The Origins and Growth of Action Learning*, Bromley: Chartwell-Bratt.

RSA (1994) *Tomorrow's Company: The Role of Business in a Changing World* (Interim Report), London: RSA.

Semler, R. (1993) *Maverick!*, London: Century.

Senge, P. (1990) *The Fifth Discipline*, London: Random House.

Serpis, R. (1998) 'Growing by learning? How effective is Self Managed Learning as a management development strategy for an organisation in change?', MA Dissertation, University of Greenwich.

Tough, A. M. (1971) *The Adult's Learning Projects*, Ontario: Ontario Institute of Education.

Urwin, B. (1996) 'Learning to learn', *Local Government Management*, Autumn, 35–7.

Webster, J. (1995) 'Self Managed Learning in Cable & Wireless', *Croner's A–Z Guide for HRM Professionals*, Issue 6 (21 November), 6–8.

Woodward, I. (1996) 'Dimensions of Continuing Professional Development', in I. Woodward (ed.) *Continuing Professional Development: Issues in Design and Delivery*, London: Cassell.

Index

A Complete Guide to Learning Contracts

George Boak

Learning contracts are valuable tools for winning the commitment of the learner, and ensuring that learners and trainers are working towards the same objectives. They play a significant part in many educational and training courses and their popularity is growing fast. Already common in work-based learning and in the development of skills and competencies, they also provide a useful way of structuring academic research projects and individual study programmes.

George Boak's timely book is based on more than twelve years' experience of using learning contracts in a variety of contexts. He begins by reviewing the different kinds of contract and looking at the advantages and disadvantages of each. He goes on to explain what is involved in preparing, negotiating, supporting and evaluating a contract and discusses related issues such as accreditation and the links between learning contracts and the competency-based approach. The text is supported throughout by case studies and detailed examples.

Anyone concerned with management development or skills training, whether as educator, HRD practitioner or consultant, will find this a comprehensive and eminently practical guide.

Gower

The Excellent Trainer

Putting NLP to Work

Di Kamp

Most trainers are familiar with the principles of Neuro-Linguistic Programming. What Di Kamp does in this book is to show how NLP techniques can be directly applied to the business of training.

Kamp looks first at the fast-changing organizational world in which trainers now operate, then at the role of the trainer and the skills and qualities required. She goes on to deal with the actual training process and provides systematic guidance on using NLP in preparation, delivery and follow-up. Finally she explores the need for continuous improvement, offering not only ideas and explanation but also instruments and activities designed to enhance both personal and professional development.

If you are involved in training, you'll find this book a powerful tool both for developing yourself and for enriching the learning opportunities you create for others.

Gower

Gower Handbook of Training and Development

Third Edition

Edited by Anthony Landale

It is now crystal clear that, in today's ever-changing world, an organization's very survival depends upon how it supports its people to learn and keep on learning. Of course this new imperative has considerable implications for trainers who are now playing an increasingly critical role in supporting individuals, teams and business management. In this respect today's trainers may need to be more than excellent presenters; they are also likely to require a range of consultancy and coaching skills, to understand the place of technology in supporting learning and be able to align personal development values with business objectives.

This brand new edition of the *Gower Handbook of Training and Development* will be an invaluable aid for today's training professional as they face up to the organizational challenges presented to them. All 38 chapters in this edition are new and many of the contributors, whilst being best-selling authors or established industry figures, are appearing for the first time in this form. Edited by Anthony Landale, this *Handbook* builds on the foundations that previous editions have laid down whilst, at the same time, highlighting many of the very latest advances in the industry.

The *Handbook* is divided into five sections - learning organization, best practice, advanced techniques in training and development, the use of IT in learning, and evaluation issues.

Gower